Steelhead Water

by Bob Arnold
Illustrations by Loren Smith

Frank Amato
PORTLAND

Copyright 1993 • Bob Arnold
Illustrations by Loren Smith
Book Design: Charlie Clifford

Printed in U.S.A.
Frank Amato Publications
P.O. Box 82112 • Portland, Oregon 97282
(503) 653-8108 • FAX: (503) 653-2766
Hardbound ISBN: 1-878175-60-2

Dedication

For the men and the women of the North Fork of the Stillaguamish, with whom I have shared the vagaries of weather and luck along a cobbled beach for more than thirty years. They deserve to have their names sung—the living and the dead among them, companions in sunshine and rain and occasionally snow; freshet, drought, and flood. And most of all for my wife, Norma, who put up with it all.

Ken and George and Ken, Jr. McLeod, Al Knudsen, Frank and Cassie Gilbert, Bill and Janice Street, Al Kolmorgan, Sparky, Elmer Olson, Frank Hedrick, Walt Johnson, Sid Pierce, Dale and Joe Bly, Ralph Wahl, Art Smith, Jim Lewis, Frank-Who-Falls-In, Frank Sass (who does not), Mike Kinney, Terry Blacker, Bill Green, Bill Tolle, Russ Miller, Bob Fleming, Bill Peterson, Lyle Gross, George and Vera Keough, Frank Snyder, Louis Marsh, Jerry and Donna Marsh, Clyde Hoyt, Dave Farrell, Phil O'Lone, Ken Ohnemus, Chris and Danny Byrnes, Clarence Middleton, Enos Bradner, Steve Raymond, Ed Weinstein, Bob Taylor, Jerry Wintle, Martin Tolley, Doug and Grace Boyer, Bob McLaughlin, Merlin Stidham, Joe and Faith Butorac, Arnold Timm, Joe Monda, Bob Strobel, Bill Ewing, Steve Fransen, John Farrar, Syd Glasso, Bill McMahon, Wes Drain, Harry Dahl, Ira Grady, Ed Nevins, Bob Bettzig, Dec Hogan, Scott O'Donnell, Pat Crane, Kenny Belk, Steve and Karen Gobin, Rock-and-Roll Charlie Gearhart, Eric Balser, Art Anderson, Loren Hansen, Clarence Tiessen, Stan Young, Marv Berg and Len from Boulder Creek, Joe, Pete, Lester, and Joel Pederson, Kenny Groshon, Jack Whitesel, Dan Lemaich, Dan Rife, Sally Pemberton, Bob Vera, Nick Gayesky, Tom Darling, Don Johnson, Dake Traphagen, Jack Sandstrom, Errol McWirt, Bob Michajla, Bill Stinson, Wendy Voit, Alec Jackson, Walt Johnson, Chris Crabtree, Catherine Clausen, Marilyn Stone, Sara Arne, Dick Sylbert, Jay Barnes, Bill Rambo; all whose names I was not thrown, or did not catch, but who shared with me a friendly word or a wave in passing. My special thanks to Curt Kraemer, who read this book in manuscript and pointed out to me the worst of the biological errors and to my son, Garth, for his proofreading.

Big party, come Saturday night, down at the Oso Fire Hall. We're gonna park the fire trucks out in the rain so there is room to dance to Steelhead Charlie Gearhart and The Oakie Drifters. Drinks are on BOB (Bring Own Bottle). Dress? Why, waders and rain parkas. Billed caps mandatory. Meet you in the parking lot. Check your flyrod at the door.

Contents

Chapter One, The Royal Family of Salmonids 7
Chapter Two, Adaptability—The Key To Survival 15
Chapter Three, My Deer Creek 23
Chapter Four, Let's Hear It For The Hatchery Fish 35
Chapter Five, Anatomy Lesson 45
Chapter Six, Probable Water 53
Chapter Seven, The Naming of Pools 61
Chapter Eight, Who Needs a Guide? 77
Chapter Nine, The Elephant's Foot Wastebasket 87
Chapter Ten, Sam's Story 95
Chapter Eleven, One Memorable Spring 107
Chapter Twelve, A Stroke of Ill Luck 115
Chapter Thirteen, Trophy Time 131
Chapter Fourteen, Smolt, Parr, and Fry 145
Chapter Fifteen, Salmonid Agonistics 153
Chapter Sixteen, Days of Puce and Lemon 161
Chapter Seventeen, The Cult of the Spade 171
Chapter Eighteen, Meristic Characteristics, Phenotyping, Electrophroesis, and Other Fun Things 181
Chapter Nineteen, Big Yellow Rock 187
Chapter Twenty, Dry Fly Dream 197
Chapter Twenty-one, Drowning in Air 211
Chapter Twenty-two, Wet-Fly Tactics: Low Water 217
Chapter Twenty-three, Wet-Fly Tactics: Mid-Water 229
Chapter Twenty-four, Wet-Fly Tactics: High Water 235
Chapter Twenty-five, This Year's Fly, Last Year's Rod, A Reel of Antiquity 241
Chapter Twenty-six, Big Round River 253
Chapter Twenty-seven, Wenatchee Mornings 265
Epitaph: Deer Creek Revisited 277

1

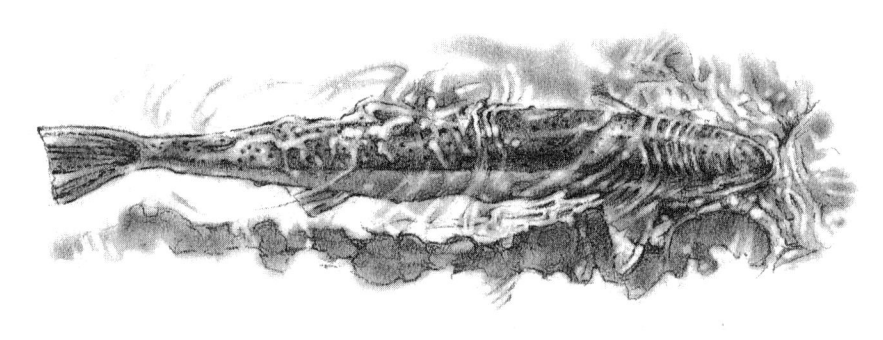

The Royal Family of Salmonids

M<small>Y</small> FRIEND ALEC JACKSON SAYS THE STEELHEAD is a prince—a prince of salmonids. The Atlantic salmon thus is "king." Well, maybe. A transplanted Englishman, Alec's roots lie deep in Yorkshire, the country of the Bronte sisters. He has at least a speaking acquaintance with both fish. The steelhead. . . only a prince? I would like to think not. He is on a par with the Atlantic. But I'm not the world's greatest authority. I decided to ask Lee Wulff, who is. I was lucky to get to know him slightly in the last few years before he died in a crash while recertifying his light plane in 1991.

Rather than be standoffish with an average "good" fisherman, I found him to be friendly and helpful. Lee loved salmonids and was respectful of anybody who shared his passion. He had long been my mentor and I had repeated a few of his many accomplishments, knowing as I did so that there was a big difference between initiating them and copying them in a different river environment.

Meanwhile I had helped found and edit a small journal for steelheaders worried about the plight of wild steelhead. It was called *The Osprey*. We were—as Lee was with Atlantic salmon—dedicated to protecting them and fished for them mostly with the fly, carefully releasing the wild ones. These were precepts he had advanced long ago and had become popularized of late. Though primarily a fisher of salmon, he made several trips to British Columbia in search of steelhead and was well acquainted with them.

On one such trip he was accompanied by Tom Pero, who edited Trout Unlimited's magazine, *Trout*. Tom spent the time taking photographs of Lee fishing for prime, wild Canadian steelhead instead of fishing himself. (Such a sacrifice!) On that trip Lee accomplished another first, the taking of a nine-pound steelhead on a Surface Stone Fly to which he attached a size 28 hook. So tiny, its bend is only about the size of the lead in a pencil. When I asked Lee about the breaking test of the tippet he was reluctant to say. But he did tell me the iron in the hook will snap at one pound of direct pressure. Later he confided the tippet was about 6X.

While Tom's photoessay was in production Co-Editor Stan Young asked Lee if he would write up the experience for *The Osprey* and he agreed to. Pushing my luck, I asked him to tell us about the comparative fighting abilities of steelhead and Atlantic salmon. He said he already had written about this, but would be happy to update the material in light of new experiences. Afterwards he cautioned me, "As a pro, it is rare that I write a piece gratis—hope this one will fill your needs." It was generous of him, but typical.

"Some years back," his letter said, "I wrote a piece comparing the steelhead and the Atlantic salmon. In it I gave the salmon a slight edge.

"It is very difficult to compare the fighting qualities of various game fish. When they are caught on the same tackle, it is easier and makes more sense. To compare an Atlantic salmon—a fish always (on this continent, anyway) caught on flyfishing tackle, with no weight on the line or on the fly, with a fish like the bass, which is caught mostly on plugs and lures, is rather difficult. Even comparing the steelhead with the salmon is tough because so many steelhead are taken deep in cold water, instead of having to remain there, safely, while the water warms enough to cause them to rise to a fly. By that time only a comparative few in many rivers are left for the fly fisherman, while all the Atlantic salmon are. In the end, the fish are cropped and the overall cropping may be as complete with fly-only as with the early deep fishing. But the fly fisherman has a whack at *all* the fish.

"I will not try to compare steelhead caught on spinning gear with those caught on a fly or with Atlantic salmon. It is a different game. I [will limit my comparison to] steelhead and salmon when both are caught on standard fly-fishing tackle. Because they come in from the sea with a lot of energy, some of which they lose during periods of starvation, a fresh run of fish of either species is likely to be stronger than a stale fish.

"In the first article I said that steelhead *did* feed in fresh water but that salmon physically could not digest food and steelhead had a chance to maintain or rebuild [their] energy and salmon did not. As a result I had letters saying that steelhead *did not* feed in fresh water and other letters which included stone fly nymphs and other stuff taken from the stomachs of steelhead and reports of salmon eggs and such. In any case, they come out about even, because steelhead apparently don't feed *much* in fresh water.

"In my own experience, which has been far more with Atlantic salmon than steelhead, I still favor the salmon by a small margin. Salmon have gone into my backing—and way, way in—far more often, in proportion, than steelhead. I believe they tend to run farther and faster by a small margin and I think that is because of their makeup. The fastest fish in the ocean are the mackerel family, the tunas, wahoos, marlin. They're hard, stiff fish, and they can and do swim with a very fast vibration. Their tails are hard, and one can lift and hold them forever by a grip at the tail. The salmon is a stiffer fish than the steelhead and, I believe, can and does vibrate faster on the run than a steelhead.

"This is a small point to mention, but if there is a difference it is small and small points can be important. The comparison in fighting qualities is essentially a draw, with individual fish giving great performances for both species and others being dogs. It is like a football game between evenly matched teams, where either one may be the winner or it may well be a tie.

"One thing does favor the salmon. It will rise to flies coming at it free drift, from either side or up from behind. Steelhead seem to me to prefer a fly that wings across their noses, and most steelheaders I know like to fish from above and at a narrow angle. In deep streams a lot of steelhead are difficult to reach and to fish for from below or well across current from them. Salmon will take a freely drifting dry fly better than a steelhead. Both, I know, will tend to take very small flies and, of course, the ratio of weight-to-hook size is a natural way to measure the skill required in landing a fish. It's why bass aren't considered to require the delicacy in playing that trout do.

"No one can compare fish without knowing them both. Most people root for the home team. Southerners seem to think that the bass is the best and gamest fish on earth. Fishermen in steelhead country or salmon country, who know their own fish well and others less well, are for their 'own' fish. Perhaps there's someone who knows steelhead as well as I know salmon and steelhead better than I do who could make a better comparison."

Not likely. Most will agree that Lee Wulff is the authority we most want to hear from. He repeatedly gives the salmon the edge, though he keeps qualifying this by saying that individuals of either species may be the better performer, and water temperatures and other environmental factors may affect either fish. So let the Atlantic salmon reign as king: The steelhead is heir apparent, a ranking member of the royal family. That is plenty good enough. He is equally game, a great fighter. And individuals of both species will vary in strength and performance.

Alec's analogy is a good one and shows how much the fish have in common. Both survive after spawning, under the best of circumstances. All Pacific salmon die. Steelhead and Atlantics take flies regularly. Pacific salmon usually are reluctant to. The degree of skill necessary for catching both fish on flies is vastly over-rated; the multiple arguments about flies and presentation are intended more to please the fisher than the fish, who usually do not seem to care.

I am an American—a Westerner—so it is the steelhead that has long obsessed me. But steelheaders have learned a lot about their fish's behavior from a study of Atlantic salmon and the literature that surrounds fishing for them with flies. Steelhead flyfishing has come into its own, a bit belatedly. Today it seems to be leading the way. Again it is the similarities, not the differences, that are important and which tend to unite us fishers, East and West. Prejudiced in favor of the steelhead I have a hunch that in the future steelhead flyfishing will make the more significant contribution to the combined lore and literature. I hope so.

Salmonids have enchanted me for nearly 40 years. They are fascinating fish—large, sleek, silvery bright when in saltwater, colorful in fresh, and all of them will take the fly at times. But as they mature sexually they darken and become single-purposed in finding suitable substrate in which to spawn. Then they are reluctant takers and in my opinion ought to be left alone to complete their life cycle. They probably should not be fished over, either with gear or fly.

The family *Salmonidae* is composed of three sub-families, all of which can be found in Western rivers. These are *Salmoninae, Coregoninae,* and *Thymallinae.* The first group includes the salmon, trout, and char; the second group the whitefish, and the third the grayling. Recently scientists have reclassified some of the *Salmoninae,* and have grouped the steelhead and cutthroat trout with *Oncorhynchus,* which is dominated by the Pacific salmon. The branching off from a common ancestor took place later than was previously thought. Thus the steelhead and cutthroat are considered taxonomically closer to the Pacific salmon than they are the Atlantic salmon and brown trout. Fishermen were initially outraged by this change, and are still having trouble accepting it and the new nomenclature. Traditionally both rainbow trout and steelhead were *Salmo*—either *gairdneri* or *irideus,* depending on when you entered the game. We still see them as trout, not salmon. It is consoling to know that our favorite fish behave exactly the same as when we got acquainted with them.

Salmonids further divide themselves into those that spend their entire life in freshwater and those that go to sea to obtain their remarkable growth. The latter are called anadromous and they are primarily what will be found in Western rivers open to the sea, for salmonids—given the opportunity—will migrate in search of bigger or more abundant food. Chief among the salmonids that provide great flyfishing sport is the steelhead.

Steelhead embody all that is wild and free. They personify what is best among game fish. They can swim the strongest current, leap barriers that will halt the migrations of all but the coho salmon. In winter on each freshet bright steelhead surge in from the sea. In summer, though they are moved along by high water, they tend to trickle in during normal or even low flows, especially the wild fish. Fish caught in or adjacent to saltwater are silvery bright with a minimum of spots above the lateral line. Often they maintain their brightness high into a river system. Two that I've caught over the years had no spots at all on their backs, and their tails were transparent and only lightly flecked. One had a blue-black back (much like a sockeye salmon) and the other's back was a peculiar light brown color. Both were remarkable specimens and fought well. And I've caught winter steelhead so fresh they had sea lice by their vents, but were all spawned out without having undergone a color change.

Most fish have spotted backs and tails, and the bright sheen of silver rapidly dulls to gray in fresh water. The males develop a wide rainbow stripe as they draw near to spawning. The females do not evidence so pronounced a color change even when ripe. Usually a slight rosy sheen is all. The bellies of both remain a creamy white. As time passes the spots grow in number and extend well below the lateral line. The fish look worn and often have scales missing from encounters with nets or seals and sea lions. Often they will evidence skin cuts from anglers's lines or leaders.

The size and shape of the head is a good way to tell males from females quickly The female's skull is smaller, neater, with a proportionately tiny mouth and a jaw that comes short of a line drawn down from the center of the eye. As she approaches spawning two distinct egg masses can be located in her body cavity and as they grow larger will be found to shift their bulk when the fish is handled gingerly; often pink membrane will extend from the vent, indicating that she is nearly ready to shed her eggs.

Males have big heads and long jaws. Often their teeth are backwards-slanting and pronounced. Their bodies are heavier and deeper, their flesh thicker and more abundant. There is more meat on a male fish of a given length than on a female and he will weigh more. Reading about the various salmonids and looking at pictures in a book will help to recognize what you see in the field. A good book is W. B. Scott and E. J. Crossman, *Freshwater Fishes of Canada*, Bulletin 184, Fisheries Research Board of Canada, Ottawa 1973.

Salmonids, the authors state, have a distinct shape and proportion. This varies slightly among species. Fins number eight—two pectorals, two ventrals, an anal, a dorsal, an adipose, and a caudal or tail. They are in the same location on all salmonids. With steelhead the head comprises about 20 percent of the fish's total length (the males a bit more) and the eye represents 20 percent of the length of the head.

The authors describe the species as "very plastic," which means races of salmonids have changed their size, shape, and coloration according to the dictates of their environment over a long period of time. Because both salmon and steelhead go to sea to attain their growth and return to their natal rivers to spawn, the Native American tribes of the Pacific coast make no distinction between them. They consider them salmon. The point has considerable validity today.

I grew up believing that the steelhead was *Salmo* and basically a trout. I am old enough not to want to change my mind if I can avoid doing so. Scientists see the fish differently from us simple fishers. Salmon and steelhead (and cutthroat trout) have a common ancestor a short ways back—short, anyway, when measured in geologic time. The branching off from the main evolutionary line took place earlier than supposed, making the Atlantic and the brown trout *Salmo*, with a common ancestor, while the steelhead and all five Pacific salmon evolved together, somewhat independently, and thus are classified as *Oncorhynchus*. So the Indians are right in a practical sense.

The Atlantic and the steelhead are a little more distantly related than I used to think. Yet they have much in common. They are more cousins than brothers or sisters. Both are noble. Fishers on both sides of the Atlantic ocean are reluctant to accept change in matters dear to them, especially concerning their sport. And nobody is more hidebound than a flyfisher. We continue to think of our fish as big trout. As the water warms in spring and throughout summer our fish become more inclined to support us in our old-fashioned notions of how salmonids should behave and will rise actively to take our flies.

2

Adaptability—The Key to Survival

THE FACT THAT THE STEELHEAD is highly adaptable may explain why he is present in so many river systems of widely differing characteristics and has so long endured. He can survive a high range of temperatures—even a few hours spent at 80 degrees F. (Juveniles will soon die at 75 degrees, however.) Only *trutta*, the brown trout, can tolerate anything near the steelhead's upper limit. And on the low end of the scale the cutthroat *(clarkii)* alone can endure the frigid temperatures that the steelhead does, ones which can remain below freezing for much of the winter. (The chars, including the brook trout, can tolerate a similar low range.)

Recently biologists have begun using a complex biochemical process to identify races of fish within a species by the proteins in their genes: these are called *alleles* and are associated with chromosomes. Fish in the same gene pool will have nearly identical allelic frequencies. By this means biologists are able to recognize broodstocks caught in nets on the high seas and can determine the natal rivers of various steelhead and salmon. The genetic make-up within a particular species, such as the rainbow or steelhead, differs only in the smallest parts, yet that is sufficient for identification purposes.

Biologists have located three main stocks of steelhead. One group is coastal in origin and ranges from Kodiak Island in Alaska to the Mad River in Northern California; in the contiguous states it seems blocked by the Cascade Mountains. The second group is found inland and includes steelhead East of the Cascades, encompassing the tributaries of the Columbia and Snake, the Fraser River, and the great Skeena system in Canada. (There is a possible additional sub-group, now entirely landlocked, located in the McCloud River drainage in California, which marks a divergence from the coastal group of rainbow trout that took place before the last period of glaciation.) And the third major group is found in remote Kamchatka near Siberia. There all the Pacific salmon and the steelhead were named by Stephan Krashnennikov in 1755; hence the validity of *mykiss* and the classification of the steelhead with the salmon, *Oncorhynchus*.

Because he transplants so well, steelhead have been successfully introduced into waters of widely different types and characteristics. There are now steelhead in the Great Lakes and their tributary rivers, extending so far East as New York State. All are successful transplants from West Coast stocks. A few rivers in Wisconsin and Michigan are able to perpetuate their runs naturally, but these came from hatchery stocks. The Pere Marquette is a famous one of these.

A good reason to think of the steelhead as a trout is because, given half a chance, he will dominate a particular ecosystem. And he feeds like a trout, unlike a Pacific salmon—first as a juvenile and later as a returning adult. Yes, steelhead feed in fresh water, though they have reduced capacity to utilize what they eat. That capability is next to nothing. Yet old habits persist. Scott and Crossman, and other biologists, describe rainbows and young steelhead as usually feeding low in the water column, that is, grubbing along the bottom of rivers and lakes, but at some times of the year they may be found cruising along just under the surface, on the lookout for food that is being blown from shore and is carried along by the current.

Steelhead divide into two classes that are identified by when they enter their natal rivers and length of time before they spawn. Though they are the same species and look much alike they behave quite differently. Winter fish are riper and will run upstream as far as necessary to find suitable redds. Hatchery fish spawn almost immediately and so do some wild fish, but other wild fish may travel up to 100 miles and wait three or four months before they spawn. The Sauk River in Washington state is a good example. A large proportion of winters spawn in the main stream and do not ascend tributary creeks more than a short distance. While remaining shy they will tolerate a little more intrusion in their environment, because swollen flows and a river grown bigger provide a greater opportunity to flee from predators. As they come closer to spawning they become less shy, for spawning takes precedence over survival.

Summer runs travel longer distances and remain in the river up to a full year before they spawn. During this time they take little or no nourishment. They tend to be more flighty than winter fish, perhaps because spawning is far off. Fish biologists tell me that both rainbows and steelhead in the wild are similarly shy, but broodstock collected each year in traps have lost much of their shyness, generation after generation. It is a condition induced by captivity and the manner in which young fish are fed at hatcheries. This bodes ill when they are released into the wild and must adapt to natural feeding conditions. Some are easily caught out, while others in streams with low biotic productivity can actually starve to death.

Returning winter and summer adults hold in deeper water until they mature. Then they move onto the redds, the female first in order to prepare the nest. She buries her eggs up to a foot deep in a shallow riffle of coarse gravel or small stones. There she lays four or five thousand eggs in a nest typically six feet square, with 800 to one thousand eggs to a redd. When she is done with one nest she moves upstream and starts a second. The first will be the deepest and best made; it is as though she becomes exhausted and careless as her spawning progresses. She continues building nests until she is void of eggs.

A cold snap generally halts fresh fish ascending a river and only ripe fish can be found until there is some rain again. For years I believed what P.D. Mallock said about Atlantic salmon on the Tay River applied to steelhead; when a river rises or floods Atlantics abandon the nests they are on and move upstream to start new ones. But steelhead are different. High water (including the very high water of a flood) may halt spawning briefly, but fish often return to the same nests. Or they will move either upstream or down to start fresh ones. This helps protect a year's spawning production from a single major disaster.

A spawned-out female is a sad thing. Her ribcage is visible, her body cavity has collapsed. The skin of her belly is loose. She is thin as death. Her lower fins and the bottom of her tail may be worn away from nest-building. She is weak and wan, and often the current carries her along with scarcely a flutter of her tail. She departs immediately for salt water. In spite of the rigors of spawning she survives in greater numbers than the male. This is partly because males tend to hang around the river to ensure there are no unspawned females left. It is usually he who you will find dead on the beach, a stripe of old wine down his flank, being eaten away by eagles, crows, and gulls.

Kelts or spawn-outs are avid takers and can be caught easily. The British call such fish "well-mended kelts." It is a nice phrase—both poetic and descriptive. There is a great need for the protection of these fish. They are poor eating besides, which helps their case some. They soon strengthen, even while in the river, and the females quickly brighten. In fact, some females have never darkened. Often a recovering fish will give a good account of itself on the end of the line.

Summer Runs

On some rivers fresh fish ascend every month, and the runs tend to blur and overlap. Generally, though, a river and its runs can be divided into two more or less distinct categories and they have different life cycles, though both spawn in late winter or early spring. Summer runs enter their rivers about the same time the last of the surviving winter runs are exiting and the progeny of the fish from a cycle two years or so earlier are leaving as smolts. Smolts are bright little fish of six-11 inches when they enter saltwater where they accomplish most of their growth. Often they return after only one year at sea; at least this is the case with wild summer runs. Hatchery summer runs mature in rearing pens after only one year of forced feeding and stay at sea two or three years; they are correspondingly bigger from having had so much longer to feed. This characteristic is the result of selective breeding of generations of early-return fish that have stayed at sea longer than is normal. This has its up and down sides.

Because they must live in fresh water for up to a year before spawning, without substantial nourishment, summer runs have characteristics more like trout than like Pacific salmon and are of special interest to anglers, especially flyfishers. Summers are an interactive part of a river's life, drawing from it and contributing to it. Until recently not much was known of substance about steelhead and much of what was believed true has turned out to be biological superstition or hearsay. Scientists had uncovered few solid facts. Fish leave their natal river environment and go to sea for some indeterminate length of time. Where they go and what they do there is part of the mystery—the vast oceanic unknown. But specific information is beginning to appear. Some of it is astonishing. Data from high-seas tagging experiments and reports from commercial fishermen obliged to report oddities in their net catches indicate that steelhead travel great distances in a short length of time.

For instance, a 21-inch summer run—one which weighed probably less than three pounds—covered 1700 miles in 37 days. This is an average of 46 miles a day! A Soleduc River steelhead was tagged by a Japanese research vessel 3700 miles from the Washington coast. That's a long way to migrate, even for a salmonid. And afterwards the fish had to swim all the way back to its native river to spawn. Simply amazing.

Much of the little that we know is deceptive, too. That is, we don't know it for a fact and may be wrong about what we observe. A steelhead may be nearer to spawning than it appears from its coloration—or it may be farther away. Color is a test, but not always a good one. Without killing a fish, or subjecting it to an examination which might harm it, it is hard to tell from appearances alone how near to spawning a fish may be. A dark male may be a long ways off, in the process of spawning, or else spawned out. With females an extended vent (the point where eggs come out) is a sure sign of a ripe fish. It is either spawning or soon will be.

In the past I've made some basic errors in fish biology based on what I thought I saw. Yet I keep learning and each year make fewer such mistakes. My hope is that my field experience is developing in a way that can be depended on. More and more I trust it and find it indispensable. When in doubt I seek out fishers with more experience than mine or with professional biology training. Fortunately there are some fine men and women in this field who willingly will share their considerable knowledge.

One man I know and trust who has looked at thousands of fish is Curt Kraemer. He is Area Biologist for Region Four of the Washington State Department of Wildlife. He is also a skilled fisher. We got to know each other during the political/environmental effort to save Deer Creek. His beat includes many of the best steelhead streams in the Puget Sound area, but he knows many other rivers well, including some in Canada and the Eastern part of our state that form the tributaries of the Columbia and Snake. He is a keen observer of what is going on in the woods, and knows his birds and animals well.

Curt has observed that summer-run steelhead ascending freshwater pass through four stages before spawning, four to 12 months later. The first is when they enter the river and proceed upstream at their own pace, lingering here, hurrying there, according to their bio-rhythms. Their arrival may take place anytime between March and September, though the bulk of the run shows up late in June. It is everybody's favorite time to fish, for the weather is mild and warm, and fresh fish are strong, beautifully bright, and ready takers.

Historically most wild summer fish have spent only one year in saltwater and are called accordingly one-salt fish. They may be three to six pounds in weight and tend soon to become trouty in behavior; they will take food and often are good dry-fly fish. Hatchery fish, selected for their larger size, have parents that have spent two or three years in saltwater and will do so themselves. Thus they have more time in which to feed and grow bigger. Two-salt fish will run from five to nine pounds, while three-salts may go eight to 14 pounds or larger. They move upriver at a rate of six or seven miles per day and sometimes do so just under the surface in daylight hours. They are most active early and late in the day, however—near dawn and at dusk.

Once they reach the area in which they will spend their long summer they look for places of security and comfort. This is the second phase, their summer staging area. Soon they become more difficult to catch. It is a frustrating time for fishermen, for as a river recedes to its summer level they can see the fish in the pools. The fish can see the anglers, too, and grow easily spooked. They are dour and strike at unpredictable times, so anglers keep casting over them, hoping for a taking period, which is infrequent. The fish are resident in the pool, very much at home there, and move about freely in their deep runs to find cool, highly oxygenated water and sanctuary lies to their liking.

As fall approaches summer-run steelhead move to staging area three. Often this is a considerable distance upstream. With the increase in water volume and turbidity their need for caution lessens and they occupy not so protected lies; they behave more as they did during stage one, when they ascended the river, and are more vulnerable during steady high flows. Fishermen have a second good opportunity to catch them now, provided the fish haven't already reached the remote high country where wild fish are born. Hatchery steelhead gang up near to where they were planted—generally within a hundred yards of their rearing ponds and tributary creeks. There they are easily found and fished over. After each high water in October, November, and early December sizeable numbers of steelhead arrive and occupy upper-reach pools and riffles. It is where hordes of anglers await them.

Meanwhile the wild fish have reached the headwaters of their parent rivers where they remain relatively inactive in cold water of bedrock canyons for five or six months until they spawn in spring. This is difficult country to reach and only the intrepid fisher will attempt to follow them there. The fish are generally safe, except for the occasional poacher who will try to snag them, dynamite their pools, or trap them in gillnets. Their rugged, remote locations protect them, for poachers tend to be lazy.

Both wild and hatchery steelhead finally reach their fourth stage, which is adjacent to the redds. Spawning time is near. In some parts of the West they become icebound all winter; in spring, with the thaw, they become active again and will take the flies or lures readily. Since they are yet unspawned they need special protection now. And after they've spawned a few may return to the sea to recover, grow, and spawn again. Winter runs have a greater survival rate than summers. In the Columbia/Snake system no steelhead are believed to survive to return to spawn again. This is a sad fact of life, because it is summer runs that especially need bolstering in most rivers.

Curt's description of steelhead and their staging areas is useful, especially to the beginning angler who knows little about the lives of migratory fish. Most of us have noticed much the same thing, but have not formulated or articulated it so specifically, perhaps because we do not have a scientific bent. Having Curt's observations at hand helps us see the process as a continuous one that repeats itself each year with only minor variations.

Winter Runs

Originally all the rivers of the West that drain into the Pacific Ocean had runs of winter steelhead, unless there was some natural obstruction to prevent them from reaching suitable spawning gravel. A boy growing up in the Pacific Northwest expected to find a river near his home with a decent run of winter steelhead in it. Time and over-fishing took its toll of the wild fish. Hatcheries were built in response to public demand for better fishing. Producing hatchery fish contributed to the decline of wild fish, because more wild ones were caught as increased numbers of anglers went out in winter in response to so many more hatchery fish in the rivers.

Today the winter run is comprised mainly of hatchery fish and the Indians get first crack at them per regulations following the Boldt Decision. Often they are allowed to take more than half the run deemed available under the concept of maximum sustainable harvest. This is permitted to compensate them for their half of the summer fish, which they do not target in Western Washington. In the Eastern part of the state there are only summer-run fish and the Indian catch is a mix of wild and hatchery steelhead. Indians are concerned over the diminished numbers of wild fish, too, and are lobbying hard for their protection.

Fishermen grew angry and became discouraged when their favorite riffles no longer produced fish early in winter. They blamed the Indian fishery. Many gave up fishing and stopped buying fishing licenses. This produced a loss in revenue just when Wildlife needed it most. Other fishers began to look at the prospect of fishing for wild fish solely for pleasure and releasing them unharmed. Many of us shifted our fishing emphasis to times when the Indian nets weren't in the river. Usually this meant late spring and early fall, instead of all winter and summer—our traditional times.

Because the runs of wild fish returning in the spring were too small to be harvested, special regulations were enacted which permitted fishing only on a catch-and-release basis. In many ways this marked an improvement in the *quality* of the fishing. Often these fish were much bigger, too. Not only fly was allowed, but fly dominated, especially during low-water flows when gear fishing lost much of its efficiency. No longer did you see a fish killed or a dead one carried up the beach. The change took some getting used to for many. Some didn't make the transition. Lots lost interest in fishing when they weren't allowed to kill a fish. This reduced the crowds considerably and the rest of us benefitted.

I found that I liked the change and caught more fish than previously. They were bigger, too. The fact that I couldn't kill them fitted in perfectly with my evolution as an angler. I had probably killed too many steelhead during the past decades; more than my share. Not to kill became—if not a form of penance—a worthwhile compensation for past actions. Others began to think as I did. This marked a major change in our value systems.

It also led to a new esthetics of angling, one in which the day's success was not measured by the number or the weight of the bag being brought home. There were other aspects to an enjoyable day spent afield and they counted for more in the broad scheme of things. There was the change of seasons, the fluctuations in the river's flow, the vagaries of the weather. Also, if you didn't kill your fish, there was no sound biological reason for closed water. New regulations permitted longer seasons. My greatest pleasure came from being able to fish anytime my schedule allowed, winter or summer.

To fish a river year-round, without closures, provides the chance to get to know one river exceedingly well. Or, I suppose, to get to know many rivers a little less well. The North Fork of the Stillaguamish was my home river and had been for decades. Now I could get to know it even more intimately. There lay a challenge that would last a lifetime. No, one lifetime was not long enough to do the job, but it was all the opportunity any of us has been accorded. It would have to do.

I rose to the occasion. From time to time other rivers called out and I grudgingly responded. But I always returned to the North Fork. It came first and occupied my primary attention. Such abiding and intense dedication produces many tangible rewards.

3

My Deer Creek

As A BOY GROWING UP in the Middle West (Chicago), never having seen a salmon or steelhead, their beautiful airflow design must have been inherent in the fuselage design of the model airplanes I built compulsively (and carelessly) out of balsa wood. The only fish I remember catching were bullheads and tiny perch. My family moved West when I was eleven and it wasn't until the following summer that I saw my first salmonid—a nine-inch brook trout caught by a fellow Boy Scout in Lake Constance, a high mountain lake in the Olympic National Park. There were so many underfed brookies present that he quickly grew bored and passed the rod over to me. I watched the single salmon egg on its hook sink down, down, into the pellucid depths, then disappear: A starving brookie had devoured the orange dot. My line tightened, the rod bowed, and I was hooked. We fried up those fish in flour and bacon grease, and they were delicious. Much of their flavor was the result of having caught them ourselves in a wilderness setting.

I began fishing in earnest the following spring and learned how to tie some basic flies, wet and dry, through the tutelage of Roy Patrick—though I fished mostly with spoons, Flatfish, and bait. Worms and single salmon eggs caught trout easily, while flies and flyfishing had an aura of difficulty or so my friends and I thought. It took years for me to learn that when conditions are right, and often they are, flies are the deadliest way of catching trout both big and small. I think my experience is typical of boys and men in my part of the country, at least those who keep fishing with deadly earnestness year after year.

A boy transported to the Pacific Northwest learns about steelhead early. They are widely known to be big, sea-going trout, mysterious in their habits. Their size, the lack of knowledge about exactly where they go in the ocean, their supposed fickleness in taking bait or fly, their great fighting ability—these qualities combine to create an irresistible appeal.

It took many years before I caught my first steelhead, but then they arrived reasonably fast, which encouraged me. Today they're about all I will fish for. All the while I pursued trout as a boy, and grew good at it, the prospect of steelhead lay in the back of my mind. I knew they were the real challenge. Someday soon I would be big and knowledgeable enough to take them on.

My father was a nonfisher, a patient man who would sometimes drive his eager son to the North Fork of the Stillaguamish River about sixty miles from Seattle over a route that was difficult and slow, for it was laced with stoplights. The trip took two and one-half hours. Since the building of the interstate it takes half that time. Instead of constituting a full day's excursion I can zoom up to the river for an evening's easy fishing.

The appeal was the series of great fishing holes that extended downstream from the mouth of Deer Creek at the hamlet of Oso. The creek was mother to a race of wild summer steelhead that brought world-class anglers to the North Fork, where the fish gathered until a rise in water levels permitted them to enter the creek's closed waters. There they leisurely moved from pool to pool, riffle to riffle, until the following spring when they laid their eggs in the gravel of some remote reach. Two months or so later the fry hatched and remained in the gravel until they had absorbed their egg-sack remnants and were strong enough to hold their own in the swift, shallow current along the edge.

At first both creek and river were fished with bait, which was deadly. A small group of anglers caught so many fish that early conservationists demanded the Department of Game (now Wildlife) enact protective regulations. Ken McLeod, Enos Bradner, and Walt Johnson led the way, with backing from the Washington Fly Fishing Club. Accordingly, Deer Creek was closed to all fishing in the late '30s and the North Fork restricted to fishing with the artificial fly during the long summer season. Since steelhead are not caught so readily as with bait, the restriction reduced the annual kill and allowed more fish to escape into Deer Creek. It provided better sport, too.

The creek is famous. Zane Grey was among the first notables to fish it. He pronounced it "the most beautiful trout water I had ever seen. Clear as crystal, cold as ice, it spoke eloquently of the pure springs of the mountain fastness." Two decades later Roderick Haig-Brown described it as "beautiful, clear, bright and fast, tumbled on rocks and gravel bars."

The North Fork wasn't the only river near Seattle that contained wild summer-run steelhead, but it was the best, for its fish would take flies and its riffles and pools were easily covered by a wading angler. About 250 to 400 fish were taken annually. Ken McLeod estimated that in the river's best year probably a thousand fish were caught and killed. He thought another thousand fish escaped to spawn. Ken's contribution to steelhead flyfishing is enormous. He became my friend and, I suppose more than anybody else, my mentor. I learned a lot from him. Many did.

Fish biologists are using Ken's figures to help establish the original size of the run. Anecdotal, they may be a little high. The run probably numbered two thousand fish at best. That's not a lot of steelhead, but is typical of good summer-run rivers throughout the West.

Deer Creek ran high enough throughout June for good escapement. Instead of piling up at the mouth the fish moved up over the lip and entered the creek. Thus fishers only had a brief chance to catch them. It wasn't until July that the fish began accumulating under low-water conditions in the North Fork. Fishing was seldom easy and reduced flows made it tougher. When fish were caught it was usually early in the morning, before the first rays struck the water's surface and made the fish wary. These conditions persisted until a good freshet arrived in mid-August. Then the fish escaped into the sanctuary water.

One night my father and I camped out near the Elbow Hole where there was a little park. It was next to the property owned by Ralph Wahl. Dad had a mattress on the ground and I the ground itself. He snored; I had forgotten how loud he could snore. To get away from the roar and find some sleep I rolled along in the opposite direction, turning over and over in my sleeping bag until I accomplished considerable distance. In the morning I was more than a hundred feet away. He was up and starting to dress. We ate some breakfast my mother had provided. I think it was cold scrambled eggs, sweet rolls, and tepid coffee from a thermos.

On one such trip I caught my first steelhead from a tiny trickle the fish would have vacated the moment sunlight struck the water. Most of the time I caught nothing—perhaps a salmon in the fall. The time I remember best was when we fished the Deer Creek Riffle at first light. We wore hip boots with slick rubber cleats. Knowledgeable fishers donned felt. Dad's feet shot out from under him and he landed on his back in the shallows, unhurt but soaked. That ended the day's fishing for him, and he was satisfied to sit on the stones and watch the sun rise in the sky while I fished until my enthusiasm at catching nothing dimmed. I never loved my father more than on that day.

My first serious girl friend, Cary, could borrow her father's old

Dodge, and she would pack us lunches and drive us to lowland lakes in the spring where we caught trout. And in summer she took me to my favorite river. She was a fine girl and even without the car I would have loved her. She took me to the river because she knew how important it was to me. And she was too wise at sixteen ever to ask me to choose between her and fishing. She thought she knew what the answer would be. Which is not to say that I wouldn't have said "her," only that she couldn't depend on me saying that and didn't want to hear the other. She didn't go to college and I did. This often marks the end of a relationship and it did ours. Soon she had a husband and a baby. I can't say I was happy for her.

In college I met a girl I liked a lot. One day she and I went to the mountains in the used Chevy I bought with my money from working for the railroad. It was March, but wintry still. We headed for the Sauk River. The Sauk runs milky most of the year, being glacially fed. Today it wore only a slight clay cast. A little creek entered the river just outside of the logging town of Darrington. True to its name, Clear Creek rarely ran dirty even in the worst of weather.

Patchy snow lay on the ground. A narrow trail followed the creek a short distance up from its mouth. At one point the trail became etched into the side of steep rock. It was not particularly dangerous, but care had to be taken to avoid a tumble into the shallows of the icy pool below. Celeste and I picked our way along the wall until we came to an easier part, which we scampered along. The stream bank was bedrock, and covered with green moss and slime; spray kept it wet at all times. The day was nippy and the wind howled. Ahead the trail petered out against a wall steeper than before.

We turned back. The light had shifted and was failing, and we were able to see well into the lime-colored water of the deep canyon pool. Just above the water entered in a white plume. Two coho salmon—each red in the body and green at the head—were spawning in the clean stones at the tail of the pool where the water fanned out. We could see the fish as easily as if the river contained no water and the fish were levitated in mid-air.

First the female prepared the nest. The motion of her body and tail were violent and abrupt, as though she were angry with the little time left on her biological clock. Her motion was surprisingly sexual; she fairly humped those stones. My girl stood near me, both because she was cold and because she was affectionate. She wasn't interested in the fish, but I was enthralled. What we were witnessing was a holy act. The cold was bothering her, I could tell. Still I lingered. Finally she tugged at my sleeve and we left.

A couple of years later I stood with a different girl at the end of a dock jutting out into Lake Washington in a part of Seattle named Windermere. It is where brain surgeons live. Our entrance to the private beach club was possible because Janet's parents owned a fine home nearby. The day was one in June and balmy. We had dated regularly for a couple of months, but lately things had turned sour. Tonight we faced a crisis. She had some points to make. My role was to listen. Her words took on a melancholy tone. I grew restless, and began to shift my weight on my feet.

Nearby on some bushes insects were hatching out and drifting in clusters onto the lake. The water was a mirror and the flies hung a few inches over the surface before they settled. Trout began rising, a few at first, then a whole lot. They made a slurping sound. I tried to listen to what Janet was saying, but my ears were filled with the sound of hungry trout. They were taking mayflies—*Ephemerella* spinners, probably. I was out of my head with fish lust. In the trunk of my car parked only a hundred yards away was my flyrod and reel. A tiny Adams dry was the order of the evening. If not, a nymph of the same coloration.

Janet continued to review our case. Yes, yes—when would enough be said? What had gone wrong, she wondered aloud? I had no idea. Let's say goodbye, she urged. I was agreeable; a rise of trout lasts but a short while. The fish get full and the insect population depleted. She began to define our problems. Soon only a few lazy rings marred the lake. The hatch was over. It was nearly dark. Dispirited I walked Janet back to the car and drove her the short distance home. She dashed into the house in tears.

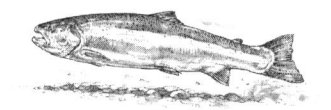

I graduated, entered graduate school in English, staved off the draft for a year, then was called for my physical and induction during the Korean War. An early discharge allowed me to return to college. I met a wonderful girl in a library and things followed the normal course. Berkeley offered me a scholarship and teaching position. I accepted eagerly. But—once away from Norma—I was filled with a terrible loneliness and longing. She drove down to California with a friend on a week's innocent vacation. We rushed back to Seattle and got married, all within the week before my classes started. I got my Master's and began writing, sometimes for a little money, but it was never much. I took a job as an editor. She entered graduate school and got her Master's in Librarianship. At the time it seemed to me we were preparing for a life of poverty. At least I would have my fishing to sustain me.

During our courtship my wife tried fishing and found it was not for her. But she was happy accompanying me out to a lake or stream on a mild day and would sit on the bank, reading. I think many new wives do this.

Five years later she was pregnant and I took a job that I hated at Boeing. They promoted me to supervisor and I hated them even more. That summer, with a baby in diapers, we came across the Oso cabin while on a day trip and impulsively rented it. We took it for "the season," which was July and August. When August ended we were offered the cabin for the following year at the price for the previous season—only two months. We snapped it up. Having the cabin restored my tranquility and promised a pastoral interlude at the end of a trying week. If we had longer than a day away my family went with me. In time she and my son each developed his own special use and affection for the river and the countryside nearby.

The camp at Oso at the mouth of Deer Creek became central to my life. Rivers are like that. Our cabins had wood stoves and rusty water that came out of a pipe from a shallow well. It was undrinkable, so we drew our day's supply from the creek. It was best to get it early, for families at the swimming hole just upstream would muddy it up by ten in the morning. The creek was pristine and the "mud" that troubled us was only a little sand that had been stirred up. We were fastidious city-dwellers, whose usual water was polluted with chlorine.

At Oso the creek was crossed by a highway and a railroad bridge about a hundred yards above the confluence. I remember standing on the tracks and looking down into a pool that must have been fifteen feet deep. Hundreds of steelhead fingerlings clotted the shallows. By the highway bridge, where the creek ran fast and the bottom was strewn with boulders, often we could make out the ghostly shapes of seven- and eight- pound steelhead lying low in the creek and awaiting rain to move them along. Upstream a half-mile or so was a box canyon that in low

Camp at Oso, Mouth of Deer Creek.

water they could not ascend; it was their furthermost point until the river became swollen with rain. The canyon was where they held until shortly before spawning. Then they moved into the shallow riffles that extended to the headwaters. This was on Forest Service land where—out of sight and sound—miles of clearcutting was taking place along roads newly pushed into the wilderness for just this purpose.

The creek closure and restriction of the North Fork to flyfishing worked well as a conservation measure for several decades. It wasn't until the early '60s that a handful of us (I was a grown man now) grew fearful for the future of the run because of environmental degradation we knew was taking place along the creek. This was due entirely to clearcut logging. The watershed had multiple ownerships, but all it was used for was the growing of timber. Until recently the cuts were entirely old growth.

Friends in camp from British Columbia raised the first alarms when the creek began to muddy with only a little rain and was slow to clear. They had seen their streams near Vancouver deteriorate and lose their summer-run steelhead populations because of ruined habitat. Jerry

Wintle was a fine fisher who regularly visited our river. He urged us to release our fish. He and Bob Taylor, another Canadian, had the cabin next to my wife and mine. We became weekend fishing friends and often took our vacations together here at the season's peak. Ed Weinstein was another friend who leased a cabin in the Oso cluster.

Jerry said that if we didn't start putting our fish back soon we wouldn't have any to fish for. He was an effective fisherman. Often he would release fish throughout the weekend, then—an hour or so before dark and a return to Vancouver—decide he wanted one for "Mum." He was single and his mother liked to eat fish. So he would fish hard into the mounting darkness and usually nail one right at the mandatory quitting time. But in the course of a season he never killed more than a few. All the rest he carefully released. This was at a time when fish were abundant and men tried to kill as many as they could. There was pride and skill involved in catching and killing large numbers of steelhead. It was your routine *macho* act.

Bob and Ed and I knew Jerry was right. Though we never caught as many as he we began following his example. I remember my first released fish and how strange it seemed. Jerry and I were fishing the Flat Water together and he watched me ease my fish onto the beach. Before I could reach it he unhooked it and sent it on its way. I hadn't so much touched it. In fact I hadn't made up my mind whether to release it or not—I was still thinking it over. Probably I wouldn't have. Of course I was indignant.

"In the future I'll release my own fish," I told him, not realizing it was a vow.

Few put back fish then. Besides our small group I can't think of anybody except Sid Pierce. It usually took many hours to hook a steelhead and the last thought in anybody's mind was to give it back to the river. To do so was antagonistic, perverse. So we were not very popular. Things changed greatly in the decades to come. On our river it started with us. Today many anglers routinely release their fish, especially wild trout and steelhead. It has grown commonplace to see it done.

In spite of Jerry's warnings we felt the chance of losing our steelhead run through over-harvest or habitat loss was remote. Logging took place far away. Rarely did we hear the chainsaw's whine. Many of the loggers were our friends and were housed in camp. We saw them drag home, weary and battered after a hot day's work off in the hills. It was a hard, dangerous way to make a living and they were only doing what they were told to do when they denuded whole hillsides. We respected them and did not envy their jobs one bit. We warm-weather sports were a bunch of sissies in comparison.

Fishing remained good. Oh, one year the run might be weak, but the next year generally made up for it. And in some years there were a great number of steelhead in the river, splashing nightly in the pools. We took their return for granted.

Up until the mid-'60s the only summer-run steelhead in the North Fork were wild Deer Creek fish. Then concurrent with a gradual reduction in their numbers a hatchery run was introduced. These fish were planted more than half a dozen miles upstream and were carefully segregated from the wild Deer Creek race to prevent in-breeding. This was vital. Equally important was not to let a run of summer steelhead start to rear in the upper river and compete with the wild winter runs for space and the limited supply of food.

The Wildlife Department urged fishermen to kill *all* their hatchery steelhead. It was an idea that greatly disturbed those of us who had discovered the great satisfaction of releasing a steelhead and watching it swim away. So we defiantly put many of our hatchery fish back, relying on others to rid the river of these fine, biologically unwanted fish.

We kept the cabin for 23 years. The run of Deer Creek steelhead entered its period of rapid decline, as Jerry had warned us, in spite of the efforts of a handful of us not to kill any wild fish. More and more the good fishing was to be found upstream—for the hatchery fish. It was a sad loss, we agreed, but an unescapable one. Logging probably caused it, but logging was the mainstay of the region.

After a decade or so in the cabin I started looking for land of my own. It took a long time. When I finally found what I wanted I continued renting the Oso cabin for a few years longer. It had conveniences that a piece of raw land did not—such as a roof when it rained, and a woodstove when it was cold, and beds when any of the three of us grew sleepy. It was not until we had implemented all of these on the new property that we gave up the rental cabin. Friends were waiting for it.

Having one's own riverfront was the fulfillment of a life's dream, but at the time it seemed nothing special, only another goal accomplished. Most of the land for sale was floodplain. Neither the sellers nor the real estate agents bothered to point this out to us. It was hard for us to discern in many cases. Floodplain often has trees growing on it. It has profuse shrubs and bushes. But it has sand deposits in its dips and some are from last winter. You can see the high-water mark in the form of a line of scummy leaves left from when the river starts to recede.

A mistake can be costly. Often the county won't let you build in the floodplain. And if you do anyway the results are disastrous. My criterion was that the land must be waterfront, but it didn't have to be on the North Fork. It could be on a tributary creek. It might be on Deer Creek, for instance—the river's most important tributary and its biggest. But Deer Creek flooded regularly and widely. This made it unsuitable for building purposes—at least for me.

The place we found was in a short-platted area called Stillaguamish Meadows—only nobody ever calls it that except the real estate people. People who live there simply say they are going "up to the river." Anybody who doesn't understand what is meant lives away and possesses a different value system.

Stillaguamish Meadows lies a mile up the Whitman Road, which deadends a few hundred yards beyond our turnoff. This is ideal. It is an area I had never fished, hadn't bothered to, for it was located in a flat region of a canyon midway up the river. Directly opposite us was a steep bank covered in alders, maples, and tall cedars. Across the river opposite us ran the Burlington Northern Railroad. The tracks began in Arlington and ended at the huge Summit Timber Mill in Darrington. However, the tracks were nicely obscured by river foliage. All we could ever see was wildness.

Each morning an empty train ran up the river, headed East to the mill; each night the train returned, laden with lumber and sawdust destined for a plant in Everett where it was made into Presto-logs. The land's natural configuration resembled a set-aside for a long narrow park. In time it will become one, because the railroad spur has been abandoned and the county is acquiring the right-of-way.

I looked at two lots before I bought mine. Both had physical drawbacks and didn't "sit" the land well. The third was not advertised in town, but had a large sign on the property stating that it was for sale. I risked a trespass and took a closer look. Like the Baby Bear's porridge bowl this one was just right, with a sloping bank and a beach that was emerging into a gravel shoal as the river dropped. Many attractive boulders rose out in the center of the river. I wrote down the phone number of the agency.

It remained for Norma to see the property, for her judgment in land matters is superior to mine. She liked it. I called the agent. He said the price was $3950. I didn't quibble. Five years later, knowing my neighbor on the upstream side rarely visited his land, I contacted him and asked if he wanted to sell. He said he didn't think so. Did I detect uncertainty? Each of our lots was seventy-five feet wide; together they would comprise a one-hundred and fifty-foot hedge against crowding.

I kept after him. Finally he said he'd sell for $5000. I said I'd pay it. He offered me a quit-claim deed. I said I wanted a title search, with the owner to pay for it, since I hadn't tried to chisel him down on the asking price. We shook hands on the deal. All along he wanted to sell, but didn't want to seem eager. Well, all along I wanted to buy. It is how famous deals are made.

In August, with earnest money down on the first piece of property, I sat on a lawnchair in the shallows, studying my domain, luxuriating in the joys of ownership. My companions were caddis creepers and salmonid fry. They were all I needed.

The first day I didn't want to leave and return to town, not even when it grew dark. So I slept down by the water's edge on an army-surplus foam mattress I had brought along for that purpose. There was no tarp or tent to cover me, nor did I need one, for it was warm, the sky salted with August's stars.

I'll swear I studied them half the night. I was up there in heaven. Gradually I calmed down and reality returned and I slept. But I never took the river property for granted. In time it came to matter rather more than less to me. I got to know every dip and swell of the land, the composition of the soils beneath the surface, the names of the trees and shrubs, the depth and rate of flow of the groundwater and its table as a separate entity from the river itself.

Since then the river and its life—flora and fauna and fish—have been subjects of my constant concern.

4

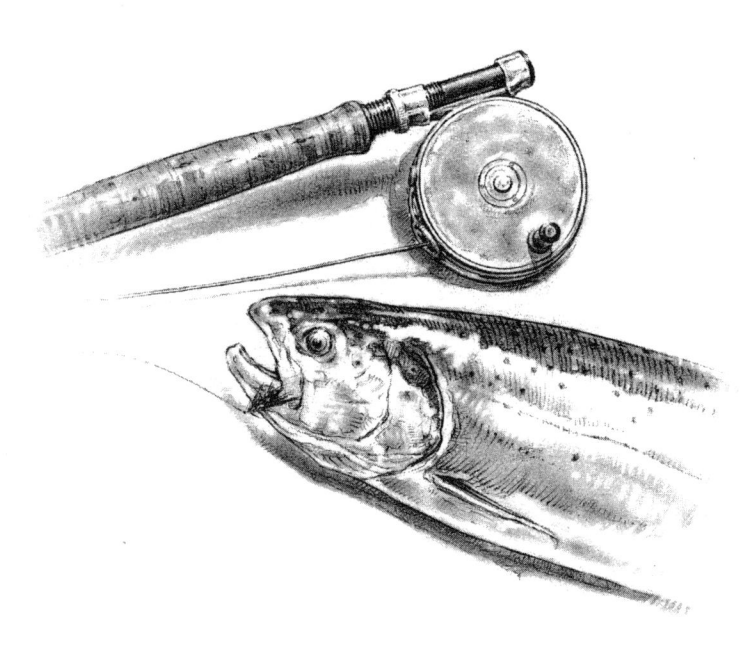

Let's Hear It For The Hatchery Fish

Fishing grows unpleasantly crowded on the best water at the height of the season. To stand in a line-up—especially one that doesn't move at a perceptible rate—takes away the joy from a day's fishing. But one can always go elsewhere on a good stream and find a fair chance of hooking fish in a run that isn't so popular or so heavily flogged. When you do this you may find your pleasure in fishing returning. At least it's worth a try before you quit for the day or for good.

You can have an enjoyable time searching out secondary water and learning how to fish it. And fishing for anadromous fish such as steelhead is always filled with hope, for a pool may be devoid of fish, one day, and the next hold many of them. A fish may be of record size, too. This is why hatchery fish—especially the summer runs—provide opportunities never previously so available.

For decades my top two summer runs weighed about eleven pounds. They were wild fish; in fact, until 1960 or so, there were no successful hatchery plants. In a given season on my favorite river the top fish often weighted no more than ten pounds. Though eight and nine-pounders were fairly common the one-salt wild fish rarely went larger. And when a bigger one was brought in to be weighed it proved to be an unspawned winter fish, which put it in an entirely different category.

I've since caught hatchery summer runs that went over eighteen pounds. Most years our local rivers produce fish of fourteen to sixteen pounds. They are big, they are strong, they are beautiful—so let's hear it for the hatchery fish. Except perhaps genetically they are in no way inferior to the wild fish. Without hatchery fish in our rivers today we'd have slim pickings.

Hatchery summer-run stocks in much of the West derive from brood developed at the Skamania Hatchery on the Washougal River. It is a dependable stock, known for producing large fish that stay at sea for two or three years and obtain impressive growth. And they often return earlier than wild fish, which is a mixed blessing. But they are disease prone. IHN (Infectious Hematopoietic Necrosis) disease—especially under hatchery conditions—will often infect a year's class of eggs and fry, and they will have to be destroyed.

Nobody knows these fish and their wild counterpart so well as Bill McMillan, who has lived most of his life on the banks of the beautiful Washougal. He despises the hatchery fish. I think he overlooks their broad appeal because of the harm they have caused to wild-fish populations on his home river. This is understandable. Hatchery fish tend to hasten upstream in large numbers on the first high water. They home to where they were planted and do not distribute themselves evenly throughout the system as wild fish do. They gang up in deep pools and sulk there until they are all caught out. They are not ready takers, but tend to "go on the bite" in the manner of trout in lakes. This produces mobs of fishers that pound a single holding pool all hours of the day.

Bill has gathered data which indicates that the planting of hatchery fish reduces the wild fish population of a river and not just through increased fishing pressure. Fewer fish return, he says, than before the hatchery fish were introduced. He urges that rivers, especially his

Washougal, be managed for their wild fish populations. I agree. But he argues that stocking with hatchery fish should be halted everywhere. Catch-and-release fishing, he maintains, can be used to stop the killing of precious wild stocks while they are allowed to rebound naturally. It is a position I respect, but do not entirely agree with.

I love the hatchery fish and believe most of our rivers would be nearly empty if it were not for hatcheries. I have seen many rivers reduced to this terrible state. Nothing is worse than a barren river. I would prefer to see hatchery stocks segregated from wild ones through intelligent management. Hatchery fish should not be allowed to spawn and compete with wild fish or take vital rearing habitat away from wild stocks, either summer or winter. But I find it hard to believe that wild stocks will rebound, given the extent of river-habitat degradation throughout the West. It is too much to expect, however devoutly it is wished for.

Most of the destruction is from timber harvest or its side effects such as road building. Wild fish populations are no longer able to recover and reestablish the levels necessary for rebuilding. The damage is too great. So we become more and more dependent upon enlightened hatchery production. And anglers expect to bring home a steelhead for the table every once in a while. It is reasonable, for they are superb eating.

Hatchery supplementation of wild steelhead runs is so prevalent that without it most rivers would have few fish in them, winter or summer, certainly not enough to allow the killing of even a small annual number. And the fisheries biologists for the various Indian tribes, especially those East of the Cascades, maintain that hatchery steelhead and salmon have been planted in such large numbers for so many years that their inbreeding with reduced wild or native stocks has so diluted the wild runs that, genetically speaking, wild fish no longer exist. For practical purposes, they say, wild fish are extinct. What we have today are progeny of hatchery fish that have spawned successfully in the rivers in which they were planted and have produced a run of adapted fish, neither native nor hatchery. These are the new "wild" fish, which are not really wild at all. But they are important because they have demonstrated the ability to survive under difficult circumstances. Arguably they are the best of what can be found in many of our rivers.

Fish East of the Cascades pose a little different situation. They are solely summer runs and have overcome great hurdles, coming and going, in the form of multiple dams. When Grand Coulee was built, and after it the many other dams on the Columbia and Snake rivers, the abundant runs of salmon and steelhead were doomed. They became fractions of themselves. Recently Snake River populations of sockeye salmon and several races of chinook salmon have been listed as threatened or endangered, a condition which has been well publicized. Most runs of coho are listed as critical. This has led to greatly increased hatchery production of salmon and steelhead in the name of dam mitigation, but has resulted in an increased awareness of the need for natural production. How to achieve it is the problem.

The Wenatchee is one stream in which the policy of supplementation through planting of hatchery steelhead is working with some degree of success. It also illustrates the problems involved in trying to increase wild runs of steelhead and salmon in a river system that is still affected by the dams and spillways that caused the runs to be depleted in the first place. To say that supplementation in the Wenatchee (and Methow and Grande Ronde and Snake) has been a success is not exactly true. But each of these rivers is experiencing a recovery of wild steelhead, bolstered by hatchery plants, that bodes well for the future. (By wild I probably should explain that I include any progeny of hatchery fish that have been born, reared, and smolted in the river, and have survived at sea to return again to the river to spawn. These are fish that have an unclipped adipose fin and consequently can be readily identified.)

The original wild steelhead of the Wenatchee looked different from its fish of today. They were a blunt-nosed, stocky race that resembled the B-race Snake River fish, but of course were smaller than those. They returned over a three-year cycle. By the 1970s they had been reduced greatly. Stocking of smolts from selected Columbia River broodstock began in 1964; these were fish trapped at Priest Rapids Dam and were destined for the upper Columbia system—the Wenatchee, Entiat, and Methow tributaries. And sometimes stock from other Columbia hatcheries was mixed in, such as fish trapped and reared at Ringold. The Ringold fish were of Skamania origin. Since 1985 stock has been obtained from fished trapped at Wells Dam, which probably narrows the genetic window of these fish slightly when compared to the earlier Priest Rapids stock.

In 1983 the river was restricted to catch-and-release fishing and returning fish exceeded their escapement goal, so there was great fishing, perhaps the best ever here. The escapement goal is a mix of wild and hatchery fish, and is determined by subtracting the count of fish over Wells Dam from those counted at Priest Rapids; these are all presumed to be headed up the Wenatchee. Depending on who you talk to in the Department of Wildlife, the escapement goal for the Wenatchee is either

Typical six-pound hatchery hen, with adipose

3000 or 4800 steelhead. (The former figure is cited in department literature for the Columbia system, while the second is Larry Brown's reasoned guess of the river's need. Larry is area fish biologist, Curt's counterpart on the East Side, and knows the river well.)

By the early 1980s the river was getting decent returns again, with hatchery fish dominating but the wild component slowly increasing. There are upper limits to what can be expected from wild production and a 20 percent return of parent stock is resulting under present conditions. This is how it works: if the returning wild run numbers 5000 fish (and I wish it did) the adults would be capable of producing about 100,000 smolts. The smolts, however, because of losses of about ten percent at each of the dams, will only return about 1000 adult fish. So to expect the wild fish to replenish themselves and build up the run all by themselves is unrealistic. For the run to increase it must be bolstered, or supplemented, by both spawning hatchery fish and the annual plants of hatchery smolts. Each year 280,000 to 350,000 hatchery smolts are planted. Most are paid for with federal money for dam mitigation. This not only improves returns of adults, but is imperative to preservation of the so-called wild run. Under current regulations some hatchery fish are allowed to spawn. And of course all the wild fish must be released for this purpose.

By early November 80 percent of the run is in the river. During the next three weeks the fishing is often at its best. Then the water becomes too cold and the fish grow uncooperative. They move around little and soon the river is locked up by ice. No more fish will be entering until spring freshets. The tally can begin. To figure out the true escapement biologists subtract the adjusted punchcard kill data from the figures obtained from the dam counts. Punchcards now require the angler to record whether a caught fish is wild or of hatchery origin (that is, whether it is missing an adipose fin). An adjustment is made for unpunched fish. Biologists also factor in a tiny figure for losses of fish from natural mortality in the river and from catch and release.

At the start of the decade the number of returning wild fish had increased to 1000 to 1500 fish. Returning hatchery adults greatly added to the numbers of fish able to spawn. This is called recruitment. In 1983 about twice the escapement goal was reached, or 9700 fish, both wild and hatchery. Another great year was 1985. The next two years were good, but not great ones. In 1988 and '89 the runs were greatly reduced, even though plants of hatchery fish remained about the same. Meanwhile the wild fish were increasing to the point where they comprised 40 to 50 percent of the run. Larry feels 1000 to 1500 fish is probably the upper limit to the Wenatchee's capability for natural production, that is, for producing fish without help from the hatcheries.

This may not be the bad news it seems at first. The Wenatchee wild fish are clearly the product of intensive hatchery production over the past several decades and may have self-selected themselves genetically for maximum adaption to the river's particular environment. With hatchery bolstering from stocks that are determined to be genetically compatible the wild/hatchery mix may illustrate supplementation at its best. It is far from the ideal of building back a wild run to the point where it is self-sustaining, however. But it is probably as close as we can come in the Columbia system, because of so many life-destroying dams. They take a great toll of fish, both going and coming. The loss is estimated at about ten percent at each dam.

There are other factors that are important for a high return of adult fish to the Columbia. A vital one is sustained high-water flows during the spring, when the smolts must migrate 500 miles or more to the sea. Not only does each dam decimate them, but the vast distances they must swim through the slack water of the reservoirs causes great loses from exhaustion. (Higher water sweeps them along better and they don't have to swim so hard.) The good returns of the 1980s were all marked by large snowpacks and steady, high spring flows; 1988 and '89 were not.

Efforts are underway to try to prioritize maximum flows during the spring, but the many competing water interests all have strong voices and tend to cancel each other out. State fish agencies and the tribes are working together on water issues to help guarantee the fish enough water each year. Biologists believe that this will help increase salmon and steelhead runs more than any other single controllable factor. The Northwest Power Planning Council is swinging its considerable weight to help get more water for the fish, too, but political concerns cause divisions and conflict.

The life cycle of the Wenatchee River steelhead differs slightly from others. Typically a steelhead returns from early September through mid-November. If the river stays warm fish remain in the Columbia and do not ascend until the water height and water temperature stir them sufficiently. This is called the thermal-block condition. Conversely, if the Wenatchee is too cold or ice-bound in late autumn, the trapped fish are apt to remain in the Columbia and over-winter there, not ascending the Wenatchee until February or March when the ice goes out, the water warms somewhat, and the amount of visible light increases.

A hatchery fish is likely to have spent two years at sea and be of appropriate size, while a wild one is smaller and has spent but one year at sea. Yet there are numerous large wild fish that have obviously spent more than one year in the ocean and I catch some annually. The hatchery fish often ripen earlier and will commence spawning at the end of March during the heavy water of spring runoff; at this time the river is so high that predation by fishermen, birds, and animals poses little threat. The wild fish spawn later—in May, June, and into July. Both races utilize the entire length of the watershed, and spawning fish have been located as low as the city of Wenatchee and as high up as the Great Northern Tunnel. The majority uses the reaches between the end of Tumwater Canyon and Cashmere. These are all fish on their maiden spawning run; there are no repeat spawners in the Columbia system, at least not for planning purposes.

Larry Brown expresses deep concern over problems arising from the Indian gillnet fishery. It is not selective and takes wild fish just as readily as hatchery ones. He thinks the use of traps by the Indian fishers would protect wild fish, but knows the Indians are opposed to the idea because it does not seem natural to them and defeats the element of individual enterprise, which is important to them. He is also worried about the dropout rate from gillnets and the resulting loss of steelhead that benefits nobody. He says many Columbia River fish show net marks and sometimes only smaller fish get through the mesh. The commercial fishery for up-river bright chinooks coincides with the return of steelhead to the Columbia and claims many of them. Hence to the toll taken by the dams must be added the numbers taken legitimately by the Indian nets, plus those lost through dropout, which are wasted. There is no way wild steelhead can be protected under these conditions.

The steelhead has survived and endured in so many streams precisely because of its ability to adapt genetically to drastically changing environmental conditions, including disasters such as the eruption of Mt. Saint Helens and ones unknown to us in the long-ago past. While not having as wide genetic diversity as wild fish, hatchery steelhead seem to have enough to provide the continuity we seek today in rivers that have lost their anadromous populations. Seen in comparison with hatchery programs conducted elsewhere results from the Wenatchee experiment are more encouraging than we might expect. But problems from the dams, the non-selective net fishery, and low springtime water flows will keep this and other Columbia system rivers from ever reaching their wild potential. Until these problems are resolved it will be the hatcheries that are keeping fish coming back, whether we like the idea of hatcheries or not.

On the West slope of the Cascades many streams carry both summer runs and winter runs. The tribes are fishing only winter runs so far. To complicate matters further both runs have remnant wild components along with their hatchery fish. The hatchery summer steelhead begin arriving as early as March, build slowly to the end of May, and peak early in July. They ascend slowly throughout the low-water months of summer and into early fall. Many lie low down in the river in unaccessible locations and are less likely to be found by bands of roving fishers. Large reaches barred by farmers to fishermen's trespass help protect the fish. When the first hard rains of fall arrive, usually in October, fish ascend in large numbers to near to where they were planted, two or three years earlier. Fishing markedly improves. Often it is superb, both East and West. This is probably the best time of the year for fly fishing over the greatest number of fish.

After the first hard rain there is no fishing until the rivers begin to recede and clear. This may take days or weeks. October and November are often great months. I can remember several Thanksgiving Day fishing trips that ended in a blizzard, but had good fishing, though towards early dark the line froze in my guides and made casting near to impossible.

The fish of autumn are colorful—stale fish, fish that have been in the river a long time, but increased water flows and cooler temperatures have reactivated them. They provide good fishing and usually are strong fighters. Often they are big.

I rarely kill a fish anymore, even when the regulations permit me to.

The need of my small family is minimal. Fish biologists want to see these hatchery fish "harvested." They aren't needed to spawn and spawning is thought to be detrimental in streams that still have a wild-fish component. So this is a good time to kill one for the table or to give to a good friend.

Though they are dark from the river environment and may look less attractive than when they entered the river, their meat is firm and pink. They have a thick layer of ocean fat next to the skin, which makes them rich and tasty. The abundance of fall hatchery fish coincides nicely with the end of the farm harvest season and seems an appropriate end to the year. The idea is—with such abundance available—not to get greedy. Take what you need for a fresh meal or two, but do not freeze many or try to feed the world. Keep your kill within reason.

If you fish a lot you will soon catch more fish than you have good use for. You will develop the habit of releasing what you can't eat within a day or two. I think this is how catch and release got started, rather than to protect wild stocks or as a form of sportsmanship. It remains a sound principle.

5

Anatomy Lesson

IT IS IMPOSSIBLE, I'VE FOUND, TO ESCAPE for long from the basic biological facts of life. Catch a fish and kill it and you are immediately plunged (up to the elbows) in the slimy mystery of its anatomy. One day in the fall a number of years ago I returned home with a pair of seven-pound hatchery fish. They were the first fish I had killed in some time and I had a good use for them. My wife and I had guests for dinner that night and they were already there when I drove up. I dropped the fish on the front porch and greeted my friends. Then, while we were having our after-dinner coffee, I remembered the dead fish. Promptly cleaning fish and setting them out to hang is a practice I am fussy about. I excused myself and went right to work.

Gwen, David's wife, was a surgical nurse, who, during her school years, had worked as my secretary at the University. She followed me into the kitchen. As I opened up my first fish—clumsily, as usual, with a dull pocket knife—she watched. I became conscious of my poor technique—I rip and tear a lot. As I cut away she provided me with a running commentary, describing various anatomical aspects of what I was removing. I realized that I knew very little about what I was doing.

Though I had gutted hundreds of fish what came out of them piece by piece remained a bloody mystery. To Gwen it was all readily identifiable. As I removed each item she named it for me. Usually it was an important organ. I began to pay close attention. What I was doing was performing an autopsy.

I couldn't resist clowning around. I was the world-famous surgeon, she my assistant. She fell into the role easily, pleasantly. Here were the heart, the guts, the liver maybe, the eggs or milt; everything else belonged to the great unknown. She indicated the spleen, then the gall bladder. Interesting, those.

"This along the backbone," she said, pointing with the teaspoon that

I used to scrape away the clotted blood, "is the central nervous system." Actually it was the kidney, I later learned, and right below it the swim bladder. But maybe the nervous system was there, as well. If so it lay tight along the spine, so subtle, so gory, so hard to see, that the naked eye (and no eye is more naked than mine) could not spot it.

A few days later, in order to learn more, I checked out a curious little book from the University library—Smith and Bell's *A Practical Guide to the Anatomy and Physiology of Pacific Salmon*. At the start the authors state: "Salmonids are one of the most intensively studied, widely cultivated, extensively distributed, and avidly sought groups of fishes in the world. It is then surprising, therefore, to find there is so little basic information about the anatomy of salmonids." They add, "The skeleton. . . has probably received more attention than any other part because the skeleton has both taxonomic and evolutionary significance." It is also easy to prepare, store, and study. But the musculature of the salmon "has hardly been examined," they say. And "illustrations of the internal organs are surprisingly rare."

This is what I was after—the naming of parts and a quick means to identify them. Usually I just ripped them out, barehandedly, and laid them aside on newspaper, later to be thrown in the garbage. On the riverbank these are the parts the fisherman flings to the current. They are offal, the most unattractive aspects of the fish. To me they had become something to wonder at.

My guidebook began by discussing the brown trout as "a typical, telost fish." Telost means it has a bony skeleton, with a well-defined jawbone. The book proceeded to discuss the head, tail, pectoral girdle, brain, eye, auditory organ, and the general visceral anatomy. I could follow much of this, but what was a "girdle," and did "auditory" mean that fish had . . . ears? Maybe not, but I knew fish could hear and were easily alarmed by noises.

My authors pointed out the shortcomings of books that came before theirs. "They show nothing of the nerves or blood vessels supplying specific organs or regions." I accepted this pronouncement as fair. But how much did I care about these elements myself? I found I did, quite a bit. It was all new to me.

I read on, fascinated: Parker in 1943 and Bell and Bateman in 1960 were wrong in their assessment of the salmonid's urogenital system. This was because they wanted to apply the term, cloaca (or urogenital sinus), to salmonids the same why they did to higher vertebrates and you simply couldn't. Thus those writers used the term "anus," when they properly should have said "vent." This seemed to me a minor point, unless you were a salmonid with a sexual-orientation problem. Much more important, my authors noted, was that "the vent, genital, and urinary openings all reach the exterior of the body separately and in that order (anterior to posterior), the latter two occurring at the end of the urogenital papilla."

This was a keen and important determination, and you did not have to be a salmonid for it to matter to you. It was basic, biological stuff and explained how a number of important things happened. Without such knowledge many subsequent processes were in doubt.

Scholars were in disagreement over something so fundamental as how a salmon or (steelhead) sheds its eggs. Kendall (1920) disputed whether eggs were first discharged into the body cavity, as his predecessors had claimed, and argued that if they were the fish would have no method of "extruding" them. Hence no baby fish a few months later. Kendall maintained that the ova or eggs were shed through the oviducts. But a couple of years later (so recently as 1967) Henderson said those weren't oviducts but "peritoneal or mesovarial folds." This meant the fish discharged her eggs into the body cavity, after all. But how did they get outside? Did anybody know? It astonished me that scientists, even this recently, understood very little about the basic bodily functions of salmonids.

The lack of knowledge about the salmonids' muscular structure contributed to this large misunderstanding, too. (I don't want to call it ignorance, but there really isn't any other word for it, even by 1967, which in terms of geologic evolution is only this morning.) My authors—with whom I tend to agree, for why else are they *my* authors?—believe muscular contractions expel both eggs and sperm through the vent, and so do I, consequently. This, sportsfans, is called spawning. It is the most important process in the lifespan of salmonids and their entire life is pointed in the direction of reproducing themselves. Without a good understanding of how they do it we can hardly claim to know our fish.

A few days later I caught another hatchery steelhead and kept it in the name of science. I felt a little less ignorant about its anatomy when it came time to clean it and approached my task with zeal. Pocket knife in hand I inserted the tip of my blade in either the anus or vent, depending on your scientific orientation, and opened up the fish. I was ready to discover new worlds and learn how fish expel their eggs. The kitchen was my laboratory, the counter my dissecting table.

There is an illustration on page 3 of Smith and Bell that looks very much like somebody had filleted a steelhead without cleaning it first. The skin and meat have been laid back from the skeleton with an incision that reaches from the belly to just above the median line. Everything else is left in place and—perhaps for my benefit—conveniently labeled.

The fish in the illustration is a female; this much was obvious; a skein of ova is visible just where it should be. I opened up my fish and the skein was in exactly the same place, only there were two of them. In the illustration the second one was obscured by the first, giving the impression of there being only one. Often, I knew, the skeins were of different sizes, sometimes one twice the size of the other. If one underdevelops the other compensates for it by doubling its volume. (This I discovered; it is called Arnold's Rule of Pregnant Biomass.) If a male fish had been pictured the effect would have been much the same. It would have appeared to have but one gonad or milt sack. I thought the picture misleading and required an explanation from my authors.

I removed the ova from my fish. They were ice-cold, as always, and dry to the touch. They had a not-unpleasant feel in my hand, firm and weighty, coated with a membrane that held the thousands of individual eggs tightly bound together. The smell was faint and not fishy. Even a small steelhead—such as this one—has huge ova for her size, as though all of her being were drawn into the act of reproduction and the rest of her sacrificed. Once the eggs were removed my fish seemed hollow, a shell of herself. Thin ribs were all that held her skin together and they were clearly visible, viewed inside or out. The meat on her flanks was paper-thin. Her metabolic processes had exhausted her body. A spirit fish, she had literally wasted away in order to spawn.

A summer fish grows similarly devastated *before* spawning, I remembered, having spent so much energy and time holding her position in the current and remaining vertical for months without usable food. Perhaps this was why so few summer runs survive, while winter fish recover in fair numbers. Once they reach saltwater both fish's chances improve vastly. (It isn't called "the nourishing sea" for nothing.)

A male has a pair of milts, which are sacks of sperm, occupying a corresponding position in his body cavity and while often large in a maturing fish they are never so huge as the egg masses. Ova put aside I am now deep inside the fish's cavernous interior, where I encounter a host of organs, all slimy pink or white and hard to handle. At first it seems the usual gory jumble, but I soon begin to discern parts, for I have Smith and Bell to guide me. I look again—which is what research is all about. Most obvious is the gut—with its pelvic girdle, pyloric caeca, spleen, and intestine. I recognize each now.

The intestine is what trout fishermen tunnel with a marrow spoon to learn what their fish have been feeding on. With steelhead it is worth a look, too, for in summer caddis larvae are often found. Once I came across a black rock bigger than an unshelled walnut. Why the fish swallowed it I have no idea. I kept it as a souvenir and use it for a paperweight. Several times I've caught winter steelhead that had devoured eggs from spawning silver salmon. I remember stories about water ouzels and baby ducks found in steelhead guts, but I suspect this was deduced from a single feather.

As my authors note one will observe three distinct gutty masses discharging their wares into the vent. A mature female has a bit of pink membrane extending from her vent and this is one way she may be easily distinguished from a male. (Fish, by the way, like people, have secondary sexual characteristics and these make for an interesting study, in both cases.) The vent is the tube through which she will shed her eggs solely by means of—and here I agree with my authors—muscular contraction. The other two discharges from the vent are digestive; one is urinary, the other fecal. (Squeeze a trout and it will punish you by defecating, but usually not a steelhead, whose intestine is probably empty.)

It is worthwhile to note all you can as you proceed through the piscatorial disassembly process called cleaning a fish. Aft lies the heart, a little thing that resembles a rose-colored bulb from the garden. The liver lives next door, and is large, purplish, and slick. There is a long fibrous mass of membrane connections that have to be cut away before the cleaning can be completed and the fish scrubbed clean. As I work along the body cavity, removing things and putting them in the discard pile, I near the head and its gills. The gills should be removed to retard spoilage, or so says tradition. I'm sure this is true in warm weather. It takes a very sharp blade and much care to get them all out. Better yet is to remove the head, as is commercially done, though it makes the fish look more like the piece of raw meat it is rapidly becoming. I usually don't behead a fish, because I like the looks of it whole. (I leave it for my wife to do, so she can fit it into the refrigerator.)

 Near the spine are a few more interesting items. One is the swim bladder. It resembles other membrane and may be easily overlooked, but its appearance belies its significance. Its function is to keep the fish upright while it swims. What could be more important? When a fish is played on rod and reel, and at last turns belly up in surrender, it is probably the result of the failure of the swim bladder. (There are other factors that exhaust the fish, too, such as lactic-acid buildup in the bloodstream.) Next to the spine is a blood-black band that runs the length of the body cavity. It *is* blood, as seen through the membrane which encloses it. This is the kidney, with ducts opening into the urinary bladder which in turn empty into the urogenital papilla. To clean a fish well this membrane has to be slit open with a knife and scraped free of coagulated blood; the blood tends to catch in pockets along the spine and is hard to remove. I use a pointed teaspoon, but a dull knife blade will do almost as well, or even a small green stick if you are streamside where cutlery is not handy. This is the most tedious and time-consuming aspect of cleaning a fish, but it is imperative. A fish not cleaned of this blood looks ugly and will spoil.

I look closely at the fish's gills before I throw them out. They are the fish's lungs and a most complicated organ that performs a variety of complex functions. Gills reflect the general deterioration of the fish in freshwater and often acquire parasites, such as copepoda. (Anglers often call these maggots, but they are wrong.) Biologists study gills to determine how long a fish has been in a river and they are a clue to whether a steelhead is summer run or winter. A fish fresh from the sea, such as a December steelhead, will not have acquired copepoda yet, though it may be carrying sea lice near its vent, which is the oceanic equivalent parasite. Gills rapidly darken when a fish is dead.

Gills do not readily leave the fish. They are tough and rarely is the knife sharp enough. So I slash away at the throat of my steelhead and tear off what doesn't readily give way to the blade clumsily until I am satisfied with the job. Then I wash the fish inside and out, running the cold-water tap hard or else using the river's current to scour the cavity. It is important to me for no blood to be left on the scales. I use a vegetable brush and rub away until the scales shine. Then I carry the fish dripping along the floor to the door and hang it outside overnight from a stout nail. Regardless of the outdoor temperature I don't refrigerate it until morning. I'm left with several layers of wet newspapers containing the fish's waste products, which I will roll up and take to the garbage can or else burn if a very hot fire is handy.

The next morning the fish goes into the refrigerator. My wife cuts off the head, which has served for hanging purposes. To do so requires a blade with a sawtoothed edge. Afterwards the decapitated fish looks up at whoever is around accusingly. I don't like to see it.

The head is a self-contained unit, very heavy for its size, inside of which is compactly housed a dense biological mass, the precise nature of which I am largely ignorant. Here are the eyes, of course, but I understand the mechanisms of its sight no better than I do my own. The iris is bright and convex in a fresh fish, with a black pupil that appears to be looking straight through you. (This is a bit unnerving to a beginner. Best glance aside, quickly.) The eyes have—forgive me—a fishy stare. There is no other word to describe the gaze that sees no more.

Once I caught a big steelhead and decided to preserve the head and mount it. This was thirty years ago. I figured this was as close as I'd ever come to a big-game trophy. I could picture it looking down from the wall of my study—if I ever had a study. I checked out a book on taxidermy and bought the requisite chemicals—formaldehyde and methyl alcohol—and put the head to cure in my wife's favorite Pyrex oven dish, taping the edges closed so the chemicals wouldn't evaporate. A month or so later I opened up the dish, planning to continue my work. I returned to the book. It said, "Now remove the eyes with a sharp knife." None we had in the house was sharp enough, I learned, and I tried them all. After half an hour I called it quits. The membrane was too tough and my hands were sore. Yet I've seen a crow or a gull remove the eyes from a fish with a few deft slashes. I abandoned the head, chemicals, and dish. When we moved from the house I left them in the basement. I've always wondered what the next occupants thought about it.

Also housed in the head is the brain, which is tiny. This explains how the fish happened to take a fly in the first place. Studying the head, I consult my textbook again. Here is not the nose but something called the olfactory rosette, which must serve to smell water with. I try to locate it. Is it these twin dents in the front of the head that look like nostrils? I think so.

The book says the spinal cord runs from the top of the skull down the back, just above the spine, and is protectively encased, but encased in what it doesn't say. The cord lies away from most of the stuff occupying the body cavity, according to the illustration. I guess I missed it. I read on. Pointed aft in the skull are the medulla, cerebellum, large optic lobe, cerebrum, olfactory nerve (with olfactory epithelium and rosette at the terminal end). All this is fed by a system of semi-circular canals enclosed in cartilage. The carotid artery serves the head and brain, along with the ophthalmic artery, and there are veins and capillaries shooting off everywhere.

Heart and lungs working together comprise the cardiovascular system of all creatures, I know, not excluding the salmonids, but their precise functioning is way beyond my ken and that of most amateur biologists. Such knowledge isn't really needed in the daily world, yet I find most of what I've acquired interesting and I shall try to remember much of it. In the future each time I approach a dead fish and prepare to clean it I will recognize that I am performing surgery. It can be knowledgeably performed or done stupidly, depending on you and how much you care about all the biological elements spread out around you on the riverbank or on the kitchen counter.

Cleaning a fish should be a recurring reminder that the essential biological process of reproduction has been interrupted. It has been terminated by man—you. The eggs and milts we discard, or the eggs steelheaders put up for bait, are what lie at the heart of the regenerative process and the future life of our rivers. Without the death we have caused this fish we are cleaning would have gone on to spawn and to suffer the meaningful death that follows in the wild for all salmon and many steelhead.

6

Probable Water

WHEN I FIRST MET BILL MCMILLAN many years ago he had driven North from Camas, Washington, where he lives on the banks of the Washougal River, to give a slide presentation to a group interested in fly-fishing for steelhead. Bill is an excellent writer and photographer, and gives about the best slide-show presentations of anybody I've seen. Stan Young and I, who were newly acquainted, watched slide after slide light up the screen, while Bill spoke enthusiastically about making summer-run steelhead come to the surface for floating or dragging flies. All the pools were anonymous ones on a river whose name was never mentioned. Afterwards there was a moment when we might ask questions.

Steelheaders are famous for keeping their favorite holes to themselves. Also their rivers, though all are many miles long. Each of us has inadvertently contributed to the unpleasant experience of publicizing a favorite hole by some rash remark, or by bragging about his fishing, and has suffered the consequences when the pool became known and exploited. So we have learned to keep our lips buttoned. But didn't steelhead flyfishers also comprise a sort of "family" and weren't Bill's rivers far away? We weren't apt to become habitues of the Washougal, I mean.

When my turn came to ask a question I said, "I've fished the Washougal only once, Bill, and had a terrible time reaching its pools. The whole river seemed fenced with barbed wire and posted with keep-out signs. I found the Bowling Alley Drift and fished it hard but without any luck, then drove eight miles upstream to the General Store and fished my way down from the bridge." He smiled and nodded, for he knew exactly where I meant. "But soon," I continued, "I was picking my way through a jungle of backyards and gardens where there was no beach to walk along. It was a nightmare. Finally I fought my way back to the road by going through somebody's pea patch. I'm not anxious to repeat the experience.

"Tell me," I continued, "aren't there some places where a visiting fisher can get down to the river and find a good hole or two without trespassing and risking his life?"

Bill looked thoughtful for a moment, then began a long discourse on the problems caused by boat fishermen along the Kalama. I listened intently, waiting for him to get back to the subject of the Washougal and the problem of gaining bank access for the wading angler, but he never did. He spoke (always interestingly, colorfully, intelligently) about landowners rushing out on Kalama porches to urge boaters to take the most rapid passage through. Often they shook their fists at the boaters, for their harsh words were providently drowned out by the river's roar. Of course the reason the fishers were using boats in the first place was because beach access had been denied them by the same landowners long ago. And now Bill—a landowner himself—was being of no specific help. Perhaps he was taking their side, even. Was it . . . a conspiracy?

On bedrock rivers like the Kalama, Washougal, Wind, and East Lewis there are few broad floodplain bars down which anglers may walk from pool to pool once they're on the river. And from many bank locations there is the prospect of a plunge into deep water if you try to move around much. You could easily drown. Problems on these rivers are very different from mine, with its many access points and places to ford the river, at least at mid-height. And it has a vast floodplain to walk along.

When he was done talking about the boating problem I thought about asking a follow-up question and trying to pin him down but decided against it. He clearly didn't want to talk about access points.

When the session was over and we were leaving I said to Stan, "Did you notice how McMillan avoided my question?"

"Yes, but he probably had good reason."

"Yeah," I countered. "He doesn't want us coming down and fishing his river."

"No doubt."

Stan was in closer agreement with the matter of propriety of withholding river access information than I was. I mean, I hadn't carried it to the fine point he had. For instance, he would tell you he had caught a fish, but refuse to name the river. It was a little different from Bill's situation but not by much. If Bill lived on the Washougal, then he—like I, on the Stilly—had probably negotiated visitation rights from fellow landowners. It was a privilege painstakingly earned and not to be abused.

A lot was at stake and much hard diplomacy had gone into getting permission. It was not to be shared. What if he told somebody and that somebody came down and caught a fish or two and kept coming back? Where would his generosity leave him? Nowhere. He would have lost something special, irreplaceable. Like most everybody he wanted to reduce the competition to zero and have the river to himself. Wasn't that what I wanted, too, in my heart of hearts?

No, it wasn't.

Later, talking to Stan, I said. "I've been brooding over this, and, as much as I respect McMillan, I think he is wrong. If a visitor asked me about reaching some good pools on the Stilly I would try to answer him directly and help him out a little, without giving away too many secrets. I could turn him on to a stretch of river, for instance, rather than a specific pool. Since he is a visitor and will be gone the next day I wouldn't be ruining my future fishing by giving away hard-earned knowledge. Of course, I'd keep my instructions pretty general."

"How would you do it?" he asked suspiciously.

"I would identify five key areas and tell the visitor how to reach them by road and by foot. I'd key him to where the trails are. Then he'd be on his own to search out the good water. If he knew anything he'd be able to read the river and recognize the lies that steelhead like. If not, tough luck. I'm not going to hold his hand for him."

Stan knows my river as well as I, and has spent many long unproductive hours walking into pools that turned out to be duds. The few pools that remain good year after year, plus the new ones, are to be cherished, not tipped off. But if a visiting angler happens upon one he's entitled to fish it and test his skill and luck.

True I might not like finding some stranger standing in my favorite pool, but he would have as much right to be there as I. It wouldn't be against the law, I mean. A principle was at stake—one of ultimate fairness. We weren't entitled to hog our favorite water. It had to be shared, however reluctantly. Anything less was not playing by the rules. I had thought long and hard about this.

I decided I would name the following five areas, or reaches: First, heading upstream, the Cicero stretch, where State Highway 530 first crosses the North Fork about seven miles East of Arlington. There is probable water that can be reached upstream and down, though upstream historically has been best. Much of the river at this point is easily accessed through a broad floodplain that is not fenced or posted. I would tell an interested angler two or three things—where to park his car, where the trails start, and where the river-crossing points are at mid- and low-water. Once started he would be on his own to find the fish.

Next would be Oso, my favorite stretch. I would mention the schoolhouse and tell him about the parking area by the firehouse and say to disregard the No Parking signs along the driveway, which are intended only to protect the routes of exiting firetrucks. Park off to the side, out of the way. Then he must literally interpret more signs along the private road leading to the water. They urge you to pick up your litter and not to have beach fires; they do not say, "No Trespassing" or "Keep Out," though they are often interpreted to mean this. The ambiguity serves to thin down the numbers of visitors.

Once you gain the beach you can go upstream or down for a considerable distance. Both directions provide easy walks, for you are on the bar side of the river most of the way. All of the water is good and any run deeper than three feet may hold fish at various times of the year. The pools are nicely differentiated, though silting has shallowed and quickened them greatly. Still, all but a rank beginner ought to recognize this as good or great water and fish it as best he can. This is a famous stretch and many anglers have caught their first summer-run on a fly here. It is never a complete waste of time.

If you walk upstream a short distance you will come to the mouth of Deer Creek where Zane Grey fished 75 years ago. If the water is low you can cross the creek and reach a couple more promising pools upstream on the North Fork. Sometimes the odd fish can be caught here when the more famous water below proves unproductive. It is worth remembering. You may now fish your way downstream for five miles, easily crossing and recrossing the river in mid-summer until you come to Cicero where I started you off. But it is a grueling journey and the sun will punish you all the way. A clue: the first mile downstream from Deer Creek is the best.

Third reach is Hazel. I don't fish it often, but it is popular and produces many hatchery fish. Access is where the river touches the road. It is easy to spot, for often there is a line of cars all slanted at the same angle like at the supermarket. Trails take off in both directions. I recommend heading upstream. The pools change almost annually and usually exist for so short a time as not to have acquired names. The river is pretty here and wild-seeming, and you will not see many signs of civilization once you get away from the highway, though you will often hear the whine of logging trucks preparing to take on the next grade. Fish where the white water turns green and slows, but in late summer, when oxygen is low, fish the fast water mainly and spend time letting the fly (either wet or dry) hang directly below you in the current.

Fourth is Boulder Creek. In fact if you follow the trail and the river up from Hazel far enough you will deadend at a tricky crossing that marks the bottom reach of the Boulder Creek run. The highway is a long way from the river, and a first-hand annual knowledge of the trails and obscure access points is vital. Waste some valuable time poking around in the scrub and following game trails to where they die out in a deadfall; some go through. Ask anybody you see for up-to-date information about routes.

This used to be one of my favorite reaches and my first trip was memorable, one February afternoon long ago. I got badly overheated under a sunny sky as I walked up and down the railroad tracks looking for the start of a trail or a break in the barbed wire and blackberry that would give me an entry point to a huge meadow. I found none. Finally a farmer across the road told me to trespass without hesitation; he had once owned the land and retained certain rights, including giving out permission to enter.

So I took a beautiful trail through the woods that broke out from the alders onto the river bar. It was a handsome run with many large rocks and deep pools that ran an exciting green. Half an hour later I had caught and killed two average-sized hatchery steelhead. How easy it was. Packing them out along the trail I came to the edge of the meadow and discovered three deer staring at me over a patch of old snow. Norma, Garth, and I overnighted at the Oso cabin at my insistence.

That night a storm moved in from the Pacific. First it began blowing.

Then the wind stopped and the rain descended in a sheet. By morning we were in the midst of a fierce storm. I returned to Boulder Creek to find the river rapidly rising and turning slate-colored. Promptly my reel jammed, and I had to disassemble it and effect a streambank repair of its drag mechanism. I got soaked in the process. By the time I put the reel back together the river was hopeless, with no chance for a fish. I left, facing into a lashing rain.

I wish you good luck at Boulder Creek. If you go there often you will catch fish. The hole at the mouth changes each year and at the start of a new season you never know what you will find. The creek itself is usually fordable year round, the river downstream not so often. In fact it is often dangerous to cross. Pools appear and disappear and the river changes course, sometimes several times during a single winter. Presently this reach is full of coarse sand, the normal riffle-pool configuration vanished. There are a few signs of recovery. Deep pockets are appearing in the rubble. They may expand into discernible fishing holes in the near future.

Upstream is a public fishing area and parking lot in a meadow at the end of the Trading Post road. It is a little hard to find. After you've crossed Boulder Creek, going East, take the second dirt road to your left. Press on and risk being told you're trespassing; you aren't. The owner, Berger Bryson, has opened the road to the public and maintains it under a contract with the state. The access he has kindly granted to the Wildlife Department and should be respected. Carry your litter out and perhaps that of the thoughtless person before you.

The road ends in a grassy circle. Park anywhere, but overnight camping is denied. Two trails branch out at right angles. The first leads to several pretty pools upstream from Boulder Creek. The second takes you to Blue Slough, but it is a long walk over a narrow, often obscured trail that provides an interesting nature walk. Boots are needed, for you will slosh through water in several places. Today this is about the only way to reach Blue Slough, for the downstream owner has closed his road to both vehicular and foot traffic. He means it.

Blue Slough is not one of my five areas, but well could be. It is more a reach of water, that is, a stretch that is bounded by line-of-sight. This makes it fairly small and limited in size. The slough is actually a pond, the site of a former winter steelhead rearing pond. Long ago it was discontinued and new, modern cement ponds were constructed at Whitehorse, a few miles upstream.

The river here is volatile. A fisher who has not visited it in, say, five years or a decade will be amazed to find it utterly transformed. All his remembered pools and riffles will be erased. In their place runs mystery water. All the same it is a favorite spot of mine and it will be mentioned frequently. I have arbitrarily grouped this reach with Boulder Creek, which is perhaps not fair, for it is fine water in its own right.

Downstream a half mile or so and just off the main highway there is a trail in to Boulder Creek that is a better route, but it is difficult to walk along because the area was recently logged and slash obscures portions of the trail. From the highway look for a tall, lonesome cedar on a hilltop. It is behind the railroad tracks and a large pulloff provides plenty of parking. The trail begins nearby, breaking away from the railroad tracks and climbing a short, steep crest. Keep your eyes peeled for recent foot traffic. The Wildlife Department posts "Fly Fishing Only" signs on the cedar each spring, but fishermen keep tearing them down because they announce the way to good fishing.

My fifth access point is Fortson. Popular and crowded, much good fishing water lies upstream and down from here—mainly down. The reach is comprised of several small pools that are widely separated and require a good walk to reach. Skeer's is one and the Maple Hole below it another. They lie nearly a mile downstream. Skeers's is where Ernie Schwiebert caught a bright winter fish twenty years or so ago, while fishing with and guided by Wes Drain and Ralph Wahl. Later he wrote about it in a magazine and in a book. This used to be Alec Jackson's favorite hole.

Fortson is nobody's great secret, so I'm giving nothing away by identifying it. It is where most newcomers head, for they've heard tall tales. Many old timers come here, too, for it is where the hatchery fish pile up. Fortson was a lumber mill back at the turn of the century. Its twin ponds remain as evidence of where the logs were stored before they were sawed into boards. The ponds are now reserved for juvenile fishing and are planted each year with hatchery trout. Additionally they hold a few large cutthroats of searun origin. Brook trout are rumored to be present, too. Parr of chum salmon overwinter in the pond as do coho. The coho are encouraged by Department of Fisheries spawning channels in the creek draining the ponds. Fishers walk back and forth across the redds in order to reach the river. This drives the salmon away from their nests and scatters them. It is the result of poor planning.

Park by the railroad tracks and follow them up or downstream, looking for trails branching off to the river's edge. There are many, and all are short and edged with blackberry that will tear your waders. Upstream along the railroad tracks is the outlet to the Whitehorse Rearing Ponds; just below its mouth both the hatchery winter runs and summer runs gang up and draw the crowds. When steelhead are newly arrived—such as after a freshet—this reach produces the best fishing on the river. But you will seldom be alone here and often the locals are nasty. They believe they own the river and the fishing belongs to them. Their style includes snagging and even gillnetting. There seems to be no law enforcement here or else the officers of both Wildlife and Fisheries are intimidated and have escaped elsewhere. The bad situation continues year after year. The locals are big and tough, and some carry guns. Everybody fears them. (Welcome to the North Fork!)

On the North side of the river, across the Whitehorse Bridge and about five miles farther on, there is a Wildlife Department public access area with a huge parking lot. One well-worn trail leads to the river. When the river is not too high the tail of the main pool can be crossed to reach the Picnic Tables Hole directly downstream, thereby doubling the amount of fishing to be had. On the far side below the ponds the trail takes off downstream for Skeer's and is presently the only way to reach this holding pool. It is a long walk, especially on a hot day.

And there you have it, my North Fork, a key summer steelhead stream, and five of its major stretches. All will produce good fishing at several different times of the year. Pick a reach and pay it a visit. The fishing may be sensational. On an off-day or at off-season you may have the water all to yourself. Then it will be just you and whatever steelhead happen to be around. What more could a fisher ask?

Now—Bill and Stan—did I give anything away? Anything we can't afford to lose?

7

The Naming of Pools

A RIVER HAS MANY POOLS, NEARLY AN INFINITE NUMBER of them, but only a few are ever good. My favorite reaches lie downstream from Oso, but more often now I fish the upper river, and I am finding these pools familiar and rewarding. Perhaps in time I will come to love them as much.

Many pools have no names or else they have names I have given them only for myself and they would be recognizable to nobody else except perhaps my old friend, Bill Peterson. I wonder about the wisdom of naming pools, though. I think of Robinson Jeffers' poem that says all the stars with names are dead. Yet people need names for things and places, for we are all closet explorers who need to attach identifying labels to the things we care about. Named, a place or a pool becomes known and orderly, no longer wild and confusing. Thus, it is a civilized thing we do. We bind our experiences to objects and they become us. In the process we grow more knowledgeable, but the wildness element is lost. When this happens an irretrievable something is gone from our lives. The loss matters more to some than to others.

Pools are truly the property of those who fish them. We are entitled to our private names and nicknames, because we have earned them through our repeated attentions and the act of caring. But the argument remains strong that pools should remain nameless and not be broadly recognized. For one thing it helps protect them from exploitation. Exploitation most often takes the form of catching fish and lugging them home and talking about it to other fishers afterwards. A pool needs to have people diverted away from it instead. Yet it is only human to give pools names, names to know and love them by. It is the most human and forgivable of vain endeavors.

Once I named a pool after a friend, Art Smith, who had suffocated the previous winter in a freak camper accident. He loved the North Fork

Art Smith, about 1968

and fished it every chance he got, coming to the river long before I knew it. He was a first-rate fisher, famous among a small circle of friends. It seemed only decent that we should have a pool to remember him by. Art barely experienced the introduction of the hatchery summer runs to the upper river. He had fished solely for the wild fish below Deer Creek. In the '60s he took a job in Eastern Washington, returning home to find the wild run diminished. He looked alarmed when I told him about the new, artificial fish. It was not so bad, I said. They were steelhead, after all.

I took him upstream in July and showed him the runs in which I'd had recent good luck. Because he was a good fisher, he immediately started catching fish at a good clip. In one pretty run below Boulder Creek he had exceptional luck. He did better there than the rest of us put together. The pool was so new it didn't have a name. When Art died I thought we might celebrate his success by naming the pool after him. Others thought it worthwhile, too. That summer it was good to me. One odd night a freak electrical storm moved up the valley. It rained like crazy for about an hour and the fish hit like that, too. One silly fish jumped ten times in rapid succession, but took out not one inch of line. I beached it in about the length of time it takes to write this sentence. Another fish ran and ran, but never jumped. And I hooked other fish that performed ordinarily. The point is, the fish hit like they never had before. Or since, I might add.

The following winter a flood roared down the valley and devastated the Art Smith Pool. In fact it destroyed all the good old pools. The river carved out a new channel to the North. The Art Smith pool became a broad, featureless riffle, which now we cross without much reflection to reach downstream lies of greater importance.

So much for my efforts to bring about your immortality, Art. Perhaps I was wrong to name the pool after you. Did I—as Jeffers warned—help to bring about its demise? I hope not, but I suspect so, and I am sorry in several ways.

On some rivers pools hardly change at all. These are generally bedrock rivers, ones with remote canyons. For instance, when I fish the Grande Ronde in October I detect no change from year to year in a famous stretch of water such as the Shadow Pool. But George Johnson, who knows the river better than I, tells me it is undergoing rapid though subtle deterioration, its pools annually receiving large bedload increases. Compared to the North Fork the change is minimal. But no river, whatever its composition, wherever its origin, is safe anymore from habitat degradation.

It is natural for a river to change, of course, but change should not be so fast or severe as to destroy it. The extent of change can be alarming. Many years ago I wrote in my journal: "The Flat Water below the Oso Schoolhouse scarcely changes over the years." This was in the early '60s. I can hardly believe I wrote it. Since then it has been buried many times over in silt from the slide at DeForest Creek. It was good for a fish at almost any time of the year. Today it lies nearly ruined.

The memory lives, however. The fishing was so good, winter and summer, that it served as a training ground for my early experiments in catch-and-release fishing. I began to think of it as my private preserve. The keep season used to run through March on this and many rivers, and no distinction was made between wild and hatchery fish. Fishers generally killed all their fish—the more the better. The Flat Water offered good fishing throughout the season, but late winter was best. Then biologists with the Wildlife Department correctly decided that the wild fish populations needed protection. They closed the mid- and lower reaches and—in order to stifle the public outcry—opened up the upper reaches where mostly spawned-out hatchery fish were all that could be found at this time of the year. Wildlife wanted them all caught out so they wouldn't be "wasted." This sudden turnabout in policy made no sense to me or a few others.

I had been fishing my own version of catch and release for years and knew it didn't kill fish to put them back. At the worst it left them with a sore mouth, which was temporary. Why couldn't catch and release be mandated—made a regulation? Then we could continue to fish and not do the river any harm. It was a number of years before Wildlife saw the wisdom in such a policy. One fish biologist told me they had to wait for public opinion to be educated to accepting a nonconsumptive (that is, a nonkill) fishery. In the meantime we endured closed waters.

Today we have such a regulation and its popularity increases annually. When the river reopened in March the fishing was often fabulous. It was as though the wait had increased the numbers of fish available and made them eager to take. I began hooking steelhead with sufficient regularity to make it seem less than a challenge. Still it was exciting. I began shortening my fishing time each day. Two hours towards dusk was plenty. Soon I was forced to pare it down to an hour and a half. The fishing held good, great. Then I fished only the hour before dark. Still I managed to hook two or three fish, beaching one or two. Finally I was fishing for just half an hour. It was just the right length of time for me. Each fish was quickly played and turned loose. None was injured or died and all swam away strongly when I freed the hook. I was confident I was doing the run no harm.

The fish were big, some huge. Though spawning fish can be expected to be caught at this time of the year, most of mine were clean. I can remember only two or three males that were ripe and a couple of females that were close to spawning. Most were bright, handsome fish. They took solidly in mid-channel with no hesitation, moving off slowly and steadily, seemingly unaware that they were hooked. Then they felt the restraint and came alive. Some were leapers, shattering the silence of a calm river with jump after jump that terminated in a loud crash; others ran powerfully instead, but rarely broke the surface. Each fish was an individual, terrific in its own right.

What I remember most is having to fight them on a long line. I didn't do this for sport, but only because I couldn't crank them in closer until they grew tired and were ready for the beach. They were slow to tire and did so by degrees. I found the half hour of daylight barely enough to hook and land a single fish. Well, that was okay, too.

Only one fish went over twenty pounds. Such a fish is invariably a male. I judged him to be 24 or 25 pounds, and he was as bright and fresh and strong as one could hope for. Of course I released him. Another big fish I lost. I kept records of all my fish. Roughly half ran 12 to 18 pounds. The others went 5 to 10 or 11, disproving the theory that all late winter fish are huge. None were late-returning hatchery fish and each fish varied considerably from the others in size, shape, and coloration. This made them interesting from a biological standpoint. (Hatchery fish tend to be all of a size and look much the same.)

I prized these fish greatly. Over five years I probably caught 75 or 80 of them. Since then the Flat Water has grown discolored, its bottom sandy, and the water rarely holds fish. I find in my journal the incredible entry: "Its configuration precludes great ravaging from floods and, though its bottom sometimes silts up, it quickly clears again with each high water, the stones on the bottom remaining in their accustomed places and the fish lying in pretty much the same places year after year." Was this only eight years ago? It seems a lifetime. The lesson is, the burdens of silt have their upper limit; too much and a stream can be seriously impaired or ruined. It can be carried to the point where it will not scour out for decades, if ever.

My notebooks continue: "The Flats cannot be fished effectively until the rains have stopped and a cool period has lowered the river level several inches." This is still true, but now it takes so long that even a persistent hard freeze may not do it with no rain for weeks. This time period happens only once or twice in a winter season.

I used to catch 20-30 fish a year from this reach, counting summers. Now it's down to one or two—though I keep trying. The tailout was my favorite place. The river flowed an even course over a bottom pocketed with clutches of boulders, then abruptly shallowed and quickened, spilling over into a riffle that led to the next pool, the Pocket. Fish came up through the riffle and rested just above the lip. They were good takers. I would fish down the run methodically, remembering the odd places along the way where I had been surprised by a taking fish and pausing there, always hoping for a strong strike. Often I got one.

The very top of the run (where we all started fishing by custom) was good, too, and so was the culvert, where a trickle coming through a field dropped six or eight feet to spew into the river. The fish liked the spot. Directly downstream were several choice lies that often yielded strikes. In its middle reaches the run became boring. A big sunken boulder on the near side marked the next good lie; I can remember a great many fish from here, winter and summer, some taking almost at my feet. The next hundred feet was excellent, too. But the tailout was best. As I approached it, it filled me with wonderful expectations. My hands began to tremble, my rod to shake.

Most of the many great fish taken here have merged in memory, creating a single, collective fish, neither winter run nor summer run, but a little of both. The fish took my fly as it swung around at the end of its drift, striking savagely and—perhaps because of the shallowness of the water—racing all over the pool, jumping repeatedly, boring straight across stream, turning abruptly, heading now toward me, then speeding away in near panic. Occasionally a fish would continue into the white water below and I'd have to follow it down to the Pocket—if it didn't come off along the way. There when I was lucky I led it ashore and studied it with much interest to see if I could find out why it gave me so much difficulty. Often it was a fish of ordinary size and I could find nothing special about it except its fighting ability.

Tailout fish from the Flat Water were not always the sleek females I dreamed of, leapers in the 9-12 pound class, but enough were to feed my soul. These were invariably active fish, slender and bright, containing an explosive energy hard to imagine if not experienced. They were the finest steelhead I've ever encountered, fish to set one's standards by. Other fish from other rivers, though good, never were this good.

Once when I first started fishing for steelhead with the fly my success in the Flat Water was irregular. That is to say, I didn't land many of the fish I hooked. And I probably hooked more fish than I was entitled to, according to my skill level. Don Ives, who was often high rod at the time, gave me some good advice—after I had cornered and badgered him into making a response to the situation I'd described.

After hooking my fish and playing them until they had lost their initial wildness—a time when they were absolutely uncontrollable—they started coming off on the short line when I still had to bring them through the slack water that stood between me and the beach. This was a goodly distance. The water was waist-deep, nearly still, and there was a lot of it to slosh through before I reached the dry sand and stones. Somewhere along the way my fish kept coming off the hook.

I told Don, "If you put a flag at every place where I lost a fish this year, and turned the river to snow, you'd have a pretty nice slalom course. What am I doing wrong?"

He gave me his look of habitual disgust. "For one thing you're rushing your fish. You're towing them through the water, rather than leading them. Also you keep your rod tip too high. This lifts their heads out of the water, which they don't like. It doesn't promote good swimming on their part. That's why they thrash around so and you lose them. You want to keep them as quiet as possible. Then you surprise them with the beach. You slide it under them."

It was good advice and I knew he was right. As soon as I began to practice it I started to land a high percentage of my fish.

T he Fortson pool is a whole different matter. It is a high-water hole in a section of the river that rarely is wiped out because of rain. If there are too many cars in the parking area I'll turn away. I'll either go elsewhere or choose not to fish today. Trails lead down to the river from either side. From the North the walk is through a pretty little alder woods where often you will encounter deer.

The main run has varied considerably over the years. The trail hits the bank a hundred feet above where it used to. The river has claimed a great chunk of the land and the woods, shrinking the run to a fractional representation of its old self. The river sharply rounds the bend at the top and just where it strikes the railroad's riprap and changes course a tiny stream enters. This is the outlet from the Whitehorse rearing ponds. It is a grassy, wandering creek that can be stepped across at most any point.

For many years there was a weir at the mouth of the creek and it regulated the ascent of hatchery adults. Now the weir is rusted and broken and does not function. Fish wander up and down, and in and out, of the creek at will. A gate some distance upstream prevents unwanted fish from entering the holding ponds. Often in April unspawned hatchery fish lie waiting, their noses pressed up against the grate. Some dumb instinct tells them to keep boring ahead. Unspawned, they don't know why. Sometimes they get admitted if eggs are needed. Usually not, for Reiter Ponds on the Skykomish is the source for all the eggs that are required for Puget Sound summer runs unless there is an outbreak of disease, in which case an emergency is declared and these fish will be needed for brood.

One April I found the river full of mud, with no fishing to be had, so I wandered over to the rearing ponds for lack of anything better to do with what little was left of the day. No attendant was present, so I made myself at home; I strolled down to the gate. As I rose up on the horizon the water exploded. A couple dozen steelhead had been milling in the creek just down from the holding pond, begging entrance. When they saw me they shot away in panic, not stopping until they had found cover downstream in their trickle of a creek.

I followed as stealthily as possible. The creek provided them scant protection, for it was open and shallow with a sandy bottom. I stood behind a tree with a thick trunk; if it hid me, a steelhead or two might come into the open and I could observe them. But I soon learned that if I so much as tilted my head they fled. How shy they were. I was 150 feet away, still as the tree itself, my face barely visible. Yet I was too close and they stayed away. Each time I moved I frighten them and they fled. But they were quick to come back. I decided to time them. It took less than five minutes for them to return to the area. The time never varied by more than a few seconds. I guess they could find no better cover than here.

On the way out I found the remains of two steelhead on the sand. They proved to be females that had been killed for their eggs by poachers—eggs that probably had already been shed in spawning; if not, they would be too loose to be any good for bait. The fish themselves were inedible, their killing wanton and useless. Birds and animals had fed on the carcasses.

The Fortson reach holds countless pleasant memories. So many times I've stood at the head of the run, ready to make my first cast, full of expectations that were met. At such a moment my mind floods with thoughts of past successes. Memories keep returning as I fish the length of the pool. It is familiar water, swift and deep, but the channel is narrow and it is always hard to get a good drift through it, for the fly and line get swept away and whip past the fish, which lie in deeper water. To catch a steelhead here you have to find an unwary fish lying in close to your side, directly downstream. This is not often the case, for usually somebody has waded well out into the current.

Today there is nobody, but neither do I find a taking fish as I side-step my way downstream, making casts toward the bank pockets opposite me. My remembering goes on. Once in early June I hooked a fine fresh fish. It took hard and raced across the river to a tiny bathtub-sized pocket that lay tight up against the far bank. There it held and would not move.

I exerted side strain, but it only made my wrist sore. The fish did not budge. Eventually it began to swim slowly upstream, keeping to the far bank, which was full of brush. I felt my line stop and catch, trapped by a snag. It proved tight. I knew I couldn't work it loose, not from my side, so I crossed at the tailout and began to make my way up along the bank, wading in water up to my waist. The fish accommodated by holding steady.

The river grew deep and gutty in places. The fish had run into the backing and I was gaining back this thin line on the reel when the rod bowed again with the fish's weight. I slacked off, for I didn't want to break off and lose my flyline, which was likely if I kept on pulling. I waded out to the place where the backing was caught on a sunken limb and pointed straight down. What to do? Reaching down into the water for the line, I wetted my sleeve to the shoulder, but could not tug free the line. It slid back and forth easily, however, so I knew it was not firmly trapped. My best chance lay in cutting it, moving it out from under the sunken limb before the fish could run, and quickly retying it. The tactic was risky but my only hope.

For a moment I had a free end of line in each hand. It was frightening. I could feel the fish pulsing quietly, but it did not run. With the slack I tied a blood knot and found I had time to trim of the ends neatly, just like on a leader, so they wouldn't catch in a guide. Then cautiously I reeled in the slack. The line grew tight and the fish throbbed; the bow in the rod increased and my wrist began to ache anew.

I was soaked. My sleeve was wet to the shoulder and, in working my way along the deep bank, I had shipped water. My feet inside my waders were swimming. Wet as I was there was no good reason not to wade deeper, if necessary. I moved up along the bank and found my line snagged again. It was caught at a point higher up in the run where the water was deeper yet.

When I had waded as far as I could go I grasped the line and tugged lightly. It came free. What luck. Still my fish would not leave the bank and swim out into the current. He moved upstream a few yards. The trailing line stopped, was caught solidly, and I was stuck again. Playing this fish was decidedly no fun. In fact it was agony. Trying to reach the trapped line I shipped more water. In my waders the level now came up to my knees.

Ahead I could see the splice that joined my backing to my flyline. It was pinned just under the surface on a stout limb. I could not budge it. So I cut and retied my backing again, this time only a foot away from the splice. Patiently the fish waited.

At last I was fast to it, with no impediments. It drifted past me, just under the surface, a silvery wedge of biomass, slightly green from the cast the river gave it. I could not see clearly, but it seemed to have considerable length. The fish came to life and shot across the river to the place where I had been standing when I'd hooked it. We'd come full circle. I slogged downstream and crossed where I had crossed before; with each step the water sloshed heavily in my heavy bootfeet.

As I drew opposite the fish it moved away from me. It swam back across the river and upstream. My line stopped again and I could not switch it free. Stuck. I was determined not to quit and so was the fish. Soaked by the river I was heavily sweated besides. It was a warm, overcast day without a breath of wind and I was wearing a closed rain jacket, for a soft rain was falling. I found myself panting like a dog.

My line was caught again on the far side, this time very high up in the pool at a point I could not wade to. Tugging gently from my side did not free the line. Tugging harder, with an upstream pull, was no help, either. I ranged back and forth through the shallows, pulling this way, cranking that, but with no success. Forty minutes into the battle I was no closer to winning it than I had been at the start. In fact I was falling behind. Why wouldn't the fish roll over and call it quits?

Upstream, people had been watching the fight. It must have been a pretty funny sight. Well, I could see some of the humor myself. A boy of about sixteen came down the beach, intent on aiding me.

"What are you going to do now?" he asked politely.

"Beats me," I responded. Then: "Wait. I have an idea. Maybe you can give me a hand." He was a big kid and looked responsible. If he took the rod for a moment I would have both hands free. Maybe I could work the fish off the snag. It was worth a try—especially since nothing else was working.

"Here," I said, thrusting the rod at him. "Just hold the rod. Don't put it down or get sand in the reel. Whatever you do keep your fingers off the handle. Let the fish go wherever he wants to run. Don't check him. Got it?"

He nodded. He was just a kid, with no experience with big fish, well-intentioned as he seemed. I didn't trust him. If he froze up on the reel the tippet would break. I had a big investment in this fish and didn't want to lose it.

He watched me take off my rain jacket and vest, hanging them neatly on a sapling that promptly bowed and dropped them to the muddy ground. I left them lying there. Freed from their weight I peered out over the river—as though from the bow of a ship. I stuffed my eyeglasses in my shirt pocket for safety's sake and found I could not see much.

"What's the plan?" asked the boy. Good question.

"I'm going to swim across the river and free the fish."

"You're kidding?"

I looked him hard in the eye. "Do I look like I'm kidding?"

I took the line lightly in both hands and began walking out into the current. The water got deeper, swifter. Over my shoulder I cautioned him, "Remember, if the fish starts to run, you let it. We'll take our chances. Right?" He nodded. Maybe he would do what he said. But at his age I wasn't very dependable.

The current grew stronger. The water neared my armpits and the point where my waders ended. This was where I literally sank or swam. I feared I was the sinker type. But I was determined to get this fish. My arms extended fully overhead, my fingers gently guiding the line and checking it from time to time for tautness, I tugged gently and—wonderful to say—found it free of everything but the fish. It drifted toward me, buoyed by the river, guided by the current. I started to handline the fish in, positioning myself between it and the boy, using my body as a protective device in case the boy pulled too hard. I guided the fish towards the bank, very gently gathering in slack as the fish washed in towards me. It was important to keep the pressure light.

As the fish swung in I backed to the beach in a hurry. The current tugged at the fish. I checked its course with the coils of line in my hand and . . . the hook came away. I staggered backwards. The fish was gone.

Freed from the tension, I nearly pitched into the shallows. The lightwire hook had gaped just enough to let go. This is why I'd lost the fish. I hadn't popped the leader, but so what? I took back the rod and cranked in the slack.

"That was a nice fish," the kid said. "I'll bet you feel awful."

"Why should I feel awful?"

"Losing your fish, after all that time. You worked so hard to land it."

"Listen, I feel great. Absolutely. I mean it." And I did. A good fish had licked me, plain and simple. I had cheated in no way myself or the fish. I had given it my all. And I had lost. I smiled widely, as wide as I could, for I was wet and starting to shiver, my teeth to chatter.

"Thanks for your help," I told him.

"Oh, that's okay."

He trudged off up the beach. I stopped long enough to pour the water out of my waders. Then—able to walk normally again—I headed for camp and some dry clothes.

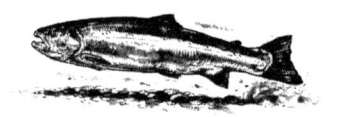

Blue Slough used to belong to Dick Bowman and he permitted me to drive almost to the river's edge. In gratitude I gave him the occasional fish. To go there now is difficult. It is posted by a new landowner who is unfriendly. He is serious about keeping fishers out. But I have found a devious way in through the woods by a secret trail. It is a pleasant walk over a path that is obscured by thick brush most of the way. Soon it will become known. On this river few things are kept hidden for long.

Coming out on the river bar I see the sky opening up and the river running at a modest height. I like this reach best when the river is so high that all the other pools are unfishable. And I dread finding somebody occupying my favorite section. What a relief it is to find the water empty today. My heart lightens in my chest.

What a lot of happy memories I have of this place. The first year there were any hatchery summer runs in the river (1966) they ganged up here in early autumn, a huge number of them. They showed up after the first freshet in September and held until there was a hard rain the following month. I first located the fish downstream in late summer. They came to Boulder Creek in June in high water and remained there as the river gradually dropped, locking them into the main pool. I had some wonderful fishing. Then early fall rains lifted them to Blue Slough. The river was smaller there and they were more confined. They jammed the three small riffles above the deep narrow pool that was shaded by a giant broadleaf maple. The lower pool was full of chinooks. The tree's low boughs made casting a challenge and claimed many flies that were snared just out of arm's reach. Fish are readily spotted at Blue Slough, but are not so easily caught. That's all right: Fishing ought not be too easy.

That first summer at Blue Slough the river and how to fish it were new to us all. It previously had been known as a winter hole. Winter fishing with gear is very different from summer fishing with the fly.

Now a handful of us had discovered that it held summer runs and were trying to puzzle out how best to catch them. This included Ed Nevins and Ira Grady, good fishers both.

I remember a badly over-weight man who had had a series of small heart attacks recently. His doctor had given him permission to fish again, but to "take it easy." Evidently the doctor didn't know anything about steelhead fishing; the strike alone might induce heart failure. The man knew the risks and was determined to die—if it should so happen—while fighting a fish. We understood his decision and applauded it. We too believed that, when the time came, we wanted it to be while attached to a huge steelhead. ("But please, God, not yet.") It was a romantic notion and not very likely to occur. The fat man talked to us frequently about his heart and of the details of its biological structure.

Each time he hooked and played a fish—and this was often, for he was a lucky beginner—he made himself sit down on a rock afterward and breathe deeply for several minutes. This was "to quiet his chambers," he told us. After about fifteen minutes of watching us fish he rejoined the lineup. His life was safe for the next hour or so, for fish hit in spurts and there was usually a long period of inactivity before we had any action again.

The steelhead were all hatchery fish, of course, and most anglers kept their catch; when they had killed their limit, which was two, they were expected to vacate the pool. On a good day it did not take long to get a pair and people were continually coming and going. That is good fishing. It wasn't for years that anglers began regularly releasing hatchery fish. It was mainly so they could keep on fishing.

The deep slot against the far bank held (and still holds) steelhead and salmon in season, but it is hard to get a fly deep enough to pass over the main lie, and necessitates an upstream cast with a sinking line and plenty of mends to allow it to settle to the bottom. Fish often take softly just before the free-swinging line begins to drag and form its deep belly. The first thing you know the line has tightened, grown heavy, and a fish is moving away from you at a rapid rate, pulling the drowned line after it. Then it surfaces and begins jumping. Once in a while a fish comes up on top and takes the fly just under the surface, which is a real surprise and a joy.

Blue Slough used to be a good place to run into Syd Glasso and Wes Drain in the spring. Alas, Syd is a decade dead and Wes recently passed away. Once at Blue Slough in late fall I found the pool full of ripe chinook. They were brutes of twelve to 40 pounds or more. Steelhead lay in the hole as well, in the faster water that was not so deep but had some rocks along the edge of the flow. The steelhead were ghostly forms, easily seen, and one had a patch of white fungus at its shoulder. It was not a good omen. In a salmon fungus marks the onset of death. The steelhead looked healthy enough, though; it held its position and showed no signs of weakness. The spot enabled us to track its position in the pool from day to day and week to week. Nobody caught and killed it, and it remained within this small staging area until rain clouded the river and drew the run upstream.

Meanwhile chinooks were spawning all over the pool, the females holding near their nests in the shallows and the males vying and chasing each other around the riffles like angry dogs. We tried to keep our casts away from the chinooks, but were not always successful for they were active. When we hooked one we tried to break it off quickly, for it was next to impossible to land without exhausting it and this might well kill it. The pool got churned into a froth in the process. We thought this spooked the steelhead and they would not take again for many minutes.

What the presence of chinooks did to the steelhead I'm not certain. They remained in their basic lies most of the day, not moving away when a monster salmon caromed by. I was impressed by their nonchalance. They refused to be intimidated or vanquished. Now if I was a steelhead I would have found another place to lie. That is, I would have moved to a more peaceful neighborhood.

One afternoon I felt the hook touch a salmon and slipped the fish some slack from a rod pointed downward, hoping the point would slide away. The first and second times this worked. The third time, the line continued to drag, the hook to hold. I tightened cautiously. The fish began to shake its head, without moving off. This is typical warm-water steelhead behavior. I tightened hard and the fish came to the surface with a swirl. It threw water and filled the sky with its rainbow. It was a ten-pound male, thick and deep, with a wide red band along its side. It remained in the pool and did not surface again. Eventually I hauled it—still upright—onto the stones, where I took its picture and released it. This was the first hatchery summer run I put back in the manner of a wild fish. The snapshot evokes a fond memory. It hangs on my study wall and is often looked at.

Blue Slough is good in spring either for late wild winter runs or fresh three-salt summer hatchery fish. But it is excellent in the fall when the river rises and holds its level. So are the other upper-river pools. Boulder Creek is best in spring and contains several places where fish repeatedly lie. But lately it has badly silted up, its pools buried in sand. I remember it fondly for its big late-winter steelhead and early summer hatchery fish, some of surprising size.

A big fish usually does something different right at the start. This tells you that it is special and you will have a problem on your hands. The fish takes control of the fight from the beginning. You must convince it that it can't win. This takes unusual patience, persistence, and luck.

One day in March at Boulder the first wild winter fish were in the river. I hooked four and landed two. That pair went about seven and ten pounds. They proved no great difficulty to play. The two I lost I never saw and do not know their size. They licked me straightaway. Each ran across the river to the snags. Trying to slow the fish only made it more determined to escape. Finally I had to break it off in the brush.

Another time at Boulder I hooked a bright, fast, acrobatic hen, which looked to be about nine pounds. She jumped and jumped. By the time I stranded her and slipped the hook free I was breathless. She was a beautiful wild late-winter fish and I badly wanted her to live to spawn so there would be more like her in the river in the years to come.

As she swam away I said to myself, "The first of the summer runs"—though of course this wasn't true. She was only *like* a summer run, a great and spectacular wild winter fish.

8

Who Needs A Guide?

GUIDES HAVE A BAD NAME ON MY RIVER, which is small and easily wadable most of the year. They belong elsewhere. Anybody can be a guide in my state. Who is he anyway but a guy with a raft or a driftboat, who states he is an expert? The only requirement is being able to fork over $150 for a license. On my river a guide is a secretive guy who will part with some of what he knows for a price. Since he deals mostly with beginners (some of them lifelong beginners) how can they properly evaluate his skills or knowledge? They can't. He takes them for a ride in several ways. For about $225 for you and your buddy, you have to furnish your own box lunch, and some guides expect you to bring along one for him. Imagine. To me and my friends being guided on the North Fork is a sucker's game.

Two guides have evenly divided the river between them. (What is there about competition in business that produces a tacit cooperation, a pact not to get in each other's way and to keep prices uniformly high?) The two men are much alike. One has a gray Achilles raft, while the other's is orange. The first sticks mainly to the river above Seapost where he parks his rig and takes out his raft. The other puts in at Seapost and takes out at the Whitman Bridge. Rarely do their territories overlap. This is by agreement. Further commercialization of this small river is possible. Several slots are still open. Is anybody interested in the two miles between Whitman Bridge and Oso? Better yet the five miles between Oso and Cicero? No takers? Thank goodness.

What on earth are they doing with a boat or a raft on a river so small, winter and summer, that the average fisher can cast to the far bank from a shallow wade? On a big river maybe they're necessary, I don't know. Here they're a water hazard, a daily mockery of what fishing ought to be like. Peter Soverel says guides have no manners and will cut in below you on a drift. This has not been my experience, but each year I encounter some foot soldier who has become enraged because one of our two resident guides has just launched his raft from the bar immediately downstream from where this man is fishing and the guide will sweep the river, taking every pool first—for a raft is a quick, efficient means of travel, much faster than a man on foot who is frequently halted by a brushpile or a pathless flight through some scrub. And those pools the guide does not stop to fish he puts his large raft over, scattering the fish. This is specially bad in summer.

It is a dispiriting experience and what makes it worse is that the guide is often chuckling up his sleeve at the discomfort he has caused the bank fishers. His clients get first consideration, whatever the price in good manners. They are paying for it.

"Clients?" I say? Yes, that's what they call their dudes, their day's wards. It makes the guide seem a little like a lawyer. (Come on, they aren't *that* bad.) Why not call their wards "patients," for it takes patience to catch a steelhead? Then the guide can appropriate the vocabulary of medicine, which is one notch up from law, speaking from the standpoint of status.

The river owes none of us a living, just as the forests do not exist to be cut down to provide jobs for loggers. But fishing today—flyfishing especially—is a business. A guide is just one of many striving to make a living off of what is essentially a solitary, pleasant recreational activity that is not meant to be lucrative.

Having said all this, I will admit to having guided a little. Let me add that I've done it only twice for fund-raising raffles of worthy conservation projects, done it for free, and done it only on foot. And I've provided my dude—in each instance a cheerful, intelligent guy, whose company was first-rate—with at least one meal, the quality of which was far above a box lunch. I thoroughly enjoyed the day and believe my guest did, too. In both cases he was soon a better caster and ended up a more knowledgeable fisher from the standpoint of learning to read water and knowing where steelhead will lie in a wide variety of reaches.

Who guides the guide? How does the guide learn what he purports to know? The same way, I suspect, that many of us did. He wasted days, months, even years, roving up and down a number of different rivers, making mistakes, taking skunks, and ultimately picking up a thing or two that proved useful. He became a graduate of the flyfishing school of hard knocks. He was almost entirely self-taught. He picked up his data on the streambank. This makes him self-educated. He is not a graduate of some special school.

So who needs a guide? Please step forward, but beware of a pratfall. The self-taught are contemptuous of those who want to accelerate the learning process by paying top dollar for a teacher of doubtful credentials. Besides, what do you learn on such a trip except a few truisms and how to tie the jam knot? Can you not learn more from a book? Books are expensive these days, but you can buy a number of them for what you will pay for a one-day guided trip and afterwards have something to wrap your hands around on a cold winter's evening. You can refer to a book later when a tactical problem surfaces or resurfaces. But if you like boats, remember—two guided trips will pay for a small sturdy inflatable of your own and even one will buy a pram.

There is deep satisfaction in learning the old-fashioned way—the same way John Houseman said he made money. Call it the hard way, if the quick way raises your hackles. I know a woman whose male friend took her on a guided float trip down the Bogachiel—a fine winter river. The guide knew where the fish were and put her Hotshot plug in front of a big one. Thus her first steelhead weighed over twenty pounds. My first one so big took me fifteen years to catch.

What did the big fish *mean* to her? What was there to compare it to? Maybe all steelhead are this big, she might have thought, until guide and friend began to whistle appreciatively. How big is big anyhow? And what did she learn on the trip? One sits still while the guide is pulling plugs and must dress warmly because of the prolonged inactivity. The guide really caught the fish—both figuratively and literally. The fish only half-tired out, the guide slips the boat net under the brute and levers it over the gunwale. Guides usually kill their client's catch, too. How else does the dude know he got his money's worth out of the trip?

All said, I'm not done talking yet. There is absolutely nothing wrong with an experienced fisher taking a novice out on a river or a lake and showing that person a thing or two. Not for money or "for future considerations," as we say in business—simply because our love of the art and the science of flyfishing *requires* us to share our knowledge. The rule of life is, "Pass it on."

So let me take you on a trip to my river. It's autumn—though it might as well be spring. The clouds are high and thinly layered; if there is a sun it is watery and far off. There is a bite to the air, but the prospect is for more rain. About half the alder leaves are down, the maples riddled with black among their faded gold. You can't see for miles and miles, as the song puts it, but your eyes will carry you remarkable distances. Underfoot is a green/black mulch, dissolving into rich brown.

Free-standing puddles throw your reflection back at you with a lot of scratchy bare branches along the top of the frame. When a breeze drifts across the surface of a puddle the universe shudders and is briefly dissolved. We slosh along, headed for a reach whose roar mounts as we near its banks. This excites us. Will it be crowded or will we have the drift to ourselves? Since it is an important pool, known to hold fish at this time of the year, probably the former.

Wind is the enemy in fall. It makes casting difficult and fills the river with big yellow leaves that mimic the strike of a steelhead—they'll even pull line off the reel if you rear back against them. The wind must blow hard for, say, half an hour before the leaves arrive in stupefying enough volume to ruin the fishing for the rest of the day.

Rain is not as bad. It is the necessary evil for a river to return to its fall high flow and be full of fish. If steelheaders aren't waterproof they soon learn to tolerate wetness. Another way of saying this is that rain cannot penetrate past your skin. When your skin is wet you're as wet as you are going to get. Time to unbunch your shoulders and relax into the cold moistness if you can.

It's better yet to plan ahead for bad weather. Chest-high waders, ones either new or well patched, a fishing vest that is worn snug and dry inside a rainjacket (one with a big hood), and a billed cap that protects your scalp and face, and is small enough to fit under the hood, is what one needs. There are no substitutes. The wrists of the jacket ought to have elastic or Velcro tape that will fasten tightly and prevent water from entering when your hands are raised, which is necessary for fly-casting. And when it is really bad out I often wear a scarf or towel around my neck to absorb the water that inevitably creeps in around the edges of the hood. It keeps you warm too when the wind is blowing.

I've directed you to a good stretch of holding water and left you on your own, with only a few words of advice and a bright fly on the end of a fresh eight-pound leader tippet. You go to the head of the pool and take up a position there, whether or not anybody else is present. You know that you're supposed to begin with short casts, perhaps even while standing on shore, but you can't help yourself and wade right into the shallows and begin casting as far out as you can reach. You may miss a close, easy fish this way, but you think you'll get to the most productive water quicker and you are right. But don't forget—there are hundreds of casts to be made on a given afternoon and it is only one or two that might engage a fish. The idea in the back of your head is that today's fish belongs to him who gets to it first and often this entails the longest cast made into previously untouched water. You expect a fish with every cast. At the same time you don't believe one will really hit. You try to remain ready for the strike, hour after hour, but you become lulled by the easy rhythm of casting, mending, drifting, retrieving. Watch an accomplished wet-fly fisherman. After his line has hit the water, and he's made a mend or two, he's still as a heron. Why, he's gone to sleep. No, he hasn't; this is the time he is fishing most intently.

The sunk line is doing its work. The fly is being swept along by the current at the correct depth—if you've done everything right. If not in a moment you'll have a chance to cast again. What you are striving for cast after cast is the perfect drift. The rest is up to the steelhead. The steelhead's job is to decide whether to take the fly or not. Mostly he won't. You are waiting for the time he drops his guard and intercepts your fly. Why he does this nobody knows. Every once in a while it happens and it is a miracle. You want to be there for it and it is why you are enduring all this wonderful discomfort.

The strikes comes when you least expect it—when you have come close to giving up hope. It happens earlier in the drift than you had thought it would. And often it is more violent than you anticipated, with the rod tip suddenly plunging into the water, the reel screaming in agony. Other times the steelhead simply stops the fly in mid-drift and it is as if you've picked up another big maple leaf. Is it a fish this time? You strike, because it is the only way of knowing for certain. Do you simply tighten, as they say in the books, or do you pull back hard? Maybe I can be of some help here.

I strike hard, whenever I can. I strike right up to the point where I think the leader is going to break. Then I give out line quickly. It is a kind of pull-push action. I figure I have but one chance to set the hook and I'd better seize it. If the fish doesn't race off I'll strike again. And again. Still I'm not certain the fish is well hooked. The remainder of the fight is conducted with great uncertainty. I believe the fish may come off the hook, right up to the moment it is stranded on the beach.

But say it happens a different way: the river is full, the strike a violent one. Your tip goes down, the reel shrieks, the fish vaults into the air. Then you strike as best you can. The rule book goes out the window. If you hit a running fish you may break it off. But if you fail to strike it and lose the fish later the fault is yours, surely, so you hang on and say a little prayer to the river gods. You'll need good luck. (Would you want it any other way? Answer honest, now.)

If you give the fish your all and still lose it you've done your level best. And a fish, in the great scheme of things, is only a fish. It's loss does not signify the end of the world. Better get this straight at the start.

A fish is not so important, say, as getting your car to start when it's time to go home in the rain and the dark. It's not so important as keeping from getting sick or hurt. That can ruin more than the day. A fish or two is the reward for a day spent happily afield, but comes as a bonus. A fish isn't absolutely necessary to "having a good day"—as people keep urging you to do—but it helps. It is possible to have a good day without catching a fish, but you can catch fish and have a miserable day. Much can add or subtract from a day's pleasure. This realization keeps you reflecting about what is involved in the act of going fishing.

When you understand that being seen carrying a dead fish up and down the beach is not the epitome of good fishing, you have come close to understanding what fishing ought to be and what constitutes pleasure, even though you may never be able to put your finger on it exactly. That's okay. Things you can easily put your finger on are frequently not worth the effort, I've found.

So what matters? Wading, and wading well, are important. To move easily through water is a joy in itself. It is a kind of ongoing baptism. I pity anglers who fish always from boats or from shore. We river fishermen are amphibians, moving eternally between water and land. There is a neither/nor quality about our life that is appealing; we are not life of the river nor life of the land. We are a little of both. Still, keeping my feet firmly planted on what passes for *terra firma* in the water, the solid substrate, is important to my well-being.

I have a healthy fear of the water and respect what it can do. It can drown you. Yet I'm never so much at home as when I'm in the water. Some of the most accomplished waders I've known are poor swimmers. I am one of these. The purpose of wading is to reach the fish, otherwise you're limited to standing on shore and making impossibly long casts. Wading is also a means of normal progression; it is how you move down and across a river. Should you make the classic mistake and fall in you must get back to land. Theoretically and practically the farthest you'll have to swim is half the river's width. It usually turns out to be much less than this. Unless you are a salmonid it is best done in a downstream direction.

Always present is the problem of hooking a big fish and having to follow it. Perhaps you have to cross the river to land it. You should never fish a river without first making a mental note of where a big fish might take you and where you would elect to play and land it. In high water you will be unable to cross the river, which means goodbye, fish. Your plan ought to include determining the furthermost downstream point you'll go before breaking off a fish. There you will plant your feet and battle it out. During a catch-and-release season it is often more important to land a fish, even if you must release it afterwards. I don't know why this is so, but it is a time when anglers take more risks, for no good reason.

Hooking and playing well a fish of substantial weight is an important part of a fisher's life experience. You want to maximize your opportunities when big fish are in the river. This is one reason to go out in the bad weather of winter.

Let's say we go out again together. It is a day much different from the previous one. The sky resembles a tent made from a down comforter. Soon it is drizzling. Long before dark it will thicken into a downpour. After putting you on some good water I go off to do my own fishing. (This is my way and no offense is meant by it.) You are standing in a pool that is crowded with other fishermen, all desperate to catch a late-summer steelhead. But the fish are not striking. Fishing now seems the most futile of acts. Running through your mind are all the profitable activities you might be engaged in: The leaves in the front yard need raking, the raingutters are clogged to overflowing, the rosebed hasn't been mulched for the winter and a freeze is due.

And then a steelhead strikes and every discomfort of the day is forgotten. The hard pulse on the line quickly grows into a living weight. The pull is vigorous and the weight begins to move off at an accelerating rate as the fish strives to rid itself of its restraint. Its flight increases speed and becomes panic. Then it takes to the air, shaking at the apex of its leap and crashing back down into the water. It runs again. (Perhaps its own leap frightened it.) The spool on the reel reveals a small core of backing, all that is left. To still be connected to a fish that has doubled, then tripled, its distance away from you, all in a wink, is astonishing. You find you want this fish badly.

After the first run or two the frenzy settles down into a dogged give-and-take. It comes as both a relief and a disappointment. When the line has been gathered back on the reel for perhaps the third time and the fish is holding steady in the current a few yards away, you presume to think it is ready for the beach. (If you are wrong the fish will immediately let you know.) To turn a fish at this point is usually accomplished without difficulty. The fish's head comes round—a little like tacking a sail—and it turns on its side, where it can be gently led into shallow water and stranded. You stand at the water's edge and admire its sleek, silvery form, the archetypal salmonid. Now you have a big decision to make. Do you release it or kill it? For a moment you are God, or god-like in your power over life and death. It being a hatchery fish you may decide to kill it for the table. The choice is yours on most rivers in the fall. Easier it is to opt for life, I've found.

If you decide to release your fish it is best to hasten the fight and end it early. It is easier on the fish and gives it greater odds for survival. So horse it in. What does it matter if the fish comes off a little early in the fight? You were going to put it back anyway, weren't you? So you wade out into the shallows and, the first time the fish comes onto the short line, you grasp the line in one hand and draw the fish in close. It planes on the surface, helpless. A barbless hook can be quickly reversed in its hold in the fish's jaw. You can use your fingers to do this, but needlenosed pliers are better, for fish have teeth.

A strong fish on a short line will begin to thrash and, if you hold it hard, to twist and roll. The leader will often break at the tippet. The fish will drift away with the current, the fly in its mouth trailing the broken tippet. Fish biologists say that this isn't harmful and the hook will fester out in a short while and not harm the fish. Still, it worries me. I know it is preferable to leave the fly in the fish's mouth than to over-tire it by playing it too long. A fish can drown, you know.

Your fish for today lies on its side in the shallows, its mouth rhythmically gaping and gasping. It pants like a sumo wrestler. You are trying to make up your mind what to do. It is a 12-pound male, a fine specimen. You've known its sex and size for some time, and you've made up your mind to kill it. It's been a long time since you've brought home a fish for the table and you have a special meal planned for this hatchery steelhead. You beach it quickly and kill it swiftly with three hard blows to its skull from a piece of driftwood. The fish shudders and lies still. It is no longer a live thing but a piece of meat.

It is typically dark, with a stripe down its sides the color of dried blood and more red along its belly, which is dark cream. Overall its hue is gray-green. If you leave it on the wet sand and come back for it at dusk it will be the same color as the beach, and you will have trouble finding it in the dim light.

A male fish of autumn looks like a ripe winter fish, but you know that the milts are small still and your fish is months away from spawning. With the river running high and salmon spawning and dying everywhere you can clean your fish in the river without causing any pollution.

What comes out of the river goes back into it without harm and becomes part of the foodchain. So you gut your fish with your pocket knife and deposit the offal and milt sacks and gill rakers and coagulated blood back in the river, though it seems a bit like dumping your garbage.

You pick up your fish with your fingers in its gill covers and head for home. Its flesh is firm and bright, a rich orange color. It will make a tasty meal. You are proud of the day's effort. You don't mind the envious stares of your fellow anglers as you pass them on the trail and find them gathered by their cars in the parking lot, chatting before they begin the long drive home.

When they ask you where you caught it and on what pattern you answer matter-of-factly, but you detect a different pitch to your voice and the tinny sound of false modesty bothers you. Well, catching a big one doesn't happen every day. God will forgive you if you walk with a slight swagger until tomorrow.

9

The Elephant's Foot Wastebasket

I AM LOOKING AT A PICTURE OF MYSELF old enough to have grey in my beard, holding up two dead steelhead. They are big, bright, beautiful fish. Coming out through a field one February I spotted George Keough's son, Steve, and bullied him into taking my picture with an old Leica. The light was just right and I pulled a good print from the negative in my basement darkroom. It hangs on my study wall up at the river.

What I was after was a memento from that wonderful day. The fish weighed 13 and 16 pounds. I've since caught bigger pairs, but so what? These two fish greatly mattered. Both were females. Between them they held ten thousand eggs. Their offspring would have helped sustain the wild winter fish far into the future. Instead, I selfishly killed them. In the back of my mind was the idea of having the picture. Well, I've got it, but I've lived to regret the deed. Today I see it for what it was—a crime against nature.

There seemed to be plenty of fish about then, fish without end. Was this only the 1970s? Was that . . . *me*? Dark hair, dark beard? The two fish have stared down at me ever since. I'm proud of having caught them, but I'm ashamed, too. I keep the picture up as a reminder of a past that I am determined will not repeat itself. I killed most of my fish, back then. I was a kill junky. My motto was, "Bring 'em back dead." I was like many other fishers, in this regard. I think I am a better person now. But . . . am I? Like most ex-junkies I fear a relapse. It is easy to kill a fish and not much trouble to clean. Cleaning them lost its squeamishness long ago. Well, it oughtn't have.

One kills out of vanity, vanity alone, since none of us is dependent upon eating steelhead to stay alive, not even Indians, who sell or barter it away. We buy most of our meat in the store, like everybody else. Why not all of it? There was a time, not far back, when men grew up expecting to be grand providers. If you lived in the Pacific Northwest or other

The pair of big, native winter-run hens

Western parts of the country you prided yourself on bringing home the bacon, but instead of bacon it was fish and game.

Men went to the woods and rivers to kill. Women baked and put up preserves for the winter. We were the Depression's children who were taught to clean up our plates, for many went to bed hungry and not just in China and India. No small part of my wife's appeal was her ability to cook. Her bread and soups are terrific. I caught fish and brought them home. It is a good thing I didn't hunt or else I would have blasted off the face of the planet any bird or animal that came into my sights.

Men emulated Hemingway and coveted expensive side-by-side shotguns. They bought big wicker creels. Their esthetic was borrowed from "Up In Michigan." Would Ernie put back a trout—to live and perhaps be caught again? Fat chance. In a similar vein I remember the photographs that appeared in Herter's catalog of fishing and hunting supplies. Men on its pages surrounded themselves with dead animals and grinned like chimpanzees for the camera. The strings of fish they held up stretched and bagged—requiring another grinning idiot on the other end for various kinds of support. And still the string sagged. The bag was what mattered—and the pictorial record of the booty.

Men have come a long way, too, baby. Even back then I am sure there were others like myself who were sickened by the sight of so much carnage. The feeling grew among some that criminal acts were taking place. Ones formerly condoned by custom were now deemed unexcusable. The youngest in the Herter line was Jacques and he was a killer without peer. I can still see him surrounded by a heap of rhinos he had killed. Herter's marketed—you won't believe this, but it is true, true as grass is green—elephant-foot wastebaskets. "Who would want to be without this handy receptacle?" the catalog asked sportsmen. Well, I would, even then. The foot was lopped off about eighteen inches from the ground and one of the wastebasket's chief attractions was the toes and horny nails, which were left attached. One elephant made four wastebaskets, if my math is right. What they sold for I don't remember, but they were pricey. Certain people would pay a lot of money for such a place to dump waste paper. And it was a great conversation piece—remember those? People at a party would stand around and admire some useless object of doubtful esthetic merit. "What's that?" they would ask. "That's my elephant's foot wastebasket," you'd say.

"You're kidding?"

And superiorly you would smile your certain knowledge that it was the genuine article.

Jacques was a curly headed kid with a smug grin—the kind bigger boys would like to punch in the nose. One picture showed him astride a giant turtle, a tortoise, which he had killed with a bow and arrow. Somehow he had fired the steel point into a soft spot between the armored plates. No, I am not setting up a strawman in order to knock it down. People bought Herter products and admired the killing proficiency of the family and staff.

The fact that I wasn't impressed showed only that I had marginal good sense, for I was subject to masculine pressure to follow the sportsman's example at an age when I was beginning to question many things. Though I did not hunt I bought capes of birds killed by others for their feathers, enabling them to kill more birds. I buy some still, but more guardedly. There is an element of hypocrisy about this. For instance, I am aware of how chickens are raised in tiny cages, force-fed, and not permitted to run around and do ordinary things that chickens like to do, such as pecking at each other and scratching on the ground. Beef cattle is a related matter and my knowledge of where a steak comes from doesn't stop me from eating and enjoying one, only from thinking much about it.

All killing is bad—the killing for food least bad. Salmon are caught in nylon gillnets—first lightly strangled, then drowned. This concerns me, but only in an abstract sense. Salmon are not my special interest. There is much cruelty to animals and people in our world and to keep functional one must disregard much of the incoming data. Yet we *know* what goes on. We are powerless to effect much of anything except how we behave as individuals and how we live our lives. It is a sad commentary. Steelhead are regularly killed in our rivers by Indians with such nets and they are incidentally taken by commercial salmon fishers in the saltchuck. Their fate is the same sad death as the salmon's. I turn my head because the political and economic factors involved are so weighty that no pious individual who protests will be listened to seriously. It would be a foolish, futile effort. But privately, in guarded conversations with men I know and trust, I will quietly question the propriety, wisdom, morality, and fairness of the killing that we do, commercially and otherwise. Which doesn't mean I still won't do any, but it will be much less than in the past and I have established some ground rules for my conduct. I may change my mind, from time to time, and even contradict myself. The important thing is to keep thinking about what we do.

 It was in March—the time of the wild fish return—that I killed a twenty-pound steelhead, my first fish so large. It was 1972 and I didn't think twice. Prime wild fish start coming into most rivers about the twentieth of February and the run peaks at the end of April. Back then no distinction was made between wild and hatchery steelhead and all steelhead were allowed to be killed until the end of March, when the river closed. This was a mistake that Wildlife has been trying to compensate for ever since through more stringent regulations.

 It was, in fact, the very last day of March, a stormy one at the end of a terrible season. Why I hadn't quit fishing before was a mystery explained only by dumb male persistence. I was on my favorite reach, The Flat Water, and dark was drawing down fast. The river was rising and had turned slate-colored. After today there would be no more fishing until the first of June, when all the winter fish hopefully had spawned and left the river and only summer runs would be in attendance. That was two months away.

The day and season threatened to end earlier, however, because of snow runoff. It was warm and raining, with the river slowly turning opaque. The rain drummed on the taut nylon hood of my parka as I slammed out cast after cast into a river that had grown decidedly brown. Only a hundred feet away and directly behind me were the warm lights where my friends Joe Monda and George Keough were sitting in front of a fire. I could join them, I knew, and George would give me a stiff drink to warm me, if only I weren't so pigheaded. But this was the time and place for big fish. I wanted one badly. Worse, I needed one.

George was a retired professor of education at Seattle University and Joe headed the English Department. George had sold his home in Seattle and bought a summer cabin on our favorite river. He had carpenters winterize and expand it at considerable expense and now lived there year-round. His retirement proved a disappointment, for he was chronically ill and unable to fish. He rarely got out of his bathrobe and slippers anymore. Joe—who loved to fish—had dedicated this afternoon to keeping George company. I thought this was a kind act. Joe knew what most of us did not, that George was dying.

I stood in the cold rain and suffered a discomfort that could easily be mended. All I had to do was go to the door and knock. But I was determined to stick it out. Since the first of December, four long months back, I had caught only two fish. They had been small hatchery hens, a pair taken late one Sunday afternoon with the river dropping and clearing nicely. It was early in the season. I expected more fish in the days to come and decided against taking a day of vacation and staying over in the rental cabin, fishing the next morning. A long season stretched ahead and if it was like most there would be plenty of fish to come. Well, I was wrong.

So I was long overdue for a fish. When I had a take it was almost dark and the river was pathetically out of shape, a muddy off-white color. The fish took tight against the far bank deep in the tailout and immediately showed himself in a splendid head-and-tail jump. I could not believe its size. An obvious male he allowed himself to be cranked in a short distance, then leisurely ran back to the center of the river and jumped again. I was confirmed in my estimate: A big, well-spotted buck, thick and quite dark. His spawning time was not far off. He ran around the pool quite calmly, up and down and across, but never descended deep into the tailout where he might cause me trouble because the current would carry him down through a long riffle and into the pool below. That was a long distance.

I was lucky. My fish ran back and forth in a narrow corridor, not greatly exerting himself or tiring. When he stopped I was quick to apply side-strain. It did not seem to have any effect. When he ran I gave him next to no pressure, but as soon as he stopped I applied side-strain as hard as I dared. He swam in slowly toward me, unresisting. He was not an unmanageable fish. In time the runs shortened and they lost their edge. What I feared most was a breakage caused by my carelessness. Soon he was tired enough to be led on a short line to the beach. He balanced for a moment on his belly, stranded, then toppled over. Mine.

He lay on his side at the edge of the water, wavelets lapping at his flank. He could still escape, I knew, so I applied more pressure on a line pointed at him like a quivering bow string and waited for his flipflops to move him up on higher ground. I guess I grew impatient and anxious to claim him, and pulled too hard, for the next thing I knew the leader snapped and I went reeling backwards, nearly falling down on the rocks. But the fish lay helpless high on the sand and couldn't take advantage of the situation. I tried to nudge him with my bootfoot a little higher, but he wouldn't move. So I grabbed him around the wrist of the tail, but it was so wide that I found no grip. I hooked a finger in his gills and heaved. He slid a little. I tugged again, he slid again. In this manner I hauled him up the beach until I came to a safe place where I killed him with several blows to the head from a piece of driftwood.

Only then did I dare speculate about his weight. He would go eighteen pounds, for sure. Would he go . . . twenty? It seemed too much to hope for. A big male is deceptive; he is so deep and wide that his weight may vary by several pounds in either direction. My fish didn't look especially thick, but he was the biggest steelhead I had ever seen.

George and Joe had witnessed the closing battle through the windows of the cabin. Over my shoulder through the streaked glass several times I saw George salute me with a raised glass. They were on my side, this said. I suspected that—in the manner of fishermen everywhere—they were secretly pulling for the fish. No matter. The fish was now dead and mine. I lugged him in the direction of the cabin. Most of him dragged on the ground. George greeted me from his front steps. The drops beat down on his scalp and bathrobe. I cautioned him about standing in the rain, but he waved off my concern. Joe stood a little in back of him.

I could see the eternal cigaret hanging from the corner of George's mouth and the raindrops had spotted it. He rolled his own—an economy he had picked up during the Great Depression. Joe had wisely slipped on a light jacket. In his hand was a Chatillon spring balance. They are famous for their accuracy. We'd soon know the fish's weight.

George took charge. It was his scales, after all, and his home. He put the hook in the fish's jaw and tried to lift the fish off the ground by raising the handle overhead. He was unable to do so. Joe took the handle and lifted the fish easily. George bent over and read the pointer in the dark rain. I stood off to the side, like a boxer awaiting the verdict.

"Twenty-two pounds," George said gruffly, the way he said most everything. "Maybe a few ounces more—I can't see because of the damn drops on my glasses. Now, can we please go inside? I'm getting soaked." I knew he only was pretending to be peevish. He was as happy as a fisher can be for another fisher's good fortune.

I went inside, too. I hesitated because I was dripping water, but George abruptly waved me ahead and in. I needn't shed my boots and jacket, he said. What was a little water among friends—as long as it wasn't poured in a glass? We were all wet to some degree. He poured me a drink from a bottle I recognized as one I had given him earlier in the week for a past indebtedness. It was Hennessee cognac.

The jolt he poured me was more than generous, more than I wanted. He gave half a tumblerful of my own medicine, you might say. It was about two dollar's worth, I figured. Absolutely first-class stuff. I didn't want to see it wasted. My money had bought it.

"Drink it down," he told me, watching to see that I did. The next thing I knew I was in Seattle, unloading the fish from the car. I remembered little of the long drive home through the storm. I had stopped at a sporting goods shop deliriously to weigh the fish again, with the same result. Twenty-two pounds. They asked me to leave it on display until the next day. Then I began to think. What would I do with such a fish? I could carve it up, bake some—freeze the rest or perhaps have it smoked. Maybe I should have the fish mounted. Wouldn't that be nice? But to mount a fish was expensive. We had a small house and where would we hang the damn thing? Could we stand to have it looking down on us every day?

Instead, I decided to make a brown paper outline of it and stop right there. A heavy-duty grocery bag is the ideal size and material. You open up the bag, being careful not to tear it, lay the fish down, and trace around it with a soft pencil. Then you cut it out. Afterwards you write down on the paper all the pertinent data—the fish's length, weight, river, reach, pool, date, and time. Fly or lure or bait. This I did.

I also took lots of pictures, including loving close-ups of its tail and head with a razor-sharp Canon close-up lens. And then I was left with a dead fish on my hands. My day of success lay behind me, fading fast. I went on with my life and caught smaller fish. Time passed.

The brown paper outline still hangs on the wall up at the river. It is one picture away from the two dead wild hens. We live in different times. Today the cutout and the picture made me think for a moment of young Jacques Herter. Where is he, and has time changed him any and his practices? His company was sold, then went out of business. He and Hemingway and all the little Hemingways—mass murderers, every one—have lost prominence in the world of sport. A different hero has replaced them. He is a kinder, gentler person. I guess in my youth I wanted to be like the others. I wanted to be in their grand company—however reduced my own status. These were the men whose forerunners shot a zillion buffalo and blew the passenger pigeon into extinction, and whose fish strung on a pole provided the original photo opportunity. (The string of fish probably ended up in the garbage can.)

Today my cutout serves as a proud and shameful reminder of the only twenty pounder I shall ever kill. It was one too many.

10

Sam's Story

I HAD TO WAIT MORE THAN TEN YEARS to hook and land my second 20-pounder. Of course I let it go. Regulations now read that we must, but I would have done it anyway. By the mid-1980s the spring run of wild fish on the Sauk and Skagit had recovered enough to permit annual special catch-and-release seasons. Often they were fabulous.

I was now fishing with a companion, a young black Labrador retriever named Sam. In fact I found him on the banks of the Sauk. His presence made imperative my releasing fish as quickly as I could or else he'd be all over them with his nose and big front paws. Controllable in most other ways he was wild whenever a fish was involved. The chance of injuring a fish grew great. So I developed and began practicing certain protective techniques. Perhaps I'd better explain about Sam, for he has changed the direction of my life and is an important part of what has happened to my fishing since.

I was on a day trip to the Sauk one sunny afternoon in mid-March and found the river low and sparkling. The Sauk is a special river and others must have thought it so, too, for, fifteen years ago it was included in the U. S. Forest Service's Wild and Scenic Rivers System. The upper watershed is managed by the Forest Service and the middle reaches where most of us fish is of mixed ownership, some of it private and the rest held by timber companies, including the state's Department of Natural Resources. The area is heavily logged and the local economy is based on timber harvest. When the loggers are on layoff in the winter they fish.

The river is beautiful and most development has kept far back, not because of any collective wisdom but simply because it floods regularly on a grand scale and homes built within sight of it are soon swept away. The river is rare in that it is undammed. It rushes through rough terrain with a good head of water and a steep gradient has kept its riffles

Author, dog, big hatchery summer-run

scoured clean, that is, until recently when it has undergone rapid deterioration from forest overcutting. The Sauk's banks are lined with tall conifers and a mix of alders and cottonwoods. In spring there is still a snap to the air and at night coyotes can be heard establishing their basic lines of communication. Often snow lies on the ground in old patches.

Not many fish had shown up so far that year and the word was out. Few anglers lined the riffles. Boat traffic from guides and others was at a minimum, and fishing was a pleasure. Late in the morning, casting from the bar at the bankside of White Creek, I took a colored male of about seven pounds. The rule was to release it and I was happy to. Its fight was only fair. I forged upstream to a place I'd never fished before, a good walk, and came out of the woods at the tail of a vast bar. Above me was a long, undistinguished pool, but I had no way of knowing what it was like until I got there. It proved disappointing to fish.

A sparkling sky stretched overhead and I was mildly content with having caught one fish so early. This bland reach yielded a fine Dolly Varden that fought valiantly for its size. It was a firm, bright fish with solid flanks, though nowhere so big and strong as a steelhead. It too went free. The Sauk is a good river for dollies and many of them are large. This was only about 20 inches. They are good eating. The rule of releasing fish held for dollies as well.

In the middle of the run a steelhead surprised me by taking with a wrench the same yellow fly as the Dolly had. It was well hooked, a bright, ten-pound female that sported about the pool but never left it. She was so slow to tire that cars driving along Highway 530 pulled over to the shoulder and watched me play it. They seemed surprised and disappointed when I slipped it back into the water.

One guy shouted that I was nuts to catch a fish and let it go. I said it was the law. He said he didn't care about the law, he would have killed it. I was a fool. He shot back to his car and drove off with a squeal. I wondered what business it was of his? He probably didn't buy a fishing license and had no right to grouse, accordingly.

It was too nice a day to be annoyed for long and I felt great. Two steelhead and a Dolly. I snipped off the fly and retired it. It had a red body and yellow marabou wing. I had never used it before. Since then it has produced only salmon. It was one of those flies that had its day, then hides in the back of the flybox. I made my way leisurely downstream, retracing my route, enjoying the sun and tranquility of the mild day. I didn't need to fish anymore, yet it was way too early to go home. At the Native Hole where my car was parked I decided to make a few casts, but my heart wasn't in them, I discovered.

Across the river I spotted a small dark form quivering at the water's edge, where there was a sandy spit. It was a black Lab puppy and it looked cold. It also seemed lost and forlorn. This was an odd place for a dog to be and I searched with my eyes for its owner, for nobody ever fishes from that side where the terrain is steep and there is no wading bar. I saw no one. I stripped some line from my Hardy reel—which makes a piercing, racheting squeal—and the dog cocked his head winningly. I was won over; this dog was for me. All thoughts of catching steelhead left my head. I now had a different mission.

The night before I had returned to my car to find a note on the windshield. "If you've lost a little black dog, it's down by the Government Bridge." I owned no dog, hadn't had one for years. Nor had I seen one. I threw the note away and forgot about it. Now the words came rushing back. Could this be the same dog?

I've since discovered the Sauk is a favorite place for people to dump unwanted dogs and I would recommend going there if you're ever looking indiscriminately for a pet. A black Lab was just what I needed. I had been thinking about going to a kennel and picking out a female pup. Now I wouldn't have to. I called across the river to the dog and tried to make myself heard over the roar of the rapids. I wasn't successful.

The dog watched me intently, though. He looked to be male. I urged him to swim across the river to me. He was a Lab, after all, and must love water. He pretended he didn't understand what I wanted. I have since learned that this is a common Lab trait. It's called simulated deafness. A swim wouldn't hurt him any—it was straight downstream, which is the same as downhill to a dog. He held at his station, there by the water's edge, and regarded me sadly. (The look may not really be sad, only the set of a Lab's ears and jowls.) Finally I could stand it no longer. If the dog wouldn't come to me I would go to him.

I left the river and drove around to the other side—to the point opposite him. A hundred yards of deadfall timber stood between us. It could be negotiated on foot only with difficulty. No longer could I see the dog and had to guess at his location. Because the prospect was for tough going I took off my waders, boots, and vest. I slipped into my street shoes. Then I began punching in through the dense woods. It was worse than I thought. With each step I found myself straddling tall deadfalls. I was always either ascending or descending some limb-riddled tree that lay on its side. Soon I was in a lather.

Finally I thought I saw the dog ahead. He was partly veiled by some brush that rose at the river's edge. This was exactly where I'd left him; he hadn't moved a yard. I called out to him and made those silly noises one makes to dogs when nobody is around, but he would not come to me. And I couldn't further penetrate the brush to reach him. We were stymied.

I talked to him sweetly. No good. I commanded him to come to me. This didn't work, either. I crooked my finger repeatedly. I held my hand out pleadingly, palm up. Couldn't he see that I posed no threat? I advanced slowly in his direction through a tight wall of limbs, pushing them ahead of me. They creaked and bent, then whipped back at me, lashing my hands and face, for it was spring. As I grew near he began to retreat, never taking his eyes off me. What was wrong with this dog? He was more than shy. He seemed downright paranoid.

The distance between us remained ever the same—about one-hundred feet. My technique was lacking, my strategy no good. What would work, what kind of trickery? I decided to feign a retreat and see if he would come after me. As I walked backwards, in the process stumbling over dead limbs behind me and being poked by branches beside me, he followed gingerly, but came no closer. Each time I stopped he stopped. It became for us a game to see if he could catch me looking back. I found myself casting him quick, sideways glances instead. The interval between us remained constant.

When I reached the deep ditch that stood between the woods and my stationwagon we had covered about three-hundred feet. He remained a hundred feet away. Why, I'd seen deer less wary. He was pathologically shy. Had he had an abused puppyhood? Had he been beaten? I crossed the ditch at the side of the road and crouched back on my heels. I called out to him. He held steady at the bottom of the ditch, regarding me with upturned watery brown eyes. (Of course they all have brown eyes. All dogs do.)

He was a handsome guy. I confirmed that he was male, about four months old, with good configuration. A tiny white star appeared on his chest like a heavenly sign. This meant, I suspected, that he wasn't a "real" Lab. About this I was wrong, as I was about many things having to do with him and the breed. What difference did it make, anyway, whether he was purebred? I wasn't going to keep him. My wife was a big stumbling block on the road to owning another dog, even one from a kennel. Besides, I wanted a female black Lab. They were known to be easier to train and more affectionate.

Three hours of daylight were left. To get this dog to cross the last hundred feet of scrub might take all of them and still I might fail to capture him. Meanwhile he held his infirm ground off in the scruff. I walked slowly away from him, not looking back. This—though slightly dishonest—proved effective. Watching me leave, he picked his way through the choked gully and up on the shoulder. He was curious to learn what I was up to, I guess. When I looked back he froze. The distance between us remained ever the same, but now we were out of the woods and on the edge of the pavement. This was civilization.

Innocently holding both hands out in front of me I tried to explain that I posed no problem, offered no threat. He let me inch toward him, warily cocking his head, not moving away. When I reached the stationwagon and opened up the back he eyed me guardedly. He was now about forty feet away. This marked a great advance in our relationship. But he would not close the distance or let me do it.

I began to speculate on where he had come from. I had spotted several signs nailed to trees announcing "Field Trials." An arrow pointed in different directions from each, depending upon where you found them. The arrows converged upon a trampled clearing. Field trials had been held there over the weekend. Had this shy dog been "worked" at too early an age? Perhaps a gunshot had spooked him. Or else his owner had abandoned him in disgust, for he was too young to be reliable at retrieving or much of anything else.

A dog lost in the woods is not a wild dog any more than a man lost in the wilds becomes an aborigine. But a dog without a human is a lost cause. He needs a family, people to belong to. I gained his trust by degrees. I won him over because—in spite of his shyness, his fear, his hunger, his Labrador pigheadedness—he wanted to belong to somebody. I was the one who had come along in the time of his great desperation. He needed a person the way I needed a dog—it was worse than either of us had imagined.

We sized each other up and a bargain was struck. We would go off in each other's company and see what happened. Later people told me Sam and I were meant for each other. This was not always intended as a compliment, though I choose to take it as one.

I let him sniff my fingers while he held far back, wary still, and after a bit more of this he allowed my hand to graze the top of his skull. Soon I was surrounding him with my arms, talking softly all the while, gently imprisoning him; I think he both wanted and didn't want me to do this. Talk about your ambivalent dogs. He still had his reservations. Then I grabbed him and tossed him in the back of the stationwagon and slammed the hatchback closed. I had him trapped—the fate he had been dreading. Or had he?

I leaped in front and drove off in a rush. He took this placidly enough, as though it were the most natural thing in the world to be cruising along in the back of a strange vehicle. People abducted him every day. It meant nothing. I wondered—was I caught in my own trap?

Now that I had captured this dog what was I supposed to do with him? My wife clearly did not want a dog; I could twist around her attitude to no other conclusion. I properly feared her anger. Maybe I should try to find him a home with others; if he lived with friends I could always go visit him. I had a number of such dog friends, ones who lived with their owners, and often I spent great lengths of time petting and talking to them.

I decided to approach people with children first. Tom and Karen Crabtree lived near me up at the river and had eight kids. They were good candidates. Mike Kinney had two kids, but only one lived with him. Benjy was just the right age for a dog.

I drove the forty miles back to the North Fork and cautiously opened up the back of the wagon. Would the dog run off into the scrub and disappear? Timidly he exited, looking from side to side, sniffing a path ahead. I inched away. He clung to my flank. As I strolled about my property he went wherever I went, sticking close. Was this the same shy dog of an hour ago? No, a connection had been made and we were bonded. I did not know this yet, only that I believed him to be remarkably well behaved for such short acquaintance.

Wherever I walked he trotted happily alongside. There was a nice bounce to his step, I noticed. I took pleasure in the rhythm of his gait. Up and down the narrow roadway we walked, my dog and I. I took him down to Tom and Karen's house and knocked on the door. Would they like a dog? They had three already; what was one more? Also, they had a lot of country space. I put it to Karen just this way.

"Not on your life." she told me.

Had I mistaken her words? A free dog? One to go with those she already had and all those children? I explained how this dog would give them a better dog-per-kid ratio—one for two if my math was right.

"Didn't you hear me?" she snapped. Then she spelled the word, N-O.

She didn't know a good deal when she saw one, evidently. Too bad. I said goodbye, loaded the unwanted dog back in the car, and drove three miles to Oso. There Mike Kinney lived in a little cold-water hut. He wasn't home. I walked down to the Oso General Store. I asked if anybody want a dog? They laughed and began congratulating me on my new acquisition.

The afternoon had lengthened into evening by the time I reached home. The dog was a perfect passenger and rode along in back as if he had done so a hundred times. It was too late to do more searching for a new owner. Tomorrow I would begin in earnest. But my resolve was weak. Already I saw this dog as mine. I pulled up in front of my house and hung over the steering wheel, deliberating. The windows were bright rectangles, but did not welcome me. Norma was coldly waiting inside. This meant I could not sneak the dog in and gain the small advantage of prior occupancy. I would have to come up with some other scheme.

"Stay here," I told the dog, "and be quiet, if you know what's good for you."

I walked up to the porch, dragging my waders and rod tubes behind me, as usual. I decided to enter alone and spring the dog matter on her later, after dinner. But I've never been one to keep secrets for long.

"Guess what?" I blurted out.

"You caught a fish?"

"Better yet."

She looked perplexed. What, to my way of thinking, could be better than catching a fish? "You caught two?" She was used to my deviant behavior and awaited an explanation.

"Come out to the car," I said. "I want to show you a surprise." Often this was how I introduced her to some new expenditure, especially a large one. I would hide it in the car until I had prepared her for it. This is called applied psychology.

She followed me out to the car and peered in back, where it was dark. She saw a shape move. "A dog?" she said. "Not a dog?" She wasn't as delighted as I had hoped. She didn't sound happy at all. She spoke the words I dreaded:

"But we don't need a dog. I thought we had decided against another dog, when the old one died?"

"Well, true, we didn't *think* we needed a new dog," I began, "but we were wrong. We hadn't seen this one. Just look at him. Isn't he a beauty? Purebred, too, I think."

I opened up the back and scooped him up. I extended him to her, holding him under what corresponds to armpits. But she wouldn't accept him. She kept her arms folded inhospitably over her middle. It was going to be difficult, harder even than getting the dog to come to me. I smiled. I had the rest of the evening in which to accomplish it.

Dinner was eaten in silence. The dog wandered about the house, sniffing corners. He wouldn't relax and lie down. I gave him some food from the can I had providently bought on the way home. He ate it right down like a good dog. Then he curled up in a ball on the rug and went to sleep. Should I wrap him in a blanket, I wondered? No, he didn't look cold, only sleepy. I remembered he hadn't been inside a house for days.

About eleven, with the TV news coming on to muffle and limit the discussion, as is often is the case with us, she asked, "What do you intend to name this . . . dog?"

"This. . . dog," I mimicked, "is a purebred Labrador retriever. I thought we might call him Sauk. Like it? It's short, it's catchy." I paused expectantly. "Original, too."

"It's a terrible name. Whoever heard of a dog named Sauk?"

"That's what I mean by original."

"Why not call him Sam?" she said.

"Okay," I quickly agreed and I had her, for you can hardly name a dog and then abandon him to the elements. It would be immoral. It turned out that everybody has a dog named Sam and eighty percent are black Labradors. But this one was ours. Her getting to name the dog was the tradeoff for my getting to keep him. Sam he was and Sam he remained over the years.

A Labrador is a peculiar breed. They are as headstrong as steelheaders and complement them perfectly. They are equally difficult, intractable, and heedless. Labs are—in the opinion of many—the only breed worth owning. Some dogs left by the side of the road head for civilization. A Lab heads for water.

Returning to the Sauk a few days later I encountered the man who had left the note on my windshield. Yes, this was the dog he was talking about. Sam had been alone in the woods, I calculated, for at least three days. The man, a river guide, was planning on putting a bullet into Sam's head so he wouldn't die from exposure or starvation. It was the humane thing to do. When I claimed him Sam had less than a day left to live. The thought still chills me.

The following year the man took our picture from his driftboat while I was playing a fish. Sam stood alongside, his eyes glued on the water, watching for the fish to show again.

The guide hailed me. "Is that the same dog?"

"It is."

"Looks like a good one. You must be feeding him right. Answer me a question, will you? I've never seen you flyfishers playing a fish before. You stand out in the river and wave your rods back and forth, hour after hour. How long has it been since you caught a fish before this one?"

I consulted my watch. "About thirty minutes."

When fresh fish are running in the Sauk the action is fast and exciting, and flyfishers are into them often. The guide had never witnessed this and thought it improbable.

He took my picture—rod bowed, dog close—and kindly mailed me a print. It is a favorite. I sent him a packet of steelhead flies, but I doubt if he ever used them. Every time I have seen him since he is pulling plugs for his clients, putting his considerable knowledge of the river to work. It is a deadly way of catching steelhead on a big river and clients like it because all they have to do is sit still and wait until a fish hits.

A dog is a constant companion—if you live right. This has both its good and bad sides. Sam ate anything I gave him and always cleaned up his plate. I experimented with dog foods until I found one that didn't give him diarrhea or cause him throw up in the back of the wagon on bumpy roads. In town Norma constructed a dogrun and a water-tight house for him. He has two areas all his own—one for his bed, the other for his water and feeding dishes.

Sam was excruciatingly slender until he turned two, when he began to fill out solidly and develop bone mass. His weight now holds at ninety-three pounds. That's big for a Lab, but he carries it well and has no fat.

Late winter and spring fishing in the Sauk and Skagit continued good and I began to think Sam brought me luck. More likely it was just an excellent season and my timing was right. When I left him back in camp with Norma I still caught fish. Without Sam I found it easier to play and beach fish, but something essential was missing from my day. Life can be too easy. Sam was my handicap. A fish hooked when he was around often had to be landed twice—once before Sam lunged after it and a second time after he did. Yet I don't remember ever losing a fish because of Sam.

I told Stan Young this once when he expressed some reservations. He replied, "Well, you might not lose them, but you will fail to raise them because he will spook them first, especially in low water."

He was right, but that is the price you pay for such companionship and devotion. Sam's faith in my ability to hook a fish borders on religion. It is flattering and I hate to disappoint him, which I often do. As I fish he keeps studying the water, no matter how long we've gone without a strike. "Any moment now," his eyes say. I badly want to please him. I admire his intensity. He has the deeply furrowed brows you see in pictures of Labs in Orvis catalogs, which make people think Labs are capable of serious thought. This—to the experienced—is a laugh.

His expectations are frankly a burden and many times I've gotten angry at him for the pressure he exerts on me. But when I hook a fish and the reel sounds alarm Sam is as happy as I. He springs into action and doesn't miss a beat of the fish's tail. The only bad thing is his barking. It is incessant until the fish is landed and released. This may be half an hour later. It is a lot of noise for a river audience to cope with. He worries the fish all the way to the beach. Who's playing it, anyway, he or I?

Because so much fishing today is on a catch-and-release basis it was many months before Sam ever saw one killed. He was astonished. He looked at me doubtfully, after I bonked it and the fish gasped its last breath. What was going on? Usually when a fish is stranded, and I get ready to release it, he enters the shallows, faces me, and waits for me to send it back to the depths. He wants to chase it, but I hold him back until there is no chance of him catching it. He believes he has earned the right of fair pursuit from all the waiting he has endured, often in terrible weather.

At first Sam had no interest in steelhead. He didn't see the connection between them and us. He thought we were just out for an outing—a simple good time. He played along the edges of the stream and occasionally went for a swim. But one evening in early June, Norma and he and I went to the mouth of Deer Creek for the last hour's fishing. They stayed on the schoolhouse side while I crossed the creek, then the river above the mouth, and began fishing back towards them. After a couple of casts I hooked a fresh summer run, a wild fish that vaulted high into the air. Sam saw me strike back and the leap that followed. Click and the connection was made. So *that* is why we go fishing, he reasoned.

Sam hit the water hard. He swam all over the pool, first this way, then that, his head held high as a cormorant, searching the air for the fish, I guess, which is where he saw it last. But now it was hugging the stones. Then it jumped again. In spite of his low perspective he didn't miss it. He headed in its direction, paws churning. But he grew confused and began to swim around in circles. Quickly I saw my chance and beached the fish and released it, sending it on its way before he could swim upstream to where I was. When he reached me the fish was back in its depths; Sam looked to the right and to the left, then at me in disgust. I had betrayed him.

Sam was never the same again, never the quiet unassuming companion out for an evening's walk and a swim. The purpose was fish hunting. It has been this way ever since. Eight years have passed; they pass at exactly the same rate for both of us, I've noticed, and now we are both middle aged. (Never say old.) Do I regret having found him? Though I hesitate to answer, it is usually solely for effect. The answer is, No.

The down side of owning such a dog is his irascible behavior. He is noisy and bothers my fish. But his enthusiasm is so keen it often surpasses my own. He is a loyal friend and companion, whatever the weather. The tactical challenge posed by landing a fish when Sam is around, frankly, is not for everyone. But he adds immeasurably to the pleasure of my day.

11

One Memorable Spring

THE FOLLOWING SPRING WAS EXCEPTIONAL. I caught four steelhead that topped twenty pounds, all in a span of three months. They measured between 38 and 39 1/2 inches. That is a tight bracket and puts them in the twenty-pound class, but none of them by more than a pound or two. I remember each fish vividly.

The first found me camped a dozen miles from the Mixer Hole on the Skagit. At mid-morning I decided to try my luck. The sky alternated sleet and wet snow. At the turnoff to the abandoned railroad grade I took the narrow, rut-lined road where trains used to run. The ties and rails were gone, but the bed remained solid. Every few yards a chuckhole yawned threateningly, its shallowness concealed by rainwater. Only having driven the road before told me it was negotiable.

Wet alders slapped at my windows and arched overhead. It was a lonely place, the drive an exact mile. If you met another vehicle you played chicken until one of you pulled off into the scrub and let the other pass. Today I met no one and there was no problem. I parked along the edge and peered down over the bank. The two-hundred yard-long hole was deserted. This was a rare treat in March.

The big steelhead nearly took my arm off at the shoulder. A moment later he was bucking out in the heavy water, joined to me by a hundred yards of thread-like backing. The big Hardy Perfect reel said it needed oil. Then the fish turned and raced downstream. I scrambled ashore and lumbered after it. Sam followed just as fast as his puppy legs would carry him. This only his first month with me, he was worried about being left behind. Half an hour later and half a mile down the beach I persuaded the fish to swim in through the boulders that jutted up out of the shallows. It was a huge buck. I wanted Sam to see him, but he had wandered off into a willow thicket and was busy sniffing around. I took a moment to study my fish—the faint pink sheen along his flank, his bodily thickness, his gigantic tail. I pulled out my cloth tape and measured 38 and 1/2 inches. I guessed his weight in the low twenties.

I should have taken a girth measurement, for that would have enabled me to calculate his weight more closely. I just didn't think of it. I righted him quickly and pointed him out into the channel. He retraced his route back to open water.

Sam returned from the bushes and wagged his tail when he saw me. He had missed the main event. By degrees the blue sky disappeared, the wind began to blow, and thick clouds moved in from the Southwest. Soon it was raining. The rain turned to wet snow. Well, that is March. Casting grew more difficult in the gale. I gave up hope of getting a second fish and returned to my car. We were dripping. Sam looked miserable. Even a Lab will wince when the weather gets bad enough. By the time we reached Rockport, wet snow was freckling the black pavement. It thickened to a half inch. We followed a blizzard into Arlington. There the cloud cover lifted. By the time we reached the interstate sun was streaming in the driver-side window. That too is March.

My second big fish came from the Sauk only a week later. I left Sam at Oso with Norma and drove to the river for an evening's short fishing. I chose the very visible run downstream from the bridge below the mouth of the Suiattle. It takes several hours to fish thoroughly. It is a sometimes hole. I hurried through the top water, which has never been very productive for me. I neared the middle bottom. The fish that took was a female and I remember her especially because, when she first jumped far across the river, the sun was nearly gone. A band of light illuminated the trees along the far bank where the current quickened and spilled over to mark the start of the next pool. When she exploded the low-angled light caught her side and turned it a brilliant pink. She was a big, bright, beautiful fish. The fight was crazy and over with fast, for she quickly wore herself out; it was the kind of fish that makes the angler look deft, when he is merely lucky to have such an acrobatic fish on the end of his line. She measured 38 inches, and weighed about 20 pounds. She was deep, deep for a female, and so I count her among the big ones, though she might have gone a shade less. The fly was a barbless red marabou with a dark blue body and silver tinsel. It is an original, though there must be many like it. Since then the pattern has caught many fish. She was easy to unpin and shot away without hesitation. I missed Sam's company, though I knew I was better off without him when playing a big fish.

It was now April. My third big fish that year came from the backside of the White Creek Drift during a period of mid-high water when the hole was difficult and dangerous to wade. A tumble into the heavy current would carry you straight down the river and into the next riffle. That is not reason enough to avoid fishing it, however. The likelihood of a big one is worth the risk.

At the top of the run overhanging branches threaten to claim your backcast and force you to wade deeper than is wise. Consequently it is an exciting place to fish. A big cedar droops overhead and a snag lies on the beach right behind where your flyline wants to go. I always use a wading staff here. Sam was on the beach today, not far away, trying to stay dry. My backcast often went where he liked to stand, which was directly behind me; I had hooked and released him several times in the course of a week. I loved the spot. From this difficult run I was used to taking 12 to 16 fish a season. Many of them were huge.

We were camped a few hundred yards away in the gravel pit and Sam slept in my stationwagon, which was mother to him ever since the day I found him. When you are feeling well the special challenges of this pool do not seem great. But I was sick, sick with the flu of the runny-nose variety, and was presently weak and in the coughing stage, which sounds awful but signifies you are getting better. You are a long ways from being well, though.

Rather than return to Seattle to recover or to Oso, where there was shelter, I decided to stay in the tent trailer and wait it out. Stan Young was camped across from me and the first night I'm sure I kept him awake with my sneezing and wheezing. He kindly brought me back a box of Kleenex from the Rockport Store the next day. So I was well provided for in most ways. I had plenty of fruit juice, packaged soup, bread, and cheese. My portable radio had fresh batteries and brought in the Seattle classical-music station. As always I had with me a stack of books and magazines.

Gradually my nose dried up, though my head remained caught in a vice. In two-hour stretches I slept through both the day and the night. The weather was fortuitously mild. I went outside only to relieve myself and to feed Sam from his big bag of puppy meal. He had the run of the camp. On the afternoon of the fourth day I felt well enough to venture out into the day's cool sunshine. In the shade it remained frigid. The prospect of some fishing gripped me. Why not slip into my waders, grab my flyrod, and drive across the bridge to the first hole, a good one, where I didn't have to walk far? I could always return to camp if it proved too much.

Even hauling on my neoprenes turned out to be a big job, however. Once they were on I was lightly sweated and puffing, but it seemed easier to go fishing than to peel them off. A long walk up the beach led to White Creek, and it was over and around big stones and involved scrambling under and over some barrier logs that had washed downstream in the last flood. By the time I reached the top of the run I was rasping and short of breath. Sweat beaded my brow and I felt giddy when I left the sun and entered the deep shade of the pool. A breeze moved across the water and I began to shiver. Go home, whispered my good sense. I began to cast.

Sam took up his station at the head of the pool and looked nervous as always. He emitted his high-pitched whine—they aren't the steadiest of breeds. After ten minutes a fish took solidly out in mid-current, ran slowly a few feet, and stopped. Grateful for the opportunity I set the hook hard. I set it again and waited for the fish's response. There was none. Oh, there might have been a faint pulse on the line that told me I had a hook up, but nothing more. Gingerly I reeled up and tightened on the line, clutching it against the middle of the cork and cautiously lifting. The fish was instantly off on a long run. It was one of those dashes that is not very fast, but is relentless and indicates a strong fish. You know better than to try to check it. Near the bottom of the pool the fish stopped and held. Cautiously I began to pull from the side in order to coax the fish into moving upstream, knowing most of my potential problems lay below.

The fish didn't budge, but gradually the line tension mounted and it must have counted for something, for the fish soon began to swim upstream, still not very fast. I gathered line back onto the spool, reminding myself not to crank too fast or too hard or else the pressure would cause the fish to race away. A dangerous riffle lay less than a hundred yards below and, if the fish entered it, it might well be lost.

The fish soon drew abreast of me and I managed to edge it out of the heaviest water and into what was relatively slack. The fish came up on top and turned over on its side and I saw it was not the giant I had hoped for but a fish of about 13 pounds. This is a very respectable size, however. It ran away again, down and across, came back up, surged at mid-channel, splashed about, and let me draw it to the rocks. While trying to work the hook free the fish began to twist and spin in the current, which was not strong. The eight-pound leader popped and the fish drifted free. My arms and shoulders were trembling from the strain. I wanted to lie down.

Wobbling as though drunk I picked my way over the big stones the long distance back to my car and drove to camp. There I flopped on my bed, still in my waders. Two hours deep sleep restored me to a sick normalcy.

The following day was clear and mild again. A watery sun hid behind some thin clouds. My nose stayed dry so long as I remained indoors. My knowledge that fresh fish were in the river was working on my mind and resolution. I had to fish, fish or die—perhaps the latter. I donned my waders and set off on foot in the direction of White Creek again. A boat was back-pulling plugs through the slack water at the bottom of the hole. This annoyed me greatly, though fishers have a perfect right to fish from boats. I decided to sit on a log in the sun until they were done. Eventually the boat drifted away to the tail of the pool, then ran the riffle below it. I rejoiced. Everybody knows that a boat manned by oars won't be back.

While we waited Sam kept casting me his expectant look. It read, "When are we going to get going?" I nodded and we started up the beach. I found the effort exhausting. The water was an inch or so lower than yesterday, for there had been no rain, but the hole remained difficult to wade even at this moderate height and the deep shade gave me an instant chill. I was running a slight fever, I suspected. I fished for about an hour without a strike. This took me to the bottom of the run where it shallowed out and became boring.

A boat passed through the water, but did not stop to fish. Another boat soon appeared and stuck to the opposite shore. Good. A bit shaky I returned to the head of the pool and began to fish through it a second time. Right away I was fast to a fish, which proved to be a bright nine-pounder. Once more I had to quit afterwards because of the chills and weakness brought on by the fight.

I returned to camp, where I slept through dinnertime, rose late, heated some soup, and constructed two mammoth cheese sandwiches. I ate them in lazy stages. I soon found myself senselessly batting my eyes at the light and turned in. I slept straight through the night. I believe I didn't once change position. I felt about the same the next day. Not good, but not too bad, either. The flu was hanging on. If anything my nose was too dry now. My cough had become theatrical. By afternoon a light drizzle was falling. There were no tops left to the trees. It was stupid to venture out, but fishermen are not known for their collective wisdom. I returned to White Creek just as a boat pulled away. I decided to fish it, even though the pool had just been thrashed by the boaters. My trip up the long bar and over the boulders was cooler and less tiring today because of the clouds and light rain. But I got wet under my raincoat from condensation. Hot, too. At the top of the run I vented my jacket. I could picture steam issuing forth from the open closure as from the backdoor of a laundry. I began to fish seriously.

Today's fish took at the upper bottom of the run just as I was mentally giving up hope. The fly simply stopped in mid-swing as the line continued downstream and bellied in toward me. It was the perfect take and hook-up, the fly lodging in the hinge of the fish's jaw. There was no way to know this at the moment, of course.

If you are fishing from the left bank (facing downstream) a fish gets hooked in the right hinge of the jaw on such a take and on the left side if you are on the other bank. At least it usually does. The fight was not as difficult as with some smaller fish I've taken from the same pool. Ten minutes into it I saw my fish for the first time. Big and broad, I knew he could have his way with me any time he wanted to. What I needed to do was keep him quiet, unexcited. If he fought against the pull of the line in the current, and I gave him unmitigated sidestrain, I might be able to land him. But if I pressured him while he was moving away, he would fight against the strain and swim faster and harder, and I would lose him. So I let him run whenever he wanted to, tightening gently from time to time to see if he had had a change in attitude. He didn't. This was a contemptuous fish. I was forced repeatedly to slacken the line to avoid excessive pressure.

I took turns slackening slightly, then tightening. It made no difference. He swam easily about as though we weren't attached. The one who was tiring was me. My nose was running anew. I felt weak and trembling, all sweaty. In fact I felt like I had when I came down with the flu several days ago. It was too great a price to pay for a catch-and-release fish. My hope was that the fish wouldn't last much longer, because I couldn't. He didn't. I soon discovered that I could move him slightly with pressure from the rod. This was the start of leading him around. I had to be careful, though, and not tow him too fast or he would rebel. He'd over-run the line and be off again in a downstream course. And there was the danger of the hook pulling out, after all this time, for twenty minutes had passed.

The run out to the current stopped just short of the heaviest water. The fish drifted in a bit before resuming his fight. This was good news. I had yet to show the fish the beach—which is tantamount to showing the bull the cape—and make him battle it out in shallow water. There I must be careful not to lift his head too high and frighten him. Now I could see the fish clearly. He looked weary. Also huge. This made me stronger. I knew the fight would be over soon. I would either have him or not.

He made one more dash back to the center of the river, but it had no authority to it, only weight, plenty of bulk and volume. There was no lightness to this fish. Since I was going to release him anyway, I was freed from the problem of having to get him to dry land. I could strand him in the shallows and release him at the edge of the beach. I wouldn't have to take him an inch out of the water.

It was tricky, though. Sam—yet inexperienced with fish—watched. I had to make the fish lie still in quiet water. I accomplished this feat and whipped out the measuring tape for a quick reading. Then I slipped out the barbless hook (it had penetrated well and was placed just where I would want it to be) and held the fish upright. His great mouth gaped and gasped as he stopped breathing air and started taking in the life-sustaining water.

Only 38 inches, but thick and male, which means heavier. It weighed more than 20 pounds, I was sure. Its gillcovers were cherry and a wide crimson stripe ran down his length. His back was greenish-brown, with a few spots below the median line. In a few more days he would be spawning. A great stud of a fish, I wondered if he would live to service a number of females, just as a bull might? Would he survive spawning and return to the sea, perhaps to spawn again? Chances are he wouldn't. Few of the big males do, alas.

I felt as though I had split a cord of wood. Is it possible to be both sick and triumphant? Licking a great fish produces an undescribable feeling. It will carry you far. In my case it took me back to camp and my customary two-hour nap. I awoke feeling hammered but great.

I was still glowing the next morning and the feeling of happy triumph was with me (like the Force) when I returned to the pool. I fished it carefully, but it rewarded me with not so much as a touch, though I was certain there were fish in the water. What was wrong—had I lost my touch? Or had my streak of luck simply run out?

12

A Stroke of Ill Luck

IF I LOVE APRIL IT IS LARGELY BECAUSE of the Sauk River and its fishing then. On the last day of the month it closes to protect its run of wild late-winter steelhead, which are spawning or about to spawn. My favorite reaches lie about 40 miles from the North Fork. The Sauk is a wild, unpredictable river and when it floods it does so on a grand scale. It washes away whatever stands in its way. The rest of the year it purls prettily within its banks. It, along with the Toutle, were the state's two premier wild rivers. With the eruption of Mt. St. Helens more than a decade ago, and the Toutle's ruination, only the Sauk is left as a thing of unravaged, undammed beauty. In the half dozen years that I've fished it I've stored up enough happy experiences to last a lifetime.

An example of the Sauk's destructive force: Dr. Nate Smith is a dedicated flyfisher who headed the Department of Sports Medicine at the University of Washington prior to retiring. He built a fine second home on the banks of the Sauk near Darrington. While he was vacationing in Egypt the river experienced one of its worst floods. The river not only took away Nate's home, it stole his land and formed a new channel. Today the river runs through Nate's former bedroom. It is an object lesson for those of us who might love rivers inordinately.

Bob McLaughlin had a cabin downstream a hundred yards or so from Nate's. The flood didn't touch it or take his land, but left his property heaped with logging debris. He had to cut his way to his front door with a chainsaw. Shortly afterwards, in disgust, he sold his cabin. He did not quibble about the price.

Untamed rivers exact a terrible toll. Love them, visit them, use them, but keep your distance. Know what they can do at their worst. Read the message of last winter's floodplain and memorize it. Sufficient respect will lead to a feeling of awe. Yet an untamed river is what I love best. The Sauk's season is short, its fish appropriately large and wild. March and April are best; during the traditional winter months it has a few steelhead, most of these hatchery plants. In summer, being glacially fed, the river turns slate-colored and is fished mostly for Dolly Vardens and their kin, the bull trout, with bait. Its small run of wild summer-run steelhead are threatened by habitat loss and must be released. The run probably numbers about 200 fish, which is its historic level. In the upper river summer juveniles may be in competition with wild winter runs—a fairly unusual situation. It is next to impossible for the river to build its run of summer fish to harvestable levels under these conditions.

The late winter run is strong for now. Habitat damage from reckless logging threatens winter fish in the lower river and it is only a matter of time before the loss of spawning reaches reduces the run's size. Once started the unraveling process is impossible to halt. This is the lesson of Deer Creek.

The Sauk contributes more than half of the Skagit's good run of fish. The substrate of both rivers has undergone progressive damage, but the worst came from the great flood of November 1990, which destroyed the towns of Lyman and Hamilton on the Skagit. Major characteristics of the Sauk changed for the worst, too. In many places the river has carved out new channels. Locals say this is usual and portends nothing serious. Many of them are employed in logging. They are immune to the sight of habitat damage, which they believe to be temporary and unimportant.

As a river declines it may continue to provided spurts of excellent fishing that resemble the successes of the past. Each year a group of dedicated anglers—many of them flyfishers—approaches the Sauk with hope and trepidation. Flowing at a moderate height and with good color, what kind of fishing will it provide? One must don waders and venture forth to find out.

The Sauk is best fished from a portable camp, one that can be vacated at a few hours notice when snowmelt starts to bring the river up, triggered by warm rain. Many fishers make day trips. It lies about 100 miles from Seattle, which makes the drive a little inconvenient for easy, daily commuting. So a number of fishers have established trailer camps in the county park at Rockport or at the old gravel pit on the Sauk by the government bridge.

Its good fishing is no longer a secret and anglers come to its riffles from all over the world. Some bring boats and motors, for motors are useful on the Skagit though unlawful on the Sauk. Both are big rivers and many important reaches cannot be reached without a driftboat or raft. At the peak of the season there is apt to be a boat-traffic problem.

A bank fisher meets a host of interesting people. I first came across the man from Idaho at White Creek in a bygone year. In spite of the many times we kept meeting and fishing together we never exchanged names. I'm sorry now. He was a dedicated and likeable person. He enjoyed surface fishing, as he was used to doing in summer back in his home state. Now steelhead in March and April are invariably taken down deep. A few skilled fishers, like Bill McMillan, will use floating lines, but tie on heavy flies that sink quickly to the bottom. The man from Idaho was determined to fish on top. We thought this dedication admirable but foolish. "Good luck," we wished him with a crooked grin. But we kept our eye on him, just in case something odd happened and he started catching fish.

The Sauk flows into the Skagit; hence the two rivers are never far apart. He alternated fishing them, which is what we did, too. Often the Sauk was dirty, the Skagit clean. Or one would be hot, while in the other you could fish a mile of water and never have a take from a steelhead. The man from Idaho suited up every day. Six weeks into the season he had not hooked a fish. But he had seen a lot of fish hooked and landed. This did not seem to discourage him. He was invariably cheerful. We considered him a colleague, almost a friend. Yet he was . . . different.

Once I heard somebody question him about his dubious practice. Was he serious? He said he was. "I'm not giving up until the guy above me and the one below me both hook a fish at the same time." These men would be fishing sunk fly, of course. What he meant was, it would take such an event to convince him no fish in a given run would come up on top to take his fly. It was a good year and I think a sunk double around him probably happened once or twice. The fact that he continued fishing on top probably meant he had modified his ground rules.

He was one of us, probably no madder than any one else except in this single odd way. We saw him so often many of us had stopped thinking of him as queer. For this season, anyway, he was a brother. We listened politely to his pronouncements and nodded our heads thoughtfully up and down (like a dippy bird) when he spoke his thoughts. He was after all only a more extreme version of ourselves. We suffered from the same malaise that brought men long distances to stand in icy water and cast stupidly into the sunset. Outsiders wouldn't understand.

The fishing that year was so good that we often felt guilty that he did not share in it. Fishing alongside the man from Idaho was spooky, a little like a curse. The curse was on him, but we began to wonder if it might rub off on us through too close association. Then we would stop catching fish.

He was trying to do a difficult thing, we recognized, however foolish. His foolishness was only a mirror of our own. I wanted to see him catch a fish and prove us wrong. At least one side of my mind did. Still, our ambivalence was such that we felt relieved each day we learned he hadn't nailed one.

He had a sense of humor, thank God, and it had to do largely with himself and his futile activity. Without it he would have been intolerable. He often mocked himself. It was good, for otherwise he'd drive us up the wall with his fierce persistence. He was out of the competition, really. He had elected himself out through the way that he fished. Whatever he might accomplish took place in a detached world, one unrelated to us. It lacked common meaning. For instance, our daily bag totals meant nothing to him. Soon they began to mean little to us. It was how he had corrupted us. He was affecting our minds, our relative balance.

Sam and I repeatedly went to the backside of White Creek. The run continued to treat us well. One day the man from Idaho joined us. "Mind if I tag along?" he asked. Of course not.

I offered to let him fish first through the water, but he declined. "No, you go," he said. "Let me watch you. Maybe I can pick up some pointers. I know you've been catching fish."

Only because I've been fishing near bottom, I thought.

So I went first. I hooked a fish at once; anyone fishing sunk fly that day would have hooked the fish. Over my shoulder I saw the man from Idaho on the bank, still stringing up his rod.

"Look here," I called out softly, just as the fish came out of the water in a flashy head-and-tail leap and showed his bright rainbow stripe. He was huge. He paused a moment, then bore straight downstream and stopped in the middle of the pool.

"Big, big fish," commented the man from Idaho.

I nodded assent. I was a little tense because so many things could go wrong at this point. For instance, the line might catch on a snap or button on my fishing vest. Or wrap around the rod butt or reel handle. I didn't want to make any mistakes, not with a fish so large.

"Sure wish it was mine," said the man from Idaho wistfully.

Then why hadn't you fished through the pool ahead of me, as I'd offered, if you felt this way?

The fish stayed in the center of the pool for about twenty minutes. Whenever I gained some line he took it right back. Then he got bored with this and ran to the bottom of the pool, stopping at the point where it quickened and shallowed and gathered itself up into a vee-groove preparatory to spilling over into a boulder-lined chute. It was a place that gave boaters pause.

The fish now came up on top and gave me a second glimpse of his size—in order to taunt me, I thought. Then he turned sideways and the current caught him and he washed out of the pool and down into the long riffle. I scrambled out of the deep water and raced after him over the loose stones that were scattered along the steep bank, slipping and sliding, nearly falling down. All the while backing screamed off my reel, whose diameter was narrowing fast.

Then the line became caught on a sunk rock far out in the river.

"Oh, shit," I pronounced.

"Too bad," said the man from Idaho. He said it as though the world were ending.

It was a critical situation. And it was a terrible place to be playing a fish. I had hoped the fish would clear the run and I could follow him down to the pool below, the Native Hole, where I had played and landed many fish. This was not to be.

"Hey, I think I know what will work," said the man from Idaho.

"What's that?"

"Watch," he said.

On our side of the river were a number of exposed boulders, each huge, and the river curled among them in a great green slick that looked deep in many place. Just out from shore in the worst place it was well over my head. Toward the middle it grew shallow again, forming an underwater island. It would be hard to reach. The man from Idaho had a plan to get there.

"I can free your line," he said, "but we might lose the fish. Shall I try?"

He was asking my permission. I said, "I'm probably going to lose it, anyway. Go ahead." The man from Idaho and I had become partners.

He put his rod down in a safe place and found a stout stick that would support his weight in the current. He began to wade out. My line he held gingerly between two fingers. I remember the way the water tried to swallow him up from the bottom. He fought his way through the gut to the shallow bar about fifteen feet out, where it was only inches deep. Occasionally the current whipped the line out of his hand, but he always managed to catch it again. Sometimes he pulled on it harder than I would have and I grew worried.

"Throw me some slack," he commanded. I obeyed.

Suddenly he let go of the line and the slack began bellying in the current. What was he up to? Was this a new stratagem? "Now, tighten," he said. I did as I was told. The fish began moving upstream, freed from the binding rock.

I fairly sagged with relief in my boots. "Here we go again," I cried joyfully. How good it felt to be tight once more to the fish, rather than to a rock. The fish began cruising back and forth across the riffle as though unsure in his mind about where he wanted to head next. This was dangerous, boulder-lined water—very swift, alternately shallow and pocketed. The fish could hang me up again at will. Instead it roamed widely. I followed its course with my rod tip. Then the line went tight and wouldn't move.

"Hung up again?" he asked pleasantly. "All right. Switch your line toward me and I'll catch it."

What, again? No doubt on his part, this mad man from Idaho could handle the problem. I switched the line and he deftly snared it. He was getting good at it. He began to pick his way out into the river again with his stick. We were a little lower in the run, where it wasn't so pockety.

He lifted the line over his head with both hands. Again he freed it. He was wonderful. My fish pulsed back into the current and ran the short remaining distance down to the Native Hole. There the water slowed and deepened.

"No problem now," said the man from Idaho, grinning insanely. "Nothing ahead but open water."

The words rang in the air like some terrible prophesy. Suddenly I hated him, this phoney steelheader. He was pretending to be my friend in order to trick me into losing this great fish. That was his goal all along, no matter how helpful he seemed. He was demonstrating the truth of what I had begun to suspect. My paranoia was only normal for the situation.

At the top of the Native Hole most of the Sauk passes through a slot maybe a dozen feet wide. It is grooved into bedrock and runs fast. On my side was a shingled beach, easy to wade out into. Below the river dropped into a slow pool. The pool posed no threat. The fish stopped his run near the top at the deepest part. Ordinarily this would produce no problem. Today I found my line fouled again far out in the deep water. Neither the man from Idaho nor I could wade so far, so deep. There must be a single snag buried there and the fish had found it. I could no longer feel the throb at the end of my line. A feeling of despair washed over me.

My line was tightly wedged. The water was about eight feet deep and swift. I waded back and forth in the shallows, pulling first hard, then gently. It made no difference. Stuck is stuck. The deeper I waded the less leverage I was able to exert and the more the current lifted me up off my feet and threatened to invert me.

A stranger came down the beach. I remember only a dark mustache. Why didn't he leave me and the man from Idaho alone? Together we had enough trouble on our hands.

"Hook a fish?" he asked.

Another time it would have been funny.

He continued, "Get hung up?"

God, this was too much. Was he looking for a bruise? I looked at him wearily.

"It's a long story," I explained. My tongue stuck to the roof of my mouth, which tasted like cotton batten.

"Too bad," he added.

Angry and in a near rage I waded out into the current until it caught and threatened to spin me around. I had the line in my hand and broke off the fish. Maybe now I would have some peace. The man with the mustache wandered off to get his own rod, I guess, inspired by the performance of my great fish. He would do better, he knew.

"I'm sorry," said the man from Idaho, my friend, my partner in grief. I should have asked him his name at this point, but the moment had passed and there would be no other.

"I think I'll fish here," he said. "What about you?"

I told him that I was going to hike back to the upper pool. I had barely touched it. All its vast length awaited me.

"Good idea," said my friend. "Maybe I'll see you later."

I said I hoped so.

I landed three fine steelhead before dark. One, a 13-pounder, fought wonderfully. It offered me no trouble, however.

When it was time to quit I found the pool below unoccupied. I looked thoroughly for the man from Idaho, but he was gone. Though I saw him a few more times before the season ended, it was always from across the river or far up a wading bar and we exchanged only waves, not words. I keep looking for him every spring, but have given up hope of finding him. No doubt he's back in Idaho, fishing on the surface for big trout, the way he likes to do.

As April drew to a close and the season ended the fishing in the Sauk slowed and I began visiting different pools, and often I drove off to the Skagit in search of fresh fish. Salmonberry was leafing and when I pushed it aside the canes slapped back at me, full of vigor. Willow wore its trident cap. When the sun came out it was fierce and I turned my face up to it, hoping for the start of a tan, but the sun lasted only moments and soon a warm rain began falling. May would soon arrive.

The Mixer Hole on the Skagit is one of my favorites at this time of the year. Unfortunately it is the choice of many. I fish it mainly in April because it runs East and West and catches the sun all afternoon. There is so much UV in the air in April that you can quickly get fried, which is what we are all after—that false glow of health. (Part of it is windburn.)

The increase in available light is what triggers the enzyme in juvenile salmonids and causes them to smolt—become those bright little fish with loose scales that migrate to the sea now. Often steelhead smolts will attack my large fly. The gape is too wide for their mouths, but they get hooked occasionally—the spearing effect, it's called—and I have to shake them off. Some days when the migration is most heavy they hit all day long, but rarely get speared.

The Mixer Hole is one of the world's great steelhead pools. It is fully a half mile long and some 250 yards wide. Upstream and within sight is the confluence of the Sauk, so this huge pool holds fish aimed at the headwaters of both rivers. This makes it doubly attractive. The lower portion of the Mixer is comprised of large rocks and boulders. It is vast and fish will hold almost anywhere in it. Flyfishers are able to cover only a small percentage of its holding water because they can't make long enough casts. Boats drift through the hole, casting lures in the direction of the wading bar or else anchor just outside the flyfishers's reach, crowding and seeming to taunt them. There is much animosity between the groups that leads to confrontations. Unless regulations are changed to protect the wading fisherman boats with big motors will continue to disturb the water he is fishing and scatter the fish. Worse, somebody will get hurt, perhaps seriously.

Each morning before sunup anglers arrive by boat, raft, or car to fish the Mixer in hopes of being the first through the pool. First man is apt to hook fish that have arrived during the night. And while the pool is probably host to hundreds of steelhead, at any given time, when they will strike is unpredictable. Even a pool of such great variety and size becomes dull after a prolonged period of inactivity and a fisher may grow anxious to be elsewhere. I try to play the law of averages at the Mixer and if I don't hook a fish in a couple of hours make myself leave. But I go there regularly, especially on bright afternoons, partly for the benefits of the warm sun in my face.

It is a place where you are apt to hook into a really big steelhead. To fish the pool alone, hook a fish unobserved, play it unassisted, and lead it to the beach where you elect to land it are among the great pleasures of steelheading. To release a giant fish to live and spawn and perhaps be caught another day is a thrill. Each season I hope for a few such experiences at the Mixer Hole and usually get more than I deserve.

Make no mistake, though, the Sauk is my favorite river. When it has risen a foot or more from rain, and the rain stops and a cool night settles down, I experience extreme nervousness while in town. The river is clearing is the message from the sky. I've had my best fishing under such conditions. Miscalculate slightly or arrive a half-day early and you will miss the whole show. Instead you'll be greeted by volumes of dirty water and a river that holds little chance of yielding you a fish.

The Sauk clears quickly if there is not too much rain. I remember driving up from Seattle one evening when there was less than three hours of daylight left. I set up my tent-trailer and rushed to the river to find it barely fishable, a shade of ugly brown. I could see about two feet beneath the surface, which is marginal clarity for the Sauk. I waded in to the shallows and began casting. The water was slow at the top of the run, and I immediately hung up and lost my fly. I saw that the color was turning green.

Excitedly I waved at the fisherman across the river, pointing downward and gesturing wildly. My gestures were exaggerated for effect. He knew what I meant and waved back with the same enthusiasm. We soon began hooking fish. The fishing held good until full dark. Since we were on opposite sides of the river and it was wide, our casts did not come anywhere near each other nor were we fishing over each other's fish. It was a nice arrangement.

I beached three prime steelhead, two of them over ten pounds. It was a typical April evening on the Sauk. Many others have had a similar experience and will confirm that mine was not unique. When conditions are right great fishing arrives often. This means high water that is rapidly clearing. The Sauk is a generous river with plenty of broad riffles to accommodate a lot of anglers. But it can become crowded, especially from boat traffic, when so many people like to fish the same run.

One afternoon at mid-month Norma and I drove up to our place on the North Fork. We planned to stay overnight and I wanted badly to fish the Sauk. It turned out to be a most unusual trip and one I've never forgotten because of an odd stroke of luck. The rain let up and the afternoon turned cool. I hurried to my favorite pool. Norma and Sam remained behind. The Sauk ran high but clear with nobody fishing it. The people in Seattle must have figured it was still too muddy to be worth the long drive. Well, they were wrong.

Many rivers go relatively unfished at mid-week. This was Wednesday. I saw a guideboat beached at the top of White Creek. Now, where had it come from? My heart sagged in my waders. Two flyfishers were casting into the best water of the pool I was headed for. I recognized the boat as belonging to a flyfishing guide. He tended to hog the water.

He sat on the rocks, watching his dudes fish, offering them no advice though they seemed to need it. The pair looked like they had not been flyfishing long; I could discern this from a quarter mile away. After a bit the guide stood up and stretched. It was the sign to reel in and get back in the boat. He would take them to the next and final pool of the day, which was the boat takeout. It was where I waited, trying to make up my mind where to go.

Rather than remain and share the lower hole with them I decided to walk up to the pool they were finishing up. There might be some fish in it that hadn't been covered. I trudged up the long beach with its rocks the size and shape of pumpkins. It was all uphill work. The driftboat passed me by. I waved, but nobody waved back. This was typical of him and how he coached his clients.

Using a very heavy line and not mending it much I fished the pool close and tight with my usual bright red marabou fly. The fish were responsive—brilliant, newly arrived steelhead and ready takers. The pool yielded me two fine fish, one 15 and the other seven pounds. The small one fought best. I released it and returned to the original pool where my car was parked. The guide's dudes had fished through it, then had winched their boat out and driven off. Halfway through the run I hooked a third fish. It went 18 pounds. The 15- and 18-pounders were the biggest back-to-back steelhead I'd ever caught. I think they still are.

It was now nearly dark. I mentally faulted the guide for not giving his clients what they had paid for, namely, the knowledge necessary to catch fish in water that unmistakably held them. The fact that it was all to my benefit was a fluke. And flukes don't count.

I could not wait for tomorrow and a possible repeat. This was not to be. I slept heavily, a smile on my face, playing and replaying the fish of yesterday in my mind, enjoying their relative performances. Norma was the first out of bed in the morning, as usual. She wore an odd expression. "Something is wrong," she said. "Wrong?" I asked. "Something happened in the night. To me, I mean."

"What?" I was still half-asleep.

"I don't know what, but I don't feel right. I'm numb all down my left side. Could I have had a stroke? I think we'd better head back to town and find out."

Which we did. We stuffed something in our mouths and threw our gear in the car. I aimed it at the Group Health Hospital in Seattle. There they performed a series of tests that lasted all day. One was where they inject dye into your bloodstream. Then they put you in a steel tunnel and photograph you as you are motored its length at an excruciatingly slow speed. The trip takes over an hour. All the while you aren't supposed to move a hair on your head. Detailed pictures are being taken of your circulatory system, clear down to the capillaries. Any jiggle will cause them to blur and be useless. They'll have to be done over again. It is bad enough the first time.

All the while I sat in the room next door and looked at magazines. I couldn't concentrate on the words. I tried to think about steelhead and whether they would be hitting today, but fish were insignificant, the catching of them a meaningless act. I kept telling myself that this couldn't be happening. Norma never gets sick.

After a bit she walked through the door, still wearing a hospital gown. She looked pale and weary. I'd never seen her unsteady on her feet before.

"How'd it go?" I asked.

"They won't know anything until tomorrow. I'm to call my regular doctor, Steven Smith, and make an appointment. They'll send him the test results and he'll explain them to me. That's how it goes. But first a radiologist has to read them."

"And what do you do in the meanwhile?"

"Go home and rest. Try to think of something else."

"You don't have to stay here? In bed?"

"No."

"How do you feel when you've had a stroke?"

"Not so great. I have a tingling feeling all up and down my left side. I guess tingly and numb is how you feel."

"It can't be anything else?"

"No," she said. I shivered. And I remembered that she had known right from the start what it was.

The tingling feeling doesn't go away, as when your arm has gone to sleep from sleeping on it and you wiggle it vigorously. It never did. She simply learned to live with it. There was no choice. Additionally she had a slight speech impediment that I didn't notice but she did. And she was experiencing a minor disturbance in vision.

"Will they go away?" I asked. "These disturbing symptoms?" Boy, I was sure full of questions.

"How should I know?" she said shortly. "I've never had a stroke before." Then a little less severely but thoughtfully, "Oh, I sure hope so. I don't want to live this way." A second chill ran down my spine.

I hung around the house, getting on her nerves, taking her back and forth to the hospital for more tests, asking my stupid questions for which there were no ready replies. I alternated between fawning over and neglecting her.

"I'm probably well enough to drive myself to the hospital," she told me once, "but—thanks—I'd rather not."

Nothing was conclusive. Dr. Smith put her on blood-pressure medicine. Her blood pressure was very high: it had been for some time. I didn't know this. She had never told me. Even in a long marriage you often don't give your partner all the news. Some facts come as a big surprise.

"High blood pressure runs in my family," she explained. Life was full of new and depressing facts. One day you are well, the next you are counted among the walking wounded. Disaster—in the form of illness—can arrive in a twinkling, or overnight on a fishing trip.

She was ordered to take an aspirin twice a day. That makes two aspirins, times 365, times the number of years you've got left on the planet.

"It's to keep my blood thin." she told me. "They don't want me to develop a clot." A clot? "In an artery," she added mysteriously.

This was a new world. You become conscious of all the mysterious happenings in your body, all the invisible, efficient things that take place

every day, without you thinking about them. Channels run up both sides of your neck, carotid arteries, and they can become plugged with stuff called plaque. It's not the same junk you get on your teeth, but comes close. The stuff lines the walls of your arteries and blocks the blood's passage, or else it coats the sides of the artery and a tiny chunk dislodges and goes drifting along its groove until it comes to a narrow opening and catches. Bump. Your blood is prevented from reaching your brain and the cells die. This is called a stroke. If the blood is held back long enough you undergo sufficient damage in your head and your brain dies. You do, too. But if it happens only briefly—as it did, in her case—a fewer number of brain cells are killed from lack of oxygen and you are disabled to a varying extent.
"You might be . . . incapacitated?" I asked.
"I already am."
"You don't seem any different."
"Take my word for it, I am."
I had to admit, if only to myself, that she seemed not quite her old self. I was not used to being around a sick person, let alone a sick wife. I disliked illness, most of all in myself. Next came my wife. Illness is a state greatly to be avoided.
She said, "If I have another stroke I could be paralyzed. Or," she smiled, "I might die."
"Don't say that."
I looked at my wife of many years. I could not imagine her paralyzed. But then I couldn't imagine her sick or suffering from a stroke, either. Nor could I imagine her dead. Suddenly I got a glimpse into a very different world, perhaps the world of the future. The planet had tipped on its side. All kinds of terrible things could happen, once the center lost its grip. God was not in His heaven—He had gone for a long walk. He had left no number where His calls could be forwarded.
A dirge of days was upon us. We read, we watched television, we talked a little. She was often mute. Was she worried? She wouldn't say. How could she not be? The test results told us practically nothing. She must rest and wait, the doctor said.
One morning she looked me in the face and said, "I think you'd better go fishing. You need some time away,"
"But what about you?"
"I can take care of myself. What will happen, will happen." This was my new, fatalistic wife speaking. The doctors had told her to take two weeks off from work and rest, but they didn't tell her how to let go or

how to sit still. She was a naturally active person. The enforced idleness was getting to her and indirectly to me. She wasn't supposed to exercise and this was making her short-tempered. We were getting on each other's nerves from prolonged contact.

"What if you have another stroke while I'm gone?" I asked.

"Worry instead that I might cut myself."

"Why worry about that?"

"My blood is so thin I might bleed to death."

"How can that be?"

"Go fishing. You're driving me up the wall with these questions." She turned her face away.

So I went fishing at last. I took Sam along, for he had been cooped up, too, and there was nothing wrong with his health. I told myself that Norma *needed* to be alone, which was true enough, though not the whole picture. An overly solicitous husband is a detriment when he isn't performing some vital chore, which he doesn't do often. He may even be a threat to a sick person's health.

We returned to the Sauk, Sam and I. It was flowing at mid-height, with just the color I liked. Its life ran on, while Norma's and mine had been turned into a side channel. April was nearly over, with it the short season. It was no more cruel a month than any other, I decided; it just seemed so this year. Norma's stroke could have happened in August or December. But it hadn't.

For what was left of April my good luck resumed as though there had been no interruption, no terrible stroke. I caught fish that day and on the next trip, too. In the grand scheme of things fishing luck is impertinent, I've discovered. But this is a fishing book, and fish is what it is mainly about, so I dutifully record these facts, these fish statistics.

Life goes on, is the message of rivers. Hope you can be here; if not, that's okay, too.

Once illness enters your life you keep reencountering more of its aspects. Back on the river I met—all in rapid succession—a number of doctors who were fishermen. It was really weird. One was a pathologist, another a specialist in sports medicine (Nate Smith) who gave me some sage advise about recovery rates and what to expect. I met a proctologist, who was not much help here, and two young emergency-room physicians from Denver, who knew everything there was to know. Patiently, kindly, they explained to me over cans of Bud just what a stroke was and what Norma's prognosis was, according to the textbooks and their own vast experience. She was fortunate in not having had paralysis. Her chances were good for a full recovery. They told me what we might encounter for the next few months. I listened as I never had to anything in my life before.

I returned home brimming with knowledge and hope. She met me at the door. She listened to everything I had to say and I said plenty. I had learned things her doctor hadn't told us about or she hadn't found mentioned in all the books and magazines she poured over in her new idle time. I felt valuable for once. Maybe fishing wasn't the great waste of time it had always seemed.

Her recovery was slow and took place in increments. She had been lucky; a stroke is usually much worse. Most people are unable to go back to work. They sit in a chair, forever looking out a window at whatever happens to be passing by on the street. Norma's numbness remains along one side of her body. I forget about it because I don't experience it directly. I think it may not be so bad, but then what do I know? For a long time she couldn't resume her knitting, which was habitual and important to her. It is how she makes dull time pass in a useful manner. Six months later she took up her needles again. Slow at first, it seems to me they fly as fast as ever. She assures me they don't. I yield the floor.

Selfishly I will always wonder about my lost day on the Sauk, the one after I followed the guide and his clients through the pools, hooking big fish behind them. Would the next day have been better or worse? But what difference does it make? There is sweet bliss in my ignorance.

Lost days are gone forever. What matters is the ones you have left. Nearly losing my wife I know how small a day's fishing is in the theater of human events. Yet fishing is good for the soul. I am vain enough to expect more good and great days on a river. I have a hunch they will take place on the Sauk, if they come. There is no finer place.

13

Trophy Time

Author, with first and only 20-pounder he's killed

IT IS APRIL AGAIN, ANOTHER YEAR, and I am camped as usual in the gravel pit down by the Government Bridge. The last week of the season is here and each passing day diminishes what already is left of the short season. A sense of finality is strong in all of our daily activities. I am not alone in camp. Stan Young has his tent trailer pitched across from mine and Bob York has pulled in his huge rig, complete with pockety-pockety generator. And there are people arriving daily from Richland, Spokane, Portland. To get to fish a given riffle requires much patience. Sometimes you have to take a number, so to speak. It is not the bank fishermen that pose the greatest problem; the long progression of boats drifting down the river is depressing. I stay up late, reading, and remain in bed the next morning to avoid those determined to be first on the nearby pools. I suit up about ten or eleven, a favorite time of mine, winter or summer. It is when the earliest fishermen weary and come in, driven by hunger. Often I can find a pool newly vacated. I fish it as though it were virginal, its fish ready takers.

The first day I take a skunk. So what else is new? That night I lie in my narrow bag, listening to the roar of the river less than a hundred yards away. Bob's generator is still; he goes to bed early and tries to be the first man out on the water. So does Stan. This creates a rivalry. But one man can occupy only one pool at one time. They will rise and cook breakfast a full hour before first light. Each morning I hear them banging around. Stan, who is hard of hearing, likes to sing so that he can hear himself. I return the favor the following evening, after his lights go out.

Sam hears the coyotes a quarter mile away and joins in the yipping chorus. Later he growls threateningly without getting up; he is curled tight in the back of my truck. (The stationwagon's been replaced by a new green Ranger this year.) It is a coward's boast. If they come one step nearer he is going to rip out their throats. Oh sure. Overhead the sky is clear and a zillion stars prick the firmament, but in a few hours big drops start to fall, drip-drip-drip on the canvas, and by daylight it is pouring. I stay in my sack an extra half-hour.

It stops raining by the time I finish my second cup of coffee. A pale sun locates itself in a thin, gray sky. I pull on my waders, lace my wading shoes tightly, pull on cleated overshoes, elbow myself into my heavy fishing vest, and take up my favorite rod from where it's been soaking all night on the top of the truck's canopy. Next there's a visit to what passes for the outhouse. Then we board the truck for the short drive to a good pool. No anglers occupy it at present, but I know a dozen lines have been through it already today.

Once I took a fish in this pool on my very first cast in filthy water. It was a dark male that was lying in close to shore and put up a poor fight. Another time, on my maiden voyage in the tent trailer, walking in to this pool to make my first cast I fell in. I went entirely under. I had to return to camp and change all my clothes. This made me so disgusted with myself that I seriously considered breaking camp and trying again another day. But I stuck it out and soon found good fishing.

It is best to go in this pool and most others as high up as you can wade. It has a stony bottom and a current that is deceptive, much stronger than it looks. It is the pool where I lost the big fish with the man from Idaho and whenever it is free I'll give it a few hopeful casts. It can produce at any time of the day, whether it's been pounded steadily or left to rest for hours. Like a handful of pools on the Sauk I greet it with great hope each year and feel I am starting to unravel its mysteries. It will produce all season.

Mainly because it is the end of April, with a lot of fish in the river, and not as a result of any special knowledge I have acquired, I hook a fish after a few casts. It porpoises twice and I see it is very large and bright. Sam barks and gives the water where it disappeared his full attention. But already the fish has moved upstream and past me. It holds a few yards above me, sawing gently in the current. My steady pull on the line has no effect. The fish tells me (from his attitude) that he can hold there for days. I know it can't be true. I am tempted to pull hard, harder, hardest, but this would mean disaster.

Already both forearms ache and I have to keep spelling off one hand with the other. I have settled on a two-handed pull, though this is a one-handed rod. It is why many anglers opt for a fighting butt or rod extension. I find that I can brace the rod butt against my navel and do just as well.

It is a fine day to be playing a good fish. The air is bright and not cold. Big white cumulus clouds creep across a sky the color of milk glass and the near mountains are rimmed in snow. The fish and I have all day to work out our problems. As I think this the fish turns and races off downstream in the direction of the wide, fast tailout. I will be able to follow it only a short distance before it is in whitewater capable of sweeping it back to the sea. Thus it is important that I keep the fish in the pool—in the head or middle of it if possible. This is my strategy or rather my hope. The fish stops its run, turns to face upstream, and is coaxed back towards me. Playing this fish is textbook stuff and will work out fine so long as the fish hasn't read the fine print.

As it comes back upstream I move in the same direction, retracing my route and urging the fish to follow me until I am high up in the pool again and playing the fish where I first entered the water. It is the ideal place, for the pool is deep and slow enough that the fish can swim along the edge of the current and tire itself out without being frightened by the shallow water. I want this fish to see the gravel and the shore only when it is dead-tired and ready for beaching.

The fight goes well and the fish—it is a big male, I am certain—is tiring by degrees. He runs out into the current briefly, but is soon persuaded to return to the slower water. There I can urge him to keep swimming where the current will tire him; when he stops I gather in line and return the strain to him fully. After ten more minutes of this he is on the short line and will stay there. I see him at last. He is huge. There is not a spot of pink anywhere on his sides. All the while I've played him—about 25 minutes—Sam has given the fish his undivided attention. That's pretty good concentration for a young dog.

The fish is now finning quietly between a couple of rocks that break the surface, his upright body a third out of the water. I wait for him to topple over on his side. Instead he scurries off one more time to the fast water. I watch the wake from his spine and give him the least pressure from the spool. Then I turn him severely and drag him to me abruptly. He is a beaten fish and obeys, even though he is heavy enough to snap the eight-pound leader like a thread. I can see the gleam of red marabou in the corner of his jaw and the hook looks well-seated, but one can never be sure. He balances on the rocks on his ventral fins, wobbles, then topples over on his side in ten inches of water: mine. Sam starts towards him, but catches my eye and decides it would not be a good plan. He's right.

Instead Sam wades out into the current and waits for the moment of release. His plan is to pursue the fish into fast water and catch it. My idea to discourage him with meaningful body language. We bump each other hard, but the message fails to get through so I block him off more thoroughly; we must have a meeting soon.

While Sam is waded out in the water, waiting, I have a moment in which to pull out my plastic measuring tape and run it down the fish's side. Forty-one inches—that can't be right. I measure it again, tip of snout to tip of tail. Yes, it's forty-one inches. It is my biggest steelhead by an inch and one-half. That probably equates to three or four more pounds. Again I do not think to take a girth measurement. The important thing is to right the fish, get his gills working right, recover him and his sense of balance, and see him swim strongly away, safe. When he does this I follow him out to the edge of the current and post-up Sam. The great fish disappears in a green slide. I straighten up, my shoulders aching, and grin at the world. There is nobody in sight. This is about as close as anybody gets to a wilderness experience today. It might have been nice to have had a witness, however.

We head back to camp, though we've been gone less than an hour. Any more fishing would be an anticlimax. I am mellow. The sun is beating down hard—hard for April, anyway. May is practically here, the season over. My plan is to have a cup of coffee and sit in the sun for an hour or more, reliving the fish experience and luxuriating in it. Camp is always deserted at this time of day. I pick up a copy of *Esquire* and start to thumb through it. Dick Sylbert arrives in his new Jeep Cherokee. He is production designer for Warren Beatty on many fine films and a fly-fishing nut. But he rarely has a free moment. Yesterday we had talked about fishing together today, but had missed connections.

"Nice fish you caught," he greets me.

"How do you know I caught a fish? Nobody saw me."

"Well, I did. I watched you playing it from the bridge. Pretty big. I knew it was you because of the dog." He reaches into his pocket and shows me his monocular. "I saw it all. What do you think the fish will weigh?"

"I have no idea."

"Sure you do. Take a guess. I saw you measuring it. How long was it?"

"Forty-one inches."

He whistles. "It might go 25 pounds or 26 pounds. What do you think?"

With false modesty I tell him that the fish couldn't have gone over 25. But that is enormous. I remembered then two 41-inch steelhead from the Snake, caught in the fall on spoons. I had only heard about them. Both touched 27 pounds. But those were hefty, B-race Clearwater steelhead, fish designed to travel long distances. Mine wasn't so thick. Still I was happy to have had Dick witness it. His estimate of over 25 pounds was good enough for me.

I am filled with a glow of accomplishment. There is no impetus to fish again soon, even though the river might be holding an even bigger steelhead. I pull off my waders and loaf away the long afternoon with my magazine. I read it cover to cover. But after an early dinner I grow restless. I decide to return to the river. By dark I haven't touched a fish, though I've gone through three pools. Things are back to normal.

April is trophy time on the Sauk and other Northwest rivers and several of the regulars have caught fish in the same class as mine. It is an exciting time to be out of doors. The Sauk is a remarkable fishery and each year poses a different set of constraints. The year previous was my best on this river. The present one is about two-thirds as good from the standpoint of the number of fish beached. The following one proved to be poor. A new slide in the headwaters is growing in severity. It pours in mud. With a little warm rain now the Sauk goes out of shape and is slow to come back in.

This season, Dan Lemaich, who has done poorly on the Sauk in the past, seems to be the only one catching fish. He chalks up his poor performance before to not knowing the river well. Now he is experiencing remarkable good luck. Or else he has learned something the rest of us do not know. What is it? He smiles enigmatically and admits he does not understand himself. "Enjoy it while you can," he confides. Words of wisdom for us all.

Tuesday is his day off and on every Tuesday he just can't miss. The river pops back into shape just in time to make him happy. The process is mysterious. Tuesday over, he goes back to work selling fishing tackle. Once he's gone the river promptly fills up with mud again. The rest of us, who have more time to fish and wait for clear water, watch his Tuesday performance in amazement. As his luck continues his confidence mounts. He becomes a little cocky. We wait for his comeuppance. There is none. He's on a roll.

The river is in such bad shape that Guide Joe Butorac cancels all his bookings for the remainder of the season; he can't guarantee out-of-state clients a fishable river after a long journey. To fly here, stay in a hotel, rent a car, hire a guide, costs considerable money. In Joe's thoughtful opinion to offer them a river the color of chocolate wouldn't be fair. Most of us have had poor luck. At mid-month many go back to the city and hang it up. Day after day the river looks hopeless. But when the last week arrives time is too precious not to return and take our chances with the river.

A host of us sits in our camp and waits for the Sauk to show some green. Other fishers head for the Skagit above Rockport, which may be bank-high but is fishable. This is the time when steelhead in good numbers are in both rivers—which is really one. Over the past few days the rains have weakened and the Sauk is capable of falling back into shape, given a little cool, dry weather. I am back in town, but I can taste hope in the air. After a cool day and night I return to camp on Sunday evening. If I'm wrong about the river I can always turn around and drive the hundred miles home.

But I'm not. High and dirty still the Sauk looks to be promising. There is exactly a week left; next Saturday the two rivers will close at dark. The Sauk is not fishable yet. It needs a few more hours to clear. I drive to the big camp at Rockport on the Skagit and find some old friends in attendance whom I haven't seen in more than a year. They are from Canada. I spend a lot of time chewing the fat. One is Jerry Wintle. It's time well spent. I drive back to my camp on the Sauk late in the day. Why, the river has cleared more than I expected. Sam runs around in a tight circle, barking enthusiastically. He knows what is up. I hurry down to my favorite riffle and hook two fish before dark, beaching both of them. So bright, they appear to be new arrivals. They take the orange marabou as though waiting their whole life for it.

Back in my tent trailer I am dismayed when it rains all night. In the morning the river is coming up fast. I start two hours earlier than usual and manage to hook and land a fish before eleven o'clock, after which my case—and everybody else's—is hopeless. The river goes out again.

But soon the rain stops, the sun comes out, and we stand around in camp, steaming in our rainjackets. We wear caps because the alders drip on our heads. I give the river a try at dark, but it is an ugly, peaty color and I soon quit. There is no party tonight and we turn in early. I read myself to sleep. The night outside my canvas is sparkling, with great portent.

The bank anglers are out early the next morning. So are the boats. At my customary hour I rise and walk down to check the river. Too high and discolored for my tastes. The report is, some of the boats have hooked and landed fish on Hotshots despite the poor conditions. Sam and I go for an afternoon outing. We see a guideboat fishing plugs take a fish in the mid-20s. They wrestle it into the net and keep it out of the water a long time photographing it. Then it is unceremoniously dumped back in the river. Poor fish.

As for me I touch nothing. By dark it is sprinkling again. During the long evening that follows hard showers drown out my portable radio and its classical music. The coyotes must have their heads under the covers, for they emit no yips, no remote howls and chatter. Shortly before dawn the rain stops; I wake to the absence of its noise. Elated I learn that the river has continued to drop and clear during the night. This is a little odd, but sometimes happens. You have to live on a river to learn just how much it will rise or fall under a variety of circumstances, and even then you may guess wrong.

In the afternoon the color is decidedly good—lime green with over two feet of visibility. The river is swarming with boats. A short time is left on everybody's calendar. I have no pulls late in the morning or all afternoon. I'm standing on the beach at the bottom of the Native Hole. Just about the time I'm ready for White Creek, which is visible from where I am, I see a boat pull in there and three anglers plus their guide disembark. This puts four men in the hole. So I make another futile pass through the pool where I am before calling it quits. All the while I keep my eye aimed upstream. The men remain for what seems to me an inordinate length of time. Eventually they pile into their boat and drift down to the takeout, which is mid-way through the pool I am fishing. I make room for them to pull ashore.

While they are winching their boat up the bank I engage them in conversation, for I know they have been up to something. Why else did they stay so long? Their day over, they have nothing to lose by telling me what happened. In fact, I don't have to question them at all; one of them blurts out their good news. They hooked four fish and beached two of them, or was it three? The story is a bit muddled. I whistle at what I hear. I am eager to go there. But I see two new men have arrived at the hole on foot. Its what you might expect on this last week of the season, with the river coming in and out of shape.

I return to camp, feeling restless. I decide to forego dinner, though my stomach is already growling. I drive to the pool and park on the shoulder. No cars and so far as I can see through the trees no boat on the beach. But as I'm stringing up my rod an obnoxious man I'll call Bill Boxer pulls up in his car. He is so competitive an angler that fishing around him is no fun. I always avoid the pool he is in, but many times he will join me and I have to endure him or else go elsewhere. Usually I leave but not today. I've waited all day for my crack at this good pool. Now here he is again. I know what to expect from him; in fact I can almost read his mind.

"Mind if I fish with you?" he says.

It makes little or no difference what I reply, he'll do it anyway. What he's doing is forcing me to invite him along. Well, there'll be no invitation from me tonight. He can be the one to go elsewhere for a change. What he's doing is legal, of course, only unethical, perhaps. There's no way of stopping him short of shooting him and I'm not yet the type.

"It's a free world," I reply coolly. That ought to be enough to dissuade anybody. Not Bill Boxer. He will persist and try to maneuver me so that he gets to go through the water first. I've seen him do it a dozen or more times. It's an old ploy and it won't fool anybody. I'm tired of having it pulled on me, as though I were a rank beginner—what we call a cracker.

I move rapidly away toward the river, taking long strides, not looking back. Boxer is on my heels. How did he get his rod out of the car and assembled so quickly? I take my hat off to him from the standpoint of speed. Yet I manage to arrive at the river first. I enter the top of the run where the current is most swift. It is running higher and faster than I expected or would like it to be. Boxer hovers on the beach, waiting for me to move down the run far enough for him to step in. And I haven't yet wetted my line.

What nerve. He's breathing down my neck. Gad, what rudeness. Well, I've completed my basic training in the same school. I make my first cast and do not move downstream afterwards.

"Mind if I cut in below you?" he asks suddenly. "Lot's of room for two. It's a big pool."

It's really a small pool, the good water all at the top, for the bottom is mostly sand and fish do not hold well over sand. The top is short and it's hard to wade out into the water very far because of the boulders and quickness of the current. The pool thus has a middle reach of about 75 feet. That's pretty little, and there are no other pools within walking distance.

"Start at the head like everybody else does," I tell him. "I don't plan on being here forever. Await your turn."

He's furious. His trick works with everybody else; why not with me? He considers *me* rude. I can hear him whipping his line angrily through the guides. The air fairly whistles. In response, rather than fishing fast as I've implied I will do, I won't move until I feel like it. That may not be until the last of the light.

Now Bill Boxer is in the water above me, tight to my flank, pressing me. I hold my ground. His cast drifts into the boulders near his feet, catches, and he has to break it off. He's lost his fly plus his tippet, which makes him madder yet. It's his problem, not mine. I think to myself, Good—serves you right, you bully. But I move down the run a little, putting a few more yards between us. I don't want to seem any worse than I have to be.

Out of the corner of my eye I see him tying on a new tippet and fly. He's fast at that, too. I haven't hooked a fish yet and it is the top of the run where they all ought to be, if they haven't been pricked by the gang that went through the pool earlier. I shuffle my feet (to make it look like I'm moving) and remain stubbornly in about the same place. Actually—with a great deal of foot-commotion—I've dropped down about a yard, which is nearly nothing.

I hear him curse softly and know that he's hung up again. He's forced to break off another fly. My own fly isn't getting very deep, I know. It may not matter here: I've found that fish in this hole will take a fly only a foot or two under the surface, even in the cold water of winter. If I overline (that is, use a line too heavy for the water) when I reach the bottom of the pool I'll be fishing so deep that I'll lose a fly on nearly every cast. So I start out light.

When I look upstream again a few minutes later there's nobody in the river. Bill Boxer is gone. This is too good to be true. Maybe he's off in the bushes, taking a leak. I search the scrub widely with my eyes. No, he's gone, all right. I sag with relief in my waders. And freed from the stress of unwanted competition I begin fishing in earnest. I cover the water like a seine.

Three fish come to my fly in rapid succession and I beach all of them. There are times like this, though rare. Sam goes wild. All the action has left me none too sane, either. None of the fish goes over 12 pounds, but that's okay. Each is bright and fights well but in a different manner. One is fast; the other two are slow but strong. The soft beach at the bottom of the pool provides the perfect place to land them and each is easily slipped onto the sand. Once freed from the hook the fish swim away without hesitation. They will all survive.

I return to camp at dark and find my neighbors enjoying a beef pot-roast dinner. They've all had several drinks. What's left over looks delicious and I am hungry, but they don't invite me to join them though there is an incredible amount still on the table. Why not? Maybe they're not really my friends. Together they form a tight little group. What they want to hear from me is that I haven't had any luck. Well, I'll happily skirt that issue. Later I coax one of them aside. He's had a poor season and needs a fish badly.

"John," I tell him, "the pool at White Creek has steelhead in it. Try it first thing in the morning and I'm sure you'll get one. Keep your fly bright and don't fish it too deep."

He regards me warily. Am I trying to decoy him to this pool, so I'll have a better one all to myself in the morning? It's what he and his friends do to each other. I see suspicion in his eyes and am sorry I brought up the subject. Then he thanks me in his usual quick, nervous manner. We're anxious to separate. I realize there's not much mutual trust here. It happens.

I'm not giving much away, though. They are all early risers, each man intent on being the first on the water. It makes no difference to me, since I will not be fishing until late morning. It might as well be John who goes through the pool first and gets the early fish as one of his friends. Then I settle down to a can of beef stew and a long evening's read. One by one I see their lights snuff out and it isn't even nine o'clock. Oh, for a little social life.

Over morning coffee I learn that John indeed took a fish at dawn. Later he comes over to my camp to tell me about it. He seems a little less guarded. He says the pool has been pounded all morning. He thinks his fish is the only one hooked there, but he can't be sure for he's been gone from it a while now. I thank him for the update. He didn't have to do this.

The rain that began at midnight as a downpour has not slackened. A fierce wind is blowing, additionally. It is a miserable day. I remain in camp, waiting for a break in the weather but there is none. The river will soon go out from this volume of water. This is Thursday and the river closes in less than three days. When it goes out it won't come back in, there is so little time left. Anglers have come long distances for these last days of the catch-and-release season. Chances are it will end early.

I go to the pool that was so good to me yesterday. It is empty, between visitors. Halfway down I hook a small fish. It is the littlest steelhead I've ever caught in the Sauk, one about five pounds. It is pretty, though. Bob McLaughlin comes down the path just as I turn it loose.

"Was that a steelhead? " he asks a bit disdainfully.

"Yes."

"Pretty little."

I agree. An old friend, I tell him the pool is his and leave though I've fished only a third of it. What I want most for Sam and me is some open space, but I doubt if we're going to find it today. In spite of the rain the crowds have increased. After lunch Sam and I drive over to the Native Hole. It's everybody's favorite and I'm not surprised to see a fly angler just leaving it. I ask him a mute question with my hands and he hunches his shoulders in a negative reply. Funny how unimportant words are for the really important things.

I begin to fish the head of this fine pool. Another angler comes down and follows me through it. This is how it is going to be until the end. So be it. Neither of us touches a fish. Is it possible to rain even harder? Yes. The river is a funny color now, neither brown nor green and not quite gray. Charlie Gearhart arrives, wearing a thick Cowichican sweater, a steaming mug in his hand. Thermos coffee. Charlie, who is bald, always wears a hat, but today for no apparent reason—when he needs one most—he is bare headed. His pate streams water.

I am fishing my big two-handed rod. It is heavy and slow, but on a big, rapidly rising river it is just the right implement. I can swing it easily and throw a long heavy line far out into current. The river is moving fast, carrying lots of fresh flotsam.

I wave my free hand. "Hurry up, Charlie. Grab your rod. River's going out."

"I'll just watch you fish," he tells me. This is unlike him, but maybe he's given up on the season. It makes sense. But why then stand in the rain without a hat on? Beats me.

Just then a fish takes my fly and vaults into the air at mid-river. It hangs briefly in the air like a bright scythe.

"Nice fish," says Charlie. "Maybe 12 or 13 pounds."

I think this, too; the pull on the rod verifies it. I settle down for the fight. The fish looks like a hen, though often a fresh-run buck has much the same appearance. The fish fights the fight of a female. Its runs are fast, but not especially strong, and it wastes much of its energy in ranging widely and going up into the air. A male's fight is more dogged and unspectacular and he takes longer to lick.

Charlie has finished his coffee, set down his plastic cup on a rock, and is standing alongside me, enjoying the fight. He seems laid-back, which is odd. A musician and a rock-and-roller with his own band, maybe he's suffering from the night before and should have stayed home. I've seen him badly wasted. He can't keep away from the river, though. If something happens he doesn't want to miss it. Now it is raining like it's time for the great Ark. Charlie's head, his face, and his sweater are soaked. He couldn't be any wetter.

I tell him, "Go in, dry off. If you won't get your rod and fish, at least put your hat on."

"I'm fine," he says. "Keep your eye on your fish or you'll lose it. With the river in this kind of shape you won't have another chance."

I know he's right, but I don't much care. I've been having fair luck all season. Charlie is a good fisherman and a casual friend of many years. He's pulled a practical joke or two on me in the past. Maybe I owe him one. A plan comes to mind—a plot, really.

"Charlie," I say, "give me a hand. You can't just stand there and watch. Take my rod. I need both hands free to release this fish." And I thrust the rod at him before he has time to reflect on what I'm up to.

What's this? He takes it skeptically. Suddenly the fish tears off on a long run and Charlie must wait for it to stop and, when it does, reel in the lost line. Only he is used to reeling right-handedly and my handle is on the left side. He must search for it before he finally finds it. This takes a few long seconds and now he must crank backwards, or so it must seems to him. When he reels it is awkward. But he is an accomplished fisherman and at last manages to bring the fish toward the beach. Sam gets excited. In fact he's been barking all the while, for he knows it is *our* fish.

I wonder: What if Charlie had to handle the dog as well as the fish? Like I do? Could he bring it off? Why not put him to the test? It is worth losing my last catch-and-release fish for.

Sam is bounding around on the beach, uttering his rapid-fire alarm bark. He knows the fish is ready to be landed. For an obedience-trained dog he has moments of major lapse. I grab him by his choker and hang on. With my free hand I dig out my needlenosed pliers. Then I put Sam on the short leash I always carry in my pocket. I turn back to Charlie and say pleadingly:

"You could make it a lot easier for me if you'd take the dog, too. Just for a minute. Then I'll have both hands free for the fish."

He looks at me a tad suspiciously. He's gullible, but trusts me when well he shouldn't. Doesn't he remember my evil ways? The big rod is bad enough to handle, but now the dog, too? Quickly I thrust the leash's looped handle at him; I'm not going to give him any time to think it over. Now I have him, poor guy. The heavy two-handed rod in one hand, the dog in the other, how is he going to reel in line? Well, he can't.

It dawns on him that he's been had. Trust another fisherman only at your peril. Sam is lunging at the fish and the fish is bucking in the current. All Charlie can do is hold his ground.

I'm tempted to leave Charlie there. I'll return to my car and drive back to camp. Afterwards I'll inquire how he made out. But this would be too cruel; it would exceed the bounds of a practical joke on a friend. So I take back Sam and let Charlie play the fish without further complications. He does a good job. In the last stage he backs up the beach and the fish follows him in and is stranded on the grassy bank. I see the line go slack.

"Shall I?" asks Charlie. The dog is tugging at me. "Be my guest," I say. I hand him the pliers. He puts the rod down on the grass. Now he slips the hook free from the fish's jaw and it swims away. Sam nearly hauls me into the river after it. How strong he's grown.

The river is hopeless. In the length of time it took to hook and play the fish it has turned a terrible brown. The season is over. Sam and I drive back to the gravelpit. People are breaking camp. I join in the activity. Bags of gear and food I stow in the back of the Ranger. Then I crank down the wet canvas of the tent trailer and clamp the lid at its four corners. It is the final act in the drama of saying goodbye to the Sauk and the season.

Already I am planning my first trip of the coming year. It doesn't matter if the season is nine or ten months away; I can hardly wait.

14

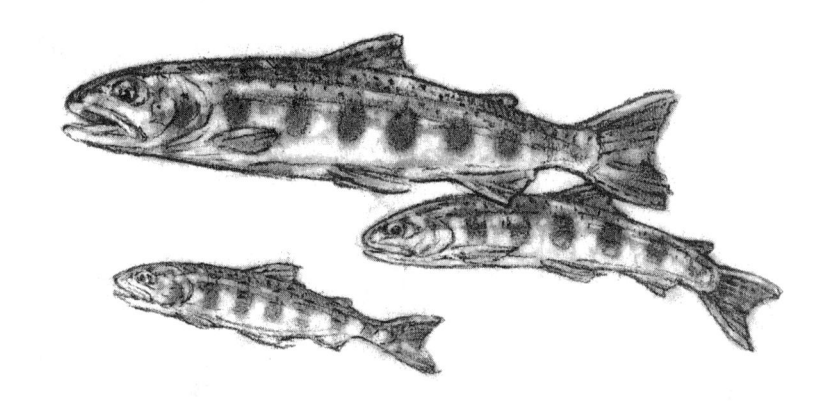

Smolt, Parr, and Fry

BRIGHT LITTLE FISH BANG ON OUR FLIES in spring when fishing for the big wild late-winter steelhead. These are the juveniles of the adult brood and are headed for the sea. Their migrations start in April, but are heaviest in May.

In spring of what is ordinarily their second year young steelhead undergo a remarkable transformation. They smoltify. "Smoltification" is the technical term for this biological process. It's an ugly word for something that is beautiful, even poetic. The word, a noun (smolt), is made into a verb (to smoltify), then is turned back into a noun again in order to describe a process. It keeps getting worse.

Young salmonids are called fry and parr by the Department of Fisheries according to their age class, but are referred to as zero-year and one-(year)-plus juveniles by the Department of Wildlife. They have a different orientation, of course. Fisheries is concerned with food or commercial fish, while Wildlife is involved with fish that have value only to the sportsman and are not to be sold or killed beyond reasonable conservation limits. The Boldt Decision has reversed some of this and things are not so simple anymore, for Indians sell steelhead, a sports fish. None of this has changed the basic facts of life. Young steelhead continue to have their years of river life before they head for the sea, where they will attain the growth required for maturation and their return to the river to spawn and replenish their race.

In *The Steelhead Trout* (1971) Trey Combs describes the Waddell Creek study that identifies smoltification by year class: the up-to-one-year-old juveniles ordinarily comprise 19 percent of a given year's migration, smolting later than older fish, and leave in June and the following summer months; the one-plus fish make up 24 percent of the migrants and leave in May; the two-plus fish constitute 53 percent and leave in April; the three-plus fish, which represent only four percent, leave in March. There are some four-plus-year-old smolts, but they comprise a tiny fraction and little is known about them.

When I asked Curt Kraemer about these percentages he said that the age of migration of juveniles is directly related to latitude and the farther North the parent river the older the juveniles are before they smoltify. The young fish need to grow to the six-to-nine inch length before they are biologically ready to change and leave. It takes longer for fish to reach this size when the climate is cold and the food supply diminished. There are small amounts of food in most rivers on the West slope of the Cascades, anyway, and this explains why juveniles make such modest growth.

Flyfishers encounter smolts during spring when fishing for adult steelhead and usually engage but a small percentage of the young fish that bang on their hook as the wet fly completes its swing or, more often, when it is being stripped back in. About half of the fish hooked will come off as they are being brought in for quick release. A few are impaled and have to be handled to get the big bend out of their small mouths. This gives us an opportunity to become briefly acquainted.

They are pretty little fish, shiny-bright. Their scales are loose and are apt to come off in your hand, so it is best not to grasp smolts if you can avoid it. They will easily shake off a barbless hook. (But there is still a moderately high loss of life from what is called the spearing effect.) They look exactly like what they are: young rainbow trout. Many still have ghostlike parr marks to remind you of their origns.

In years past, with the minimum size of six inches on many streams, trout fishers pursued these fish and returned home with big bags of shiny "trout." So regulations were changed to protect the steelhead smolt migrations. Streams were closed at the end of March. This also saved spawning adult steelhead from human predation. Today the common wisdom is that spawning steelhead are reluctant takers and those nearing spawning can be played and released safely. Smolts that get impaled on flies represent a small percentage of the ones in the river; even they can be hooked and let go safely, most of the time. (Now bait and small hooks are a different matter and mortality is much higher, for often they will swallow bait.) All their lives juveniles have been undergoing great reduction by predation and natural causes. About a tenth of the fish hatched from eggs will live to smolt size and less than a tenth of those will return after two or more years in the Pacific.

The smolting process is fascinating. It's a complex biological one, rife with mystery, for it is necessary for the small fish, which have spent about two years of their life in a fresh-water environment, to make the transition to saltwater. It is thought that enzymes are triggered by growth and various external factors to bring about this change. Increased daylight (especially important with its available UV), greater food supply (both in the river and awaiting them in the sea), a rise in river levels from spring rain or snowmelt—all these factors help achieve their transformation.

Oddly, mass movements of smolts are hinged to the dark of the moon. Just before the new moon rising thick clots of smolts descend their natal rivers and head out to sea. (In 1989 those of us fishing the Skagit were met by lots of smolts battering our flies in the week of April 26, when the moon was dark.)

May sees the greatest migrations and they last through the month. The fish are in transition between environments and it is vital for them to preserve their blood-salts level. They have not had much food, if any, during the long winter and are ravenous. Like kelts they will eat just about anything, including bait or flies. They are not fair game.

When they reach the estuary they find an abundance of forage food unfamiliar to them. There their body salts are easily replenished and they reverse the salt-retention process. Their scales firm up and their new, bright color makes them hard to see. The parr marks—those dark oval bands that stripe their flanks and make them difficult for predators (including man) to view against an algae-coated river bottom—are gone. Later when they return as adults to spawn they will assume a darker hue again, making them less visible but easier for them to sort themselves out by species and by sex from other salmonids.

One of the joys of being on a stream in the spring is to recognize and respond to the vast renewal process. Fresh redds are easily observable wherever there is coating of algae or silt on the stones, for the overturned stones glow brightly. In a few weeks the algae grows back and redds look like the other gravelly reaches, but under the stones the eyed eggs will be incubating. By then smolts born nearly two years earlier will have cleared the river and be on their long journey across the Pacific. Only recently have scientists learned that they routinely travel thousands of miles.

As one generation leaves the river as smolts a former one is spawning (some of them surviving afterwards) and the next one is starting life as an egg buried in the gravel. What a wonderful process. These fish will emerge in roughly two months. I am frequently on the river in July and keep my eyes sharp for the first baby steelhead. They are something to behold, these tiny transparent-looking creatures. They are about three-quarters of an inch in length and appear in large numbers in the shallows where the current isn't strong. In a few days they will be able to hold their own in faster water that approximates, except for its tiny scale, where they will be found as adults.

You have to be sharp to spot them, though. They dart around in small numbers and look much like other fry that have emerged about this time. There are coho fry present, but steelhead fry are a little smaller and can be identified by their extreme shyness. They seek faster water. Pass your hand over the water and cause a shadow to form and just watch them scatter. Coho say ho-hum and remain steady and unfrightened. They go about their constant search for food undisturbed. The steelhead's flight is temporary, though. They are not so much frightened as alarmed. It is a big difference. A moment's quietness will return them to their original lies or very near to them. They are completely at home in their riverine environment. When they move to deeper, swifter water their smoky appearance and dark backs camouflage them and make them nearly invisible. But you can see them if you try and are willing to spend many minutes staring into the broken depths, looking for their telltale shadows.

This year the fry were late. Cold water delayed their hatching, I think. Or else I simply missed them emerging. I kept my eyes peeled at the end of June and all through July. They were not where I expected them. Then on July 24 they were everywhere in good numbers. Spotting some about 1 1/4 inches long, suddenly I started seeing many others, some a shade smaller and a few larger. I reasoned that the different sizes meant that some had hatched out at different times and had longer in which to grow. Then I became confused. The ones I was sure were steelhead were not shy at all. Great clouds of them covered what was left of the spawning flats and did not scatter when I approached, but only moved leisurely upstream and away from me, maintaining a six or seven foot distance. Either steelhead had lost their shyness or I was looking at coho.

I decided to pursue the matter further. This meant closer. A week earlier, walking down a silty strand on my way back from fishing, I came upon a small net with a handle. It looked like a child's toy—something used by a beginning insect collector. I thought it would be fun to nab butterflies with, but a little short-handled and flimsy for the job. Since nobody lived along the reach and might have only set it down I picked it up and took it home with me. I figured I could find a use for it.

The net lay by my rain gauge with a heap of other things waiting for an opportunity. One morning I returned from my morning's fishing—productive for a change—and saw large numbers of fry ganged up in the shallows at the foot of my beach walk. I decided to try to trap them with the net. I enlisted Norma in my cause. "Come on," I said, "let's see if we can catch some fry."

My idea was to have one of us hold the net and the other chase the fry into it. So I stationed her at a likely place—alongside a swift narrow mini-channel that might become their escape path when I came charging after them with the net. But the net wouldn't work, at least not the way I intended. It would have to be starched and have its mesh reversed first. Pointed backwards in the current it wouldn't trap a single fry.

Meanwhile Norma was poking around two boulders that had water rushing between them, where tiny pools had formed in their lee. She picked up my net and dipped it into the slack. Soon she had a fry wriggling at the bottom of the white mesh. She held the net in the river, while I collected some water in my rain-gauge bowl so the little guy would feel right at home and wouldn't be subjected to a moment's dryness.

I filled the bowl fractionally and—quickly—she inverted the net. The fry dropped with a plop. His agitation soon ceased and he finned quietly an inch off the bottom. I saw that his fins were orange—a coho characteristic. How wonderful it was to behold my own fry at close range. (It's called pride of ownership.) His snout was transparent. Later Curt Kraemer told me that this was typical of all newly emergent fry and would soon disappear.

The fry's eye was tiny; I was expecting a huge eye, as with salmon parr, which is the next stage up. His dorsal and tail were as clear as the water he swam in. I looked for discernible fin rays, a sprinkling of spots, or some telltale coloring. All were missing. His tail was deeply forked and spotless. It waved in the water much as a goldfish's does. In fact my fry looked very much like a goldfish, though it was smaller and of a different shape. While I was studying him, junior-scientist style, Norma dipped the net again and came up with six or eight similar fish. I dumped back my little guy, drew some freshwater, and received the new batch of fry.

They looked at home in the bowl even though packed tight. They related to each other as they had in the eddy. That is, they occupied fixed spacial locations and held them. They were as alike as peas in a pod; perhaps the adage should be changed to read, "Peas are as alike as fry in a pool." The fact that some of them actually bumped into each other without any panic and held stations lightly brushing each other was interesting. They were social creatures, perhaps even gregarious ones.

I remembered how hatchery-raised parr had their fins worn away from repeatedly rubbing against the cement rearing ponds. Some of the damage was from contact with the others, though. They would nip at each other under crowded conditions as they competed for food. Their proximity in my bowl didn't seem to bother them at all. Steelhead might be quite different. For some reason I thought of steelhead as rugged individualists. They would move away from each other (as I would), meanwhile keeping track of each other's relative positions as they held together in the current. Touching was something they wouldn't endure. I was attributing to them my own personal characteristics, of course.

I recalled Annie Dillard's warning in *Pilgrim At Tinker Creek*. Locust were grasshoppers metamorphosed through wild and crazy mass-behavior. They became killers through overcrowding. The individual grasshoppers developed spots and assumed gross behavioral characteristics. They collected in colonies and migrated by the trillions to greener pastures, which they immediately ate up. Crowding was the cause and the effect, too. But coho were not grasshoppers. To them crowding was the natural condition. They lived happily in tight little groups such as my bowl provided. If separated from the others they would soon begin a search for new relatives and join the clan, I supposed. No sense of disruption would result.

Could a coho die of loneliness, I wondered?

Meanwhile Norma was busy with the net. She chased a solitary fry into deeper, stiller water. The fish kept moving away from her. He was not of a school. She sensed he was different and persisted. I could see her wading through water up past her knees. I turned my eyes back to my bowl of coho. In my peripheral vision I saw her swoop. She missed. I smiled; netting fish was not intended to be easy. She swooped again and nailed the little guy. While she restrained him (I make this sound difficult, as though a struggle were taking place between them but it wasn't and whatever struggle there was belonged to the fry in the net) I took the bowl of coho fry and upended it in the slack. Home, you little guys. I expected them to shoot away like the spokes from a wheel, each flashing off in a different direction. They did no such thing. They remained exactly where they landed. Each fanned away with its minute tail, marking time. They held as a cluster, their fins quivering. Why, if I was a fry, I would have highballed it out of there.

We transferred the solitary fish to the holding bowl and lowered our heads over it. He was certainly different—and the differences were outstanding. He was agitated. He didn't quite batter his tiny, transparent skull against the Pyrex, but he swam around wildly, first here, then there, searching for the exit, investigating every round corner. There was no way out and he soon realized it. But he wouldn't quiet down. An inch and a quarter long, much the same size as the coho fry, he was a wild man. Perhaps he was even a wild fish.

This was no coho. There were superficial similarities, however. His fins did look a bit orangish and were transparent. His eye was about the same size, and in the same place, as a coho's. But he was an untamed creature, with a fierce will to survive and dominate his environment, even if it was but a ceramic bowl. There was a muscular vitality about him that the bowl's previous occupants lacked. If he was a man I'd sure hate to meet him in a dark alley.

His parr marks were fewer, but bigger and darker. I wanted to invert him and examine his anal fin for size and shape, but he was not the type to put up with such treatment and I respected this. A squared-off anal fin would confirm he was a steelhead. All the while he never stopped fighting for his life—though it was in no real danger from the likes of me. (I love baby steelhead—didn't he know?) Then I grew worried. He'd been in the bowl less than two minutes and it didn't look like he was going to quiet down short of death.

"Let's put him back," I said to Norma, though I was really speaking to myself. I got no argument out of her.

But I wanted to get a better look before I said goodbye. Was he a steelhead? I wanted proof positive. I drained the water from the bowl, trapping him in a corner. He didn't like this one bit and wriggled like mad. He beat at the bowl with his small body's full length. This alarmed me. I plopped him into the palm of my hand for a final try at an inspection. Instantly he leaped into the river, disappearing in a flash.

Four days later I returned to the spawning flat, now gone over to a nursery, planning on visiting the young coho and spotting a steelhead fry or two if I was lucky. Maybe I'd collect some specimens for an aquarium experiment I had in mind. But the fry were gone; they had migrated to deeper water. I searched and searched, but all I could detect in all that turbulence were one or two slender shapes. My eye was trained to spot them by now. There they lay, thin as knife blades, ghostlike, about the same color as the water. The river here was too swift for my dipnet, even if I knew how to use it.

I can't say for a fact they were steelhead, but I think so. Young coho wouldn't be able to hold in so strong a current.

15

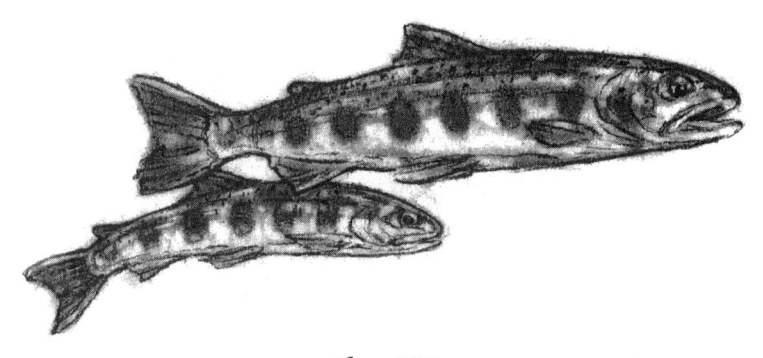

Salmonid Agonistics

Crossing the long slack riffle below Blue Slough, I come out in a big back eddy created by a drowned log. It is deep, with a sandy bottom, and alder and willow boughs arch overhead. A dark cloud of coho fry moves leisurely out of my way and into the still deep, water. This year's batch, they are a couple of months out of the gravel, and all of one size. They may have hatched out at slightly different intervals, starting back in March, and then spent several more weeks as alevins in the gravel before digesting their egg sacks (they are called sackfry at this stage) and becoming free-swimming juveniles. Since then they have fed voraciously on whatever they can find—the larvae of these tiny Mayflies, for instance, presently hovering like Lilliputian helicopters, or on bigger caddis creepers. Coho fry are mid-depth drift feeders. They are reluctant to come to the surface, but in a month or so I will catch a few on dry flies. They swim in small schools and intercept whatever the current brings them in mid-stratum of the water column; if it is not something edible they quickly eject it.

They are pretty little fish and I am always glad to see them, for they indicate a healthy river ecosystem. I identify them entirely by size and behavior because I cannot see them individually or well. I know they have olive backs with eight or ten heavy dark parr bars running down their sides. Their fins and forked tails are orangish and by this can they be told from young steelhead, which will have hatched out later and be smaller, at least by the start of the summer. And they will have long, whitish anal fins with dorsals very similar in shape and coloration to a steelhead's. It's a pity I can't see this much as the fry scatter and regroup, but knowing about it adds immeasurably to the day's pleasure.

I don't see any steelhead fry at the Blue Slough crossing, but am not surprised; if there were any now they'd be the progeny of early winter fish, either wild or hatchery ones that weren't caught out and had spawned successfully. The bulk of the steelhead fry are from later-spawning wild fish and are yet to come, eggs or alevins buried still in the gravel. I've seen fresh redds early in June and know the last of these fish won't have finished spawning until July. Their prolonged season and the emergence of fry over a staggered length of time is nature's way of protecting them from any single short-lived disaster.

As I leave the water and make my way through the deeply shadowed woods the image of the scattering and regrouping coho fry stays with me. Partly because of their difference in size there must be a pecking order, and I can only guess at how it works from what I see and know about them. It would be size-dependent. The bigger fry would determine the outcomes of confrontations and face-offs, where each fry's station will be, and who defers to whom. These relationships will be maintained almost inviolate as the school grows and moves from one location to another, following its food supply. The school will form and break apart and reform, with individuals drifting away and new ones being added to its numbers over the long summer. Predation will take its gross toll. Size-based dominance within the species will exist for more than the one year coho remain in fresh water and grow to migrating size.

I wonder if this principle of rank and order holds true in saltwater and if it is retained during their long ocean journey? And does it continue to exist or is it recreated all over again at the time the fish enter freshwater and begin to ascend their rivers to spawn? If some fish give way to others, what are the rules—the determining factors? And what is the relationship of pecking order to choosing partners and mating as the fish mature, come to recognize each other by sex, and sort themselves out on the redds? Does anybody know?

In *Fisherman's Fall* (1964) Roderick Haig-Brown tells about what happens to salmonids when they are forced to live with each other in a confined environment. This he created for himself. Once he saw an ad in a magazine for an aquarium and remarked on it to his wife. Then he forgot about it. On Christmas Day he opened a large package from her and the children. It was the aquarium. He was taken back, but quickly grew enthusiastic about its possibilities. He hurried to a nearby creek and came back with clean gravel, stones, and river moss. He bought a minnow trap with which he caught nymphs, larvae, and small scrapfish. He rebuilt the intermittent pump that came with the aquarium and put it to work in continuous cycle in order to provide the oxygen-rich water nontropical fish require. Then he introduced the first occupants—bullheads and sculpin. The bullheads became permanent residents and adjusted well; the sculpin were too openly hostile and had to be removed.

In April the minnow trap produced young coho fry from the river. They and the bullheads proved compatible in the aquarium. Haig-Brown watched the coho establish an order of dominance and take up feeding stations. There were three fry and—as one might guess—size seemed to be the determining factor as to who got the choicest locations. Once they sorted themselves out each coho seemed content with his position in the hierarchy and thrived. Haig-Brown fed them experimentally and found beef scrapings and dried daphnia best.

The coho ignored the daphnia that floated on the surface; they became interested in it only after it had begun sinking—which is in keeping with their established mid-depth feeding pattern. When the daphnia fully sunk they ate it hungrily. In time they learned to adapt and come to the surface for their food, but this wasn't natural.

Haig-Brown added a fourth young coho to the mix and after a brief period of some difficulty it was accepted. All adjusted happily to the new world order. Efforts to introduce sticklebacks and chinook and chum fry were unsuccessful. In the case of the other salmon the coho dominated them to the point where they cowed and Haig-Brown decided to remove them before they sickened and died.

A year passed in relative coho harmony.

In spring of their second year it was time for the coho to smoltify. They didn't. Instead they became agitated and stressed, their fins fraying, their flanks darkening, and their feeding coming to a stop. He watched them closely and after a while thought he saw the start of recovery, for their sides brightened and they started eating again. He had a vision of them living out their three-year span in the aquarium without any need to go to sea. But he was curious, not content to leave matters alone. This is a common trait among scientists. The minnow trap produced a three-inch steelhead in March. Haig-Brown says it was "a dark, powerfully built fish, smaller than the big coho, and I thought he might settle in quite readily without causing too much disturbance." Guess again.

The steelhead dominated the aquarium. He fed on top with a satisfying, noisy rise to the floating daphnia; he fed at mid-range with the coho; and he munched along the bottom all by himself. He was much faster and more active than any of the salmon. At first the biggest coho chased after him "in a rather dignified way," Haig-Brown reports. The steelhead, though smaller, saw this as sport, for he was the faster. The big coho gave up pursuit—which was no doubt an effort to drive away his competitor.

The steelhead then decided he wanted the feeding station occupied by Coho Number 2, which was behind a rock. He took it. The Number 2 Coho moved to an inferior site. The smallest coho now began to exhibit stress signs similar to the smolting period—frayed fins, darkened flanks, loss of appetite, etc. Haig-Brown records these with clinical detachment. The demise of Coho Number 3 took place on April 22, after one year and eleven days in the tank.

The second largest coho next started showing distress signs. Within a month he was dead. Haig-Brown summarizes: "Whether these deaths were caused by the frustrated need for salt water, by the disturbance of yielding to the steelhead, or by a combination of both factors I am not sure." That was the voice of the careful scientist. The naughty little boy who thought to put the steelhead fry in with the healthy coho in the first place had a pretty good idea what would happen. But he had to see it for himself.

There were two coho left, including the big one. He looked healthy enough—Haig-Brown uses the words big, plump, placid, velvety, to describe him. The big coho "ruled" the center of the tank. Two months passed. Haig-Brown continued his observations. "The change came overnight," he writes. "One day the coho was supreme, the next day he was a beaten and dominated fish. In a way it was not surprising." All the usual signs of failing health manifested themselves plus one other. Unobserved, the young steelhead had attacked the coho's tail and bitten it to the quick. Haig-Brown decided to act: he had all the evidence he needed to prove the steelhead's will to dominate—to survive at any and all costs.

Quickly he transferred the coho to an isolation tank. No help there.

"It was too late. Fungus attacked the wounded tail and, though I scraped it away and applied ointment, he died." There was but a single coho left, the small one. For a couple of weeks there was harmony. Then "the murderer returned to his attacks." Haig-Brown netted out the steelhead and hastened him back to the river. He notes that the fish took the change in environments "without the slightest discomposure, holding calmly against the current, seeming like any one of the several dozen small pre-migrants that hold behind the wing dam." Haig-Brown watched through his snorkel mask for ten or fifteen minutes longer, after which time the "murderer" mixed in with his peers and became indistinguishable. The remaining coho survived in the aquarium environment. Haig-Brown loses interest in the experiment at this point and doesn't chronicle the fate of the last coho. It seems a kindness.

Other writers who fish have looked into the matter of competition among species. Pat Trotter addresses inherent aggressive responses in his fine book, *Cutthroat: Native Trout of the West* (1987), and what he sees closely parallels behavior patterns others have observed in rainbows and steelhead. Like Haig-Brown Trotter has an interest bordering on the morbid in what happens when a competing fish is introduced to a confined population of another species. It is not unlike the fascination men have for boxing, knowing that one or the other is going to beat the other one silly. Trotter states, "The most dominant fish in a population assumes the best lie, the second most dominant fish occupies the second best lie, and so on down the line. But this dominance is put to the test from time to time. The term for the nipping, chasing, and direct fighting, and for the ways fish have of challenging and threatening one another, is *agonistic behavior*."

He continues, "Agonistic behavior patterns are pretty much the same for all salmonids. What's more, the different species of trout, salmon, and char seem to understand each other's threat displays. It is in these threat displays that a trout's pigmentation seems to come into play. There are two types of threat display: the frontal and the lateral." And here differences between rainbows and cutts can be detected, for in frontal display the cutthroat gives his opponent a full, head-on view of his red throat slashes.

Steelhead have none to offer, but yield no other ground. Frontal threat behavior is similar but deadlier than the approach from the side. Trotter states: "The threatening fish approaches its opponent with its back arched, dorsal fin flattened, all other fins fully extended, gill covers flared out, mouth opened, and the bottom of its mouth pushed downward. As it fixes its opponent with its eyes, its head appears to be enlarged, much as a dog or a cat would look with its hair standing on end." This is the monster-from-outer-space look, we might call it. Little kids develop it to an art.

Trotter says, "In the lateral threat display, the fish turns side-on to its opponent, assuming a parallel position, both fish facing upstream. It stretches out its body and assumes a rigid pose with the line of the back straight, the mouth and gill region dilated, and all fins, including the dorsal, fully extended. Sometimes the fish may actually appear to quiver." He states that in such a position the throat slashes are not easily seen, but the red rainbow-like band along the lateral line clearly stands out and this may be a substantial part of the threat.

Pilots of jet fighter planes—at least in movies I've seen—do this, too; they pull up alongside each other and waggle their wings furiously. And I've seen dogs raise their hackles and shoulder each other stiffly. Parallel threat behavior says, "Get out of my space, buster. Do it fast."

What would happen, asks Trotter, if steelhead and cutthroats of about the same size were introduced into a confined area and asked to co-exist? It is the same question Haig-Brown posed with the coho. It is the kind of question that occurs to a boy of a certain weird temperament. I too, am interested. I would put my money on the steelhead every time.

Trotter writes, " . . . in study after study of mixed populations, rainbow trout are the more aggressive species. Rainbows dominate cutthroats almost totally, even though they use the less aggressive threat display. Only when the cutthroat is a markedly bigger fish than the rainbow does it ever dominate. Even cutthroats that have dominated other cutthroats are stressed to death, often in less than a night, when paired with a rainbow trout of similar size." And a footnote tells us to see Nilsson and Northcote for more instances, but I have had enough. [If you haven't, this is N. A. Nilsson and T.G. Northcote, "Rainbow Trout and Cutthroat Trout Interactions in Coastal British Columbia Lakes," *Canadian Journal of Fisheries and Sciences 38:1228-46* (1981).]

There is a familiar cartoon that shows how the food chain operates. Progressively larger fish swallow each other up from the rear. Everybody who sees it laughs. But this isn't quite how it happens in nature. Sure, one fish eats another, but that isn't all. One fish sets out to systematically destroy another—not because it's hungry, which would be understandable, but just for the fun of it. This is hard for me to comprehend. Yet I know it is true.

Here is a wanton universe. It is killing in excess of what is needed to survive. It doesn't fit in with our established concepts of evolution or ecology. It is harsher, crueler, than it need be. Ruthlessness is the guiding precept, life robbed of any rational plan. Thus, all we are is subjects for prolonged cosmic play.

I'm still thinking about this in June. I look into a pool down from Blue Slough and see clots of month-old coho fry dissolve and reform and move apart again. Most of them will die short of smolting. A powerful force is at work in nature and it shows no mercy. To me today it seems horrible. That's just a word, I know. To another it may seem haphazard and without any cruelty involved.

Wantonness is all around us. It prevails. It is the daily news, but it is not new. In the morning paper I read about sea lions killing wild steelhead headed for their spawning grounds in the Cedar River. Soon the run will be destroyed. The sea lions are not hungry. They have already eaten their fill. Now they are destroying—solely for pleasure—steelhead as they mill about at the foot of the fish ladder at Chittenden Locks. They are biting and maiming fish at random. They abandon what they've injured, often fatally. The public is evenly divided over whether to protect the sea lions or the steelhead. The National Marine Animals Act saves the sea lions from retribution. Instead of shooting them, wildlife agents throw firecrackers at them. Later, agents capture them and truck them off to remote locations. In a day or two they're back. They've had a nice vacation. They're maiming and killing again.

Similarly killer whales—*orcas*—slash through schools of salmon in the San Juan Islands. They have already eaten all they want. What they are doing now is playing. This part of nature is real and can't be dismissed. It is frightening in its very randomness. It makes me think about the effects of what I do. Of course I catch and release steelhead, which I have no need to eat, not really, no great hunger they will sate. Friends who do not fish question the motives of those of us who do. They see my hooking and playing fish as applied cruelty. The fish's fright and panic are what excite me, they argue. It's not just getting them to take my fly. I partially agree.

Am I any kinder than the sea lion or *orca*? I have to believe I am. There is a big difference between us and it isn't just my opposable thumbs or that I worry about what I do. My fish is not seriously injured as a result of my actions and should not die. Yet I am indeed practicing a form of agonistic behavior.

Indians say we sportsfishers (a term they don't accept, by the way) are "playing with our food." They dislike us for not eating or bartering or outright selling our catch. It is a bitter denunciation. It hurts the way it was meant to. There is much truth in it.

I believe myself to be a civilized person, a man of some perception. I earn money and go to the store, where I buy the food that other people have grown or killed and butchered for me. Thus I do not harvest directly. But I enable others to do so. In fact, I make their livelihood possible. Is this so bad? I take pride in fitting in with the economy and playing my part in bolstering it. This means I consume and I spend. Death and killing remain far off. I do not see the daily blood spilled in my behalf. For this I take much credit and pat myself on the back until my arm aches. But I'm kidding myself, I know.

My sport is separate from my life. Or is it? It is extraneous and unessential. It is a happy escape. It is frivolous. I pretend that what I do with a fish is noble and call it sport. But it is noble only in that it avoids inflicting death and involves killing, if I so will it. I have that choice to make—whether my quarry will live or die—and I enjoy making it. I invariably opt on the side of life. But one deserves no credit for a bad deed left undone, a life not taken. Life matters—even if it is only a dumb fish's.

It may well come down to the exercise of power. Live or die—I am a god and I shall say. But a terrible sense of responsibility comes with the territory. And sometimes shame comes, too. My power is awesome and frightening. Is my behavior any less reprehensible because the pain I inflict is short-lived, my quarry cold-blooded? Afterwards my fish goes on about its fishy life with only a sore mouth to show for its encounter with man.

What matters most to me is this: The only time a human comes in contact with a wild steelhead (whose life goes unrecognized, unexperienced, otherwise) is when the fish takes a fly, etc., and is hooked. Then it is briefly known. Just this once—and then no more. It is a moment of epiphany. (I know, I know—not so for the fish.)

A steelhead is too spectacularly beautiful a creature not to be encountered at least once in a lifetime. It provides a moment of excitement and wonder. Yet it is fraught with moral complications and evokes cardinal questions involving the multiple sources of pleasure and pain. Each fisher for himself, I suppose; that is what is commonly believed in the realm of sport. But I am going to continue to think hard about what I call sport, and examine and reexamine what I do in the name of sport, and keep reflecting on the daily consequences of my actions in my sporting day on the river.

16

Days of Puce and Lemon

By THE LAST WEEK IN MAY fresh summer runs may be found in many Western rivers. They are wonderful fish. Biologists believe that the first *wild* summer-run steelhead travel the farthest and will spend the longest time in the river, during which time they do no serious feeding. These fish need to have the maximum strength and endurance. They must swim to the remotest reaches of the watershed and remain there without nourishment until they spawn the following spring, nearly a year away.

The early *hatchery* fish also enter the river now and are great fish in their own right. They are apt to be bigger, having remained at sea a year or two longer. They have a vigor and strength that surprises me each new year. When hooked they are apt to go out of control, and all the angler can do is hang on for the ride and pray there is no breakage. I've had both wild and hatchery fish run 100 yards without a pause. Almost always you lose such a fish. While you listen to the reel spin, the length of line remaining on your reel diminishing, you have a long moment in which to marvel at what you have encountered. Then the fish is gone. Usually it simply comes off the hook.

The speed and power of fresh summer fish is remarkable. The best will clean you; if they don't come off of their own accord they hang you up on brush along the far bank and you must break free. Or—after a couple of superb jumps that seem to go over your head—they swim upstream past you, turn and bolt downstream, putting so much distance between you two that you run out of beach on which to follow them. Again you must break off. More losses occur at this time of the year than at any other and stories about monster fish abound.

The number of fresh fish in the river increases throughout June and I pursue them at every opportunity. I try to arrange my work to give me maximum free time then. I love to fish at most any time of the year and keenly look forward to April. But it is June and early July I enjoy most, mainly because it is shirt-sleeve weather. The fish are prime. Even if I don't get one a day afield is special. The trees are newly leafed, the river strong and sparkling. But the fishing is often great. On my best Junes I find I hook a fish about every third pool and land one every six. That may not sound like much, off hand, but I cover a lot of water. One June I beached 20 fish, another 15. But other years have been near busts.

Gradually the weather warms and becomes oppressive. Sensible fishers go out early in the morning. They come in at ten, shedding down jackets. The temperature is rapidly soaring. All at once the snow in the hills is gone, the rains have stopped, and the river descends to its summer low. From day to day it shrinks disturbingly. I lose interest because of the heat. The big pools become small ones and the small ones nearly disappear. I stay inside more. It is a good time to work on a book.

The Fourth of July is fast approaching. Across the street from my house in town two ten-year-old boys are solemnly setting off fireworks. These are the "safe" kind, the only ones allowed within the city limits—but who's kidding whom? Occasionally I hear the blasts from bigger ones that have been smuggled in from the Indian reservations. Someone is daring the police. "Catch me if you can." Fat chance.

It's hot enough to melt your wax and leave you puddled on the concrete. Would you believe 92 degrees? After dinner an early dusk settles down. A few skyrockets lance the sky and afterwards their plumes droop low. Their colors are puce and lemon. The streaks are slow to disperse and remain banding the horizon in a sickly fashion. It will be midnight before they are gone.

Today is July 2. Tomorrow we are going up to the river. Hooray. When it grows really hot we're better off there. We can always plop into the shallows anytime the urge overtakes us. It brings the old body temperature down in a flash.

Most of the summer people have arrived for the long weekend. They have invited friends; friends of friends have cleverly tagged along. The noise element is high. Things aren't going to quiet down until the long holiday is past. At twilight the first rockets thud in the distance like door slams, fired by those who cannot wait for full dark and maximum effect. Teenaged boys try to impress each other with their bravery by darting in close with red-eyed punks. Rockets have short fuses, I recall, so perhaps the darting is necessary for safety's sake. The sky is all lit up with colors. A cloud of gunpowder smoke hangs in the air like an angry thought. There is no breeze to send it scurrying. By six P.M. the temperature hits and holds in the mid-nineties. The promise of a cool evening is not kept.

Everybody stays out-of-doors, hoping for a breeze and not wanting to miss it should one arrive. Nobody builds a beach fire tonight. The kids in one of the cabins have been playing rock-and-roll all day. It is greatly amplified, the sound mostly bass. The brats look stoned: They walk along the top of the riprap, all goggledy eyed, with dim smiles on their faces. I identify the blare as The Grateful Dead, who I've always liked. But didn't this kind of music end two decades ago?

The river is full of fish. (This, you understand, is a few years ago, perhaps 1984.) The steelhead are mostly wild ones, slated for the headwaters of Deer Creek. They will tarry in the North Fork and ascend the creek whenever they feel like it—probably on a freshet in mid-August. Meanwhile we take our individual cracks at them. Fishers observe the long-established protocol of never stepping in front of each other. The rule is regularly violated, though. If somebody is waiting for the pool you are expected to move along briskly, dropping downstream a couple of yards after every cast. It is only your basic politeness at work in a crowded environment. If you forget to move, somebody will remind you.

An hour before dark I pry myself out of my hammock and head for the Flat Water. The need to fish is irresistible. Norma agrees to tag along. She loves the heat and can't get enough of it—damn her hide. It's all I can do to put one booted foot in front of the other. A lineup of anglers is stretched out in the run, but I see an opening at the top and step in.

It's the part of the pool I like second best; the tailout is usually where I get my fish. On about my sixth cast a steelhead takes a wet fly with a bit of orange in it. The lineup below me moves reluctantly towards shore to give me room to play it. This too is protocol. The fish takes me downstream past them until I am abreast of my wife. She is sitting on the sand with a Doris Lessing novel.

"Not a fish, already?" she asks brightly.

"'Fraid so. Feels like a good one, too. Want to play it?"

"No, I guess not." She is a little reluctant so I have to insist. I thrust the bent rod into her hand. "Be my guest," I urge. She accepts as though it were another domestic task in a long day.

Soon I have to explain that she is turning the reel handle in the wrong direction, giving the fish line when she should be taking it in. I fear for a backlash. The fish is strong and is into the backing, which becomes a mild tangle. The fish bucks out in the current, then jumps in close on a slack line. I bite my lip and swallow some good advice.

Actually she's doing a fine job of playing it, for a woman who doesn't want to get her shoes wet. Gradually the fish comes under control, goes over on its side, and is stranded on the sand. A sleek female, it lies half out of the water and immobile.

"Nice job," I tell her.

"That was fun," she says.

I work the hook out with my needlenosed pliers, right the fish, and scoot it into deeper water. It swims off as though pursued. I follow it out to the edge of the current to make sure that it remains upright and strong. It does.

Already she's returned to her book. She isn't standing tall, beaming the way I would. I guess women are different. I see the lineup reforming and rejoin it at the top. In the remaining twenty minutes before dark nobody touches a fish. We disperse with a word and a wave.

That night it is hard to sleep, the air is so still and close. It leaves me breathless. In the morning it is the Fourth of July. At noon, though scorching, I venture out as lightly clad as I can get away with. My reasoning is that in all this heat and brightness nobody else will be so stupid as to fish. I am wrong. The pool upstream from the Elbow—it's called The Pocket—has six anglers jammed into it. Waves of heat rise from the sand between us. The air is molasses. Rock and roll is loud again. It sounds like Country Joe and The Fish, and the "Fixing To Die Rag." So help me, we're caught in a time warp.

The fish last night had taken high in the run—much higher than people ordinarily fish it. Maybe in all this heat the fish are shunning the deep part of the pool, which is warm and has lost much of its oxygen content. The place to fish today is up in the fast shallows, not the deep slow stuff where the others are all lined up.

They are wasting their time, if I am right. So I wade out into the quick water, where the footing is difficult and discouraging. The sun burns a white hole in the sky. I begin laying out a floating line a short distance in front of me. It is hard to keep my balance, the boulders are so large and tightly packed. At first it seems silly to be fishing such thin water. The fishers down below look up in astonishment, unsure what I am up to. Is it a stratagem? The water is only six to eight inches deep.

Gradually it slows and deepens. As I inch downstream I begin to lose faith in the tactic. Last night's fish was a fluke. Soon I'll be in the water the others have been pounding. They are all friends of each other, narrowly spaced out only a yard or two between them as though their ankles are in leg chains. I see one crank in his line. Then a wonderful, astonishing thing happens. As a body they quit the pool. It is more than I could have hoped for. I watch them move up the sand like a camel procession.

Rather than drop deep into the hole I decide to wade back upstream and fish again through water I have just vacated, but to fish in tighter near to where they had been wading. I tie on a drab little fly—a forerunner of Spade. I stand quietly for a moment to let the water calm down from my feet. On my first cast, nothing happens. But the grubby fly is moving at just the right speed to imitate a drifting insect, I think.

On my second cast a fish nails it, leaping high into the air where it shines. Five times it does this, each time crashing back on its side. This is much to my liking. Then it runs a short distance and turns over on its side, forming a bright crescent. I crank it in to my feet. There it rests in 18 inches of water. I back up to the beach and draw it up on the sand.

Soon I hook another. About fifty people are watching from the shade of the trees where the cabins are. A teenaged boy detaches himself from a knot of comrades and hurries over to where I am playing the fish. I put the rod in his hands. "Here," I urge, "have some fun."

I settle back on my haunches to watch the boy handle the fish. Not bad, I decide. But—just like Norma, the night before—he wants to turn the handle in the wrong direction. Twice I have to point out this practical error before he gets it. I tell him to keep his rod tip high, so there will be no breakage; for the leader to break the rod has to straighten out enough to allow a direct pull. Otherwise the bend in the rod will cushion the leader and protect it. This is right out of the Edward Ringwood Hewitt songbook. The kid gets it; he's not dumb. From then on he has no difficulty playing the fish and bringing it in to the beach. He does and I release it.

He seems disappointed, though. "This is too fine a fish to kill," I explain. "It's a wild one and there aren't a whole lot left." I snip off the fly and hand it to him for a souvenir.

"Keep it," I say. "You did a nice job."

Swimmers are waiting for the pool. I understand; I am in a lather myself. It is time to leave—to go back to camp for a dip in my private river. Two fish is plenty anytime.

At twilight I am back. There is no breeze. The air is thick and close. Rockets arch overhead, leaving trails widening and fading. Their colors—like the ones in town—are puce and lemon. The pool is deserted; everyone is off having fun. I slip into the water, feeling a little like a poacher. A moment later a fish takes with a series of sharp jerks, but holds in place and does not go off on a run until I set the hook hard and haul him around a little. Then he becomes a bullet. Again it is at the top part of the pool where I find him. There are a number of steelhead there, evidently just waiting for somebody to put a fly over them. I wonder why the others haven't figured it out yet?

A dark-haired woman in a sundress is sitting quietly on the sand not far away. She is alone. On her head is a broad-brimmed straw hat. It is white or nearly so. She is slim and attractive. (Even when playing a fish, I don't miss the vital data.) She is somebody's wife, doubtless, probably some man I know, a denizen of the Elbow. Her station is the only place where I will be able to leave the water when it is time to land the fish.

The fish runs upstream into the riffle at the top of the run, necessitating that I follow it; when I regain all the line I am opposite her again. I wade ashore. Just then the fish begins a long run straight out from the beach. The woman puts down her magazine and gets to her feet.

"My, aren't you the lucky one," she tells me.

Lucky, I think? It's all skill, lady.

She continues, "I mean, didn't you catch a fish earlier today? Wasn't it you?"

I won't deny it. I smile consent.

"It was nice, the way you let that boy play it. He was very proud. It was all he could talk about this afternoon."

"Would you like to play this fish?" I blurt it out. I had no idea I was going to say it, I swear. "The fish still has plenty of fight left."

"That might be fun. Yes, thank you. But you must tell me what to do. It's my first fish, you understand."

She makes it sound like a sexual experience. At the same time she might be putting me on. It is a distinct possibility. If I am showboating (and I am), I would deserve it. She's not the kind to put me down directly, only in a subtle manner. It would be the kind of wound where you don't feel the blade entering. She is pretty, but old enough to have teenaged children. This puts her ten or fifteen years younger than me. That's not out of reach these days.

I put the rod in her little hand and step back. Again I repeat the Hewitt routine—rod tip up, let the fish run off the reel when it pulls the rod tip down, crank in line when you can raise the tip again. It's beginning to sound original. Did Hewitt ever give his rod over to a woman? Hardly. Did he ever have lewd thoughts about women, or only about fish? Whatever, he was a grand old man.

This woman makes every mistake in the book. It doesn't matter. The fish is well hooked and the leader is stout. The fish continues to fight well. Maybe this is because it is being played, well, inexpertly. Or maybe it's just a great fish.

The lowering sky is aflame from natural causes, that is, the sinking sun and the residue of fireworks in the air. It is the smog effect and very handsome. Bright particles streak the firmament and fresh bursts are continually adding hues to it. Purple and gold are the dominant colors. Another fine run from the fish, but a shorter one, and the line suddenly slackens. I fear we've lost the fish. No, we haven't. The line tightens and the rod bows again. The fish turns over on the surface.

"You have to put a little more pressure on the fish," I tell her.

"But I don't want to lose it for you."

"Oh, come on, just pull," I say. "The leader is plenty strong. The fish is tired. Haul it up on the beach."

"I'm afraid. I'll break something."

What, this woman afraid? A bear wouldn't faze her. I put my hand over hers to give the rod a little more lift, which is needed to move the fish in from where it is foundering. Her hand is cool. How can it be cool on such a day? My own is red-hot. (Can she feel it burning?) We move back up the beach together and slide the fish onto the sand. I hear the crinkle of organdy. My arms lightly encircle her from behind. I'm trying not to touch her too hard, too much. How badly do I need a bath? Is anybody watching? Only the 50 denizens of the Elbow.

Women, I think, would make great anglers, if only they liked to fish.

The steelhead lies obediently down on the beach and doesn't wriggle a fin. Is it a sign of supplication? If I'd landed it it would be thrashing now. We study it, head to head. It is sleek and beautiful. She's not so bad, herself.

"I suppose you're going to release it?" she asks.

"Yes."

"Because you don't want to see it killed?"

"Something like that."

Suddenly my motives are suspect, even to me. I don't quite know why.

"Do you take the hook out or do I?" she asks.

"You don't want to get your dress dirty."

"I'm not worried about getting my dress dirty. What do you take me for?"

It was the wrong thing to have said. I tell her, "I'll do it, anyway."

She gives me an odd look as I twist out the hook and guide the fish back into the water. I don't know what it means. It is obscure, without measurable content. We stand side by side and watch the fish swim off. We might be on an excursion liner. It is an intimate moment, without being a sexual one. A rocket scuds overhead. It's in no way a Freudian rocket.

Smoke curls across the sky. She walks away. Our moment is over. I know I will never talk to her again. She is ordinary looking, I discover. The chief thing she has going for her is her slimness. Also, she is immaculately assembled and groomed. Nowhere can I find a careless touch. Her manner proclaims pride of ownership. Not only a mother but perhaps an early grandmother. Nothing she has seen or heard for a decade has astonished her. Her sex belongs to her husband. She is right where she wants to be in life.

I'm done fishing for the night. I feel drained. There is, in fact, not a cast left in me. The Fourth is winding down in an orgy of bombs and flares. I feel so alone; I want my wife, not somebody else's. It is nearly ten o'clock and everybody who envisions himself young is firing off his last explosives in a flurry of desperation. There is no tomorrow, not on the Fourth.

The zebras sound like small-arms fire, while the cherry bombs are mortars from over the knoll. A purple flower opens overhead and is followed by a gold one, in an intense bouquet of sparks. People move around like specters through the smoke that hugs the ground. I have to pass through this shadowy corridor to reach my car. Ahead is a circle of teenagers. They loom like savages in a Golding novel. I see adults touching butane lighters to sparklers held by tiny people. The air is alight with a frenzy of trailing zigzags as the children whip their sparklers around in tight arcs that seem to devour their tails.

As I enter the line of trees, I hold my rod tip high to avoid snagging it and breaking it off. When I duck under a cottonwood limb my back creaks. The air stinks of cordite. The ring of teenagers does not break apart as I draw near, but neither does it widen for my passage. I call out, "Friendly forces, friendly forces." I don't want to get fragged, you see.

Somebody in the deep dark shares my bemused sense of displacement. Perhaps it is Steve Raymond, whose Camp Bucktail is next door. I hear a deep bass voice reply, "You may pass through, Friendly Forces." And the terror of the Fourth won't come round for another year.

17

The Cult of The Spade

By AUGUST THE RIVER HAS DROPPED to its seasonal low flow, but in drought years it arrives there earlier and continues to shrink incredibly. A river becomes a creek, a creek a trickle. One year on the North Fork the river held a substantial run of steelhead; anybody with eyes could see them in the pools. You could make out suckers and whitefish as, well as the odd chinook.

Fishing was tough. Steelhead and angler were eyeball to eyeball and neither blinked. Few fish were being taken. The water was crystal. Most of my flies—bucktails—were comprised of bright colors. Standing midway through the Manure Spreader Hole, I watched my sunk fly swing the width of the river. If it or the sinking line crossed their bow the steelhead moved away. If not they held stock still. They missed nothing.

What bothered me most was color. Bright colors were not required; in fact they seemed to alarm the fish. So I devised a fly that had no color to it. Of course, this is impossible. What I wanted was a fly with no bright colors or flash of tinsel. Most flies of the day were red or orange, intended for dirty water. It would be a sunk fly, I decided. Dry flies were not producing well, and I and others were fishing lines that sunk—the slower the better, for rocks lined the bottom of the hole and claimed plenty of flies. I needed a fly that was quick and easy to tie, one made of readily available, inexpensive materials. For fishing in the slack water it needed to be designed so the bend of the hook did not swing down and let the fly drift upside down through the pool. Like an aircraft it required a horizontal stabilizer. I thought and I thought, and finally came up with what I hoped might be the right combination: a drab fly that looked like something found in the river and would ride along, whatever the speed of the current, in an upright position.

I found a 1X-short, 1X-strong hook that was suitable—the Sealey 1736J. (It is no longer made, and there is no adequate substitute on the market, though Alec Jackson says he is going to reintroduce it.) Size 6 was just right, though I tied it in 4s, also; the wire gauge changed with 4s, producing a hook that behaved differently and was not so good for my purposes. And I found no Sealey 8s; 8s would have been just right. To produce an artificial 8 I tied the 6 smaller and a shade shorter on the hook, and I selected a smaller soft hackle for the front.

The pattern was simplicity itself. The fly had just three parts. The tail was grey-brown deer body hair. The body, medium black chenille. The hackle, grey Plymouth rock, usually the saddle from a cock. Later I decided hen was better. In 25 years, the materials have changed only slightly to fit different conditions, but the basic fly and its lackluster colors remain the same.

What I concocted belongs to a long tradition. If I didn't know it then I know it now. There's not much new to be uncovered. The English soft-hackled nymph and wet fly, including some ties specially for seatrout (teal and orange, partridge and silver, etc.), were important antecedents to Spade. So were the Oregon and California steelhead flies—Burlap, Brindle Bug, Boss, and the Comet series. Spade contains colors already proven in Hoyt's Special and the Black Woolly Worm (the one with orange tail). But it differed from most in the total absence of flash and brightness. What I wanted was a fly that would sink rapidly to fishing depth and not alarm the fish. I wanted it to look so natural, so lifelike, that a steelhead might open its mouth and sample it, thinking it food.

Better yet, if it looked natural enough, a dour steelhead might actually be *moved* to eat it.

I sat out in front of my rental cabin at Oso in the shade of some huge cedars and Douglas firs (since cut for timber), enjoying the coolness and the invariable breeze that makes August bearable there. I tied Spade flies solely. What need had I for others? With just three parts I could crank them out production style. Quickly I made up a dozen. Brushing my arm accidentally across my makeshift desk, I sent them scattering. I bent over to pick them up off the ground, but could find only a third. Their colors were so much like the needles from the conifers that covered the ground that the flies had disappeared. This became a frequent problem. A fly easy to tie, it is equally easy to lose and not be able to find again.

I took the flies out the next day, not to the Manure Spreader Hole but to Boulder Creek. Waded out into the current I dropped the leader and fly to the water in preparation for making my first cast. A coho juvenile grabbed it and hooked himself. Admiring his parr marks and pretty orange fins, I shook him off. I made my first true cast and hooked a second little coho. A few casts later I hooked my first steelhead. It was a juvenile of about the same length as the young salmon. I knew I had something here. The fly proved to be a problem with juveniles, however. I snipped it off and tied on a conventional bright pattern. The young fish left it alone, but so did the big ones. I kept fishing with the bright fly and watched it swim through the tiny pools of the upper river. I caught nothing. I didn't know what else to do. Whenever I put Spade back on I hooked more babies.

The next day I tried Spade downstream, in the hole it was designed for—the Manure Spreader. Jerry Wintle was there. I hooked an adult steelhead and lost it. Jerry wanted to see my fly. I showed it to him.

"That's Hoyt's fly," he announced with a cursory glance.

"It is not," I countered. "Hoyt's fly has a red tail and a gray wing. Mine has neither."

"It's *like* Hoyt's fly."

"It's like a lot of others," I admitted. "But it's mine."

I caught fish regularly on it for the rest of the season, but Jerry made his contribution to its success by (inadvertently) passing on a bit of low-water lore. It happened this way. Bob Taylor and I had watched Jerry hook and play a fine fish just before dark in the Elbow Hole. When he was done, there was no time left for another fish. Afterwards I saw him whisper something to Bob. I was highly curious. What did he tell him—what secret? I had to know.

Jerry Wintle

"What did he say?" I asked Bob, as soon as I had a chance.

"Tell you later," he promised.

Back in camp, drinking a beer, I cornered him. "What's Jerry doing? What's his trick?"

"He's working his fly."

"What do you mean, 'working it?' How?"

"If you watch closely at the end of the drift he lets his rod tip bob up and down. And he'll release or else take in a few feet of line. Not a lot. It isn't necessary to work the fly much. Even if you are watching closely it's easy to miss seeing what he's doing."

"He's a sly one, all right," I agreed.

So I began working Spade and I caught fish like crazy.

Most often they took it softly. The take was much like foul-hooking

Steelhead Water **175**

a scrap fish or a salmon. Tightening on what I sensed to be a fish, it would swim upstream slowly against the pressure, with little or no resistance, but I could feel its weight growing. Tighten hard enough and the fish exploded.

At Oso few juveniles attacked my fly. I could not understand why not. When I went back upstream it was like feeding candy to the children. People heard of my success. I was happy to show them my fly. Ed Weinstein and Bill Stinson were two good fisher looking for a drab fly. Both tied Spade and caught fish on it that year. Stinson wrote about it in his book, *Flyrod Steelhead*, in 1982. He remembers the fly's origin a little differently. The story has been retold a number of times, and each time some of the details come as a surprise to me. None of them exactly true, this is one reason why I am writing my own account.

The first published mention of Spade is in a Canadian magazine. My friend Ed Weinstein has moved permanently to Vancouver, B.C., and sends me back a clipping. This is prior to 1975 and long before Stinson's book. The article is by Jack Vincent. He recounts a fishing trip to the Bulkley and Morice rivers near Hazelton. There he encounters Jerry Wintle and his wife, Jean. Jerry is fishing a new fly that he has made popular because he's caught so many fish on it. It is my Spade, but it is called, "Wintle's Western Wizard." Later Jerry confides the name is a joke. Well, I can appreciate it.

One fall soon afterwards I meet an angler from British Columbia who comes down to fish the North Fork for its fall run of big hatchery steelhead. He shows me his Wheatley fly book. One half is filled with Spades. The other contains a fly very much like it, but it has two turns of light orange hackle tied in front of the grizzly. He explains, "The orange helps in off-color water."

"What do you call this fly?" I ask.

I don't remember his answer. It is neither Spade nor Wintle's Western Wizard. I resist telling him it is *my* fly, that I had originated it. I doubt whether he would believe me. Besides, what difference does it make?

In 1976 Trey Combs lists it among hundreds of others in his book, *Steelhead Fly Fishing and Flies*. About the same time Pat Trotter quotes me on its origins in an article in *Salmon Trout Steelheader Magazine*. As usual Trotter is accurate.

The ground lies fallow for years, and I doubt if many people tie and fish Spade. When the water is low or dropping on the North Fork I bring it out and give it a try, but more often fish a fly of the same shape or design, with different colors. I'm back to brighter flies now and I don't shun tinsel. I think it comes from the fact that I am a long-time steelheader and I put my faith in brightness, along with everybody else. It works. But when the water is low I switch to small flies with horizontal stabilizer tails. The style comes out of California and was developed for the saltwater flats caused by tides off the mouths of winter steelhead rivers. Spade, per se, I rarely tie.

Some patterns from that time include: Eclipse: tail, dark moose; body, black chenille; hackle, red and yellow, mixed. The idea behind this fly is why not combine the best qualities of the dark (that is, black) flies and the bright ones? What would happen, for instance, if George McLeod's Skykomish Sunrise (a great fly, perhaps the best of them all) is overcome from behind by . . . night? By total darkness? But the darkness stops short, just before it reaches that brilliant hackle?

Similarly, Boss is such a logical pattern that I "invent" it again, long after its original time. This happens with patterns. I fish it successfully for many years before I know it already has a name. A 16-pound summer succumbs to it one June at Boulder Creek. The way I tie it is thus: tail, black bear or dark moose; body, black chenille, ribbed with flat silver tinsel; hackle, hot orange. It is a wonderful fly and I've caught more than 100 steelhead on it. It doesn't need bead eyes, which makes it fish upside down.

Another good fly from that time, and one that produces today, is simply Spade with a red body. Rib it with silver tinsel, if you must, but it is fine without. And, in the fall, but before the yellow leaves fill the river, a plain bright yellow body works well, with or without a rib. It will catch searun cutthroats, too.

Spade and Eclipse went into eclipse, at least for me, and I began fishing other flies, often on the surface, during these late summer months. One fly that evolved about the same time as Spade, and has strong similarities, is Harry Lemire's Greased Liner. Harry and I have not discussed this, but I suspect both of us would acknowledge a parallel development at the least. Maybe he has sunk his fly when the need arose, or accidentally, and caught fish on it. I know for certain that I've floated and riffled Spade and caught fish. Fish like it worked both ways.

The two flies are hard to see on the surface, however, especially in broken water when the sun is glinting off the surface. I often tie a white ruffle on the head of Spade (or on Greased Liner), just for my benefit. If it spooks steelhead it is a risk I am willing to take so long as I can keep my eye on it and spot a fast-water rise. I call it "The Risible," which mean it's laughable.

Dry-fly fishing produces eye strain. No wonder so many anglers like Jerry Wintle enjoy fishing a sunk fly on a floating line. The fish take it solidly with a wet fly strike, very decidedly, and you don't have to keep watching the damn thing all day long. You go home without feeling your eyes have been burned into your head with a cigaret butt.

Meanwhile Spade went on with its buggy life independent of me. People used it in Canada, but little in Washington State. They who caught fish on it originally brought it out again when conditions warranted it. I credit Guide John Farrar with its resurgence. It became a good producer on the Wenatchee. John changed it a little—not the basic dressing but the materials—making it much more attractive. Seeing one of his I fell in love with it again. John substituted reddish-brown hair from the top of the tail of a white-tailed deer for the grey body hair, which was brittle and subject to breakage. Body hair is hollow and gives the fly a tendency to float, which I don't want in a wet-fly dressing.

For the body John used black dubbing. That made a huge difference. Dubbing—with the guard hairs left in and the softer underfur picked out—brought the fly to life. And by using soft hen neck feathers for the hackle (which I didn't *have* to use, originally) he gave the fly a soft collar and a lot of action in the water. This made it more like the English wet flies and nymphs I drew on but did not fully understand.

John fished the Wenatchee long before I did, and so did Joe Butorac, Bob Aid, and Bob Strobel. Some fishers there—like up in Canada—used it almost exclusively. When I started making trips to the Wenatchee I fished a sunk line and marabous or hair-winged wet flies. Oddly I never gave Spade a thought. My success was irregular. Other people did better than I, most times, and I became frustrated. It wasn't until I began using a floating line that I took fish regularly under a wide range of conditions. And the use of Spade soon followed. I learned that all of its derivatives would produce solidly. These included Eclipse and Boss.

Alec Jackson has long been a champion of Spade. Like many good tiers, the fly is so simple, so plain, so drab, that he can't refrain from "improving" it. One of his modifications has a claret hackle, another, one of olive-dyed grizzly. I've told him he should retain the original grizzly and only tie a turn or two of colored hackle aft, if he must. Blithely he ignores my suggestions and goes on turning out "creative" Spades. They get reproduced in magazines and their colorful lives prolonged. Of course they catch fish; any fly shaped like that will do so.

Spade asks for a short-shank hook. Mike Kinney says that "Spade doesn't look right unless it's tied on the old Sealey." I agree. But Alec's version on his own hook is an interesting innovation. Dressed in classic low-water style, with the tail and body leaning well forward as on a Logie or Jock O'Dee, it takes on a different configuration and becomes part of another tradition. By degrees I'm getting used to this version and accepting it.

Today Spade shares common ground with Skunk, which is a dark but bright and flashy fly. Steelheaders often feel lost with a drab fly on the end of their leader and fear they will lose effectiveness. (This may be based on the fallacy that steelhead don't see very well, especially in off-color water. For them Skunk fills the bill and they fish it longer and more confidently.)

The origins of Skunk are clouded, surrounded by mystery. It may have been first tied in Oregon or it may have started out as a bass fly used in Washington by Wes Drain. Probably the ties were logical ones and developed concurrently. It wouldn't be the first time two minds came up with the same solution to a problem independently, at about the same time. Skunk is one of two or three of the most popular steelhead flies, and deservedly so. Fishers argue whether it is a bright or a dark fly. I think it is both. I've caught a lot of fish on it. It gets fished because of its fame and its strange appeal, for it is a dark fly that hedges in the direction of brightness, eg. the red tail, the silver tinsel rib, and the brilliant whiteness of the wing. Yet its body and hackle are black. The original version had a black wing overlaid with white. (A skunk's tail provides both colors.) Today the wing is simplified to white and often polar-bear body hair or mask is used. These are bright materials with a lot of translucence and flash.

I've found, and for years been told, that Spade will out-fish Skunk under a wide range of circumstances. (I'm sure there are some where it won't.) Ed Weinstein introduced Spade to the Grand Ronde river in the '60s. It was so effective that he began tying Spades on the riverbank, trading them for meals and drinks. This was when the Ronde's run of wild fish was nearly gone and the hatchery product wasn't yet available.

When it came my turn to investigate the Ronde, many years later, unmarked hatchery fish were returning in droves, and both they and the wild ones were one-salt fish, not easily distinguished from each other except by the rule of "the tall dorsal," which wasn't foolproof. I decided to take Weinstein's final modification, which was giving the fly a conventional white bucktail wing, and then rib the body with silver. This was a far cry from the original Spade, but it caught fish nicely. Actually

Ed's and mine were the first Spade/Skunk hybrids. Many followed. To list them all would be meaningless and exhausting. Suffice to say most give Spade some brighter characteristics of its companion—a red tail (ugh), a white wing, a red or chartreuse butt, etc. Joe Butorac is responsible for some of these bastardizations. It is best not to stray too far from the original of either fly, or else you are tying something else.

Joe's Golden Spade is a good, legitimate variation. He first tied it on the Wenatchee when he noticed caddis flies laying eggs on the water. So he gave Spade an egg sack. The fish liked it and it has become an important fly to use on certain rivers, especially in October when there are steady hatches of large caddis. The best known Butorac bastardization is Skapade. When he gleefully showed it to me one day, I dove into my flybox and produced another version. "This is Spunk," I told him with a chortle.

Other people's variants followed. Stan Young dresses it with a brown hackle for the North Umpqua and catches fish on it. This as much acknowledges its Oregon sources, and links it to Brindle Bug and the imitation bee flies. And Jimmy Hunnicutt has two versions, according to Trey Combs who fished it with him on the Dean. One has an orange butt—which I believe Jimmy picked up from Bill Ewing—and another a blue-dun dubbing body and tail of white polar. (This is hardly a Spade.) His hook sizes are the same as mine: 4 and 6. They balance the fly well.

Jimmy's polar version brings me back full circle to some ties I made years ago. I'll pass them on for whatever they're worth. They're based on the idea that Spade is a style, not a pattern, and one might rightly refer to The Spade Generic without much exaggeration. It works like this: throw away the standard tail for a given fly and substitute the wing material in its place; thus, Skykomish Sunrise would be tied Spade-style with a tail of white polar. It is a good material because it is bright and stiff, and won't easily wrap around the bend of the hook and cause the fly to whirl like a plug-cut herring in fast water. Keep the body the same as the original (or else make it red dubbing, which is better yet) and the hackle the same, but soft and "henny." Skykomish Sunrise (Spade style) will then have a stiff white tail and a body of red or fluorescent orange chenille, with a flat silver rib. The hackle, as always—and very important on this fly—is red and golden yellow, wrapped together and fully mixed. A nice variant is to replace the red with orange in the hackle and wind it mixed with the yellow.

Skunk (Spade style) is: tail, white polar (mask ties best); body, black chenille; rib, flat silver tinsel; hackle, webby black. (Note: black-dyed Chinese pheasant rump is good stuff and has an iridescent green cast that fish like.)

Spade variants are infinite—and almost meaningless, for soon they leave the original pattern behind and become new flies in their own right. This is well and good, but runs the risk of producing many one- or two-fish flies—flies that have no proven value and soon fall by the wayside with the countless hundreds that preceded them.

To have produced—by accident; it is how all good flies are created—a fly that is in wide use is satisfying. It will catch fish anywhere. But I know that if I hadn't come up with it, another fisher would have, given a little more time, for it is a fly tied in response to a common situation—low, clear water and spooky fish. I'm sure other people tied flies very much like it and found—to their delight—that they caught fish. There was a great need for such a drab, dark pattern for steelhead. If it continues to catch fish under a wide range of conditions and in many places it will deserve to live. But if not it should fail.

I'd like to see it up there with the Bomber, Adams, Skykomish Sunrise, and its odd complement, Skunk. But it may travel the route of neglect that leads to oblivion. That is okay, too. I can't help its case any at this point, for Spade has a life separate from mine. Like the prodigal son it has gone out into the world and must make its way there. If it succeeds nobody will be prouder than I.

18

Meristic Characteristics, Phenotyping, Electrophroesis, and Other Fun Things

It is satisfying to learn to tell the various salmonids apart—the salmon from the trout, the char from the salmon, the trout from one another—but this is quickly and easily learned, especially if you fish rivers a lot and observe the salmon and trout in their spawning dress. To tell the various parr from each other is more difficult. There is a good illustration in Haig-Brown's *The Western Angler* (1947), but it really shows their great similarity. I've always thought salmon juveniles had an embryonic look—big eye in disproportion to the rest of their bodies, and bodies that were slender and seemingly not fully developed. To tell steelhead from coho juveniles is useful, if you are going to be around rivers much, and you should be able to do it by eye soon after the fry are free-swimming. They behave differently, are smaller and quicker, and occupy faster water, etc.

Both coho and steelhead live in the river for about two years and have trouty characteristics, moving to intercept food aggressively and often on summer evenings dimpling along the edge of a glide. To sort them out visually and get to anticipate their annual regularity is one of life's small pleasures. It gets keener by the year. If you catch a juvenile on your barbless hook it will probably be over four inches in length and easy to study. Steelhead fingerlings look more fully formed, more complete, their eyes more in proportion to their heads. Their parr marks are similar to those of the salmon, coho especially, and not unless you have two specimens side by side (which is not likely) are you likely to see much difference.

The coho parr's orange fins, forked tail, absence of spots on the tail, and elongated anal fin set him off from young steelhead. Or, if you reverse the characteristics, steelhead pre-smolts have squarish tails, fins that are not so orange, tiny spots on their tails, and anal fins that are short and squared off.

Adult salmon and steelhead are easier to tell apart, though when you hook one in a river you might fool yourself during the first stages of the fight. A fresh-run humpbacked (or pink) salmon often fights well and some are terrific performers, in no way inferior to a steelhead, and it is not until you get them on the short line that you see with disappointment that they are salmon. Coho can put up a great fight, too. Though often salmon have a telltale beat to their tails throughout the battle, there are times when they move so swiftly that the beat is not noticeable and the doggedness of the usual salmon fight is missing. Most of the time a salmon feels and behaves like a salmon and is always to be released on the North Fork, for there is no keep season. The hooking of salmon is something special and gives us a handshake acquaintanceship with the various salmon when they are running at different times of the year and often dominate the river briefly.

It can be a pleasant experience. You soon get to recognize individual differences. You learn how one male coho differs from another, or a female from a female, in color, shape, size, etc. These are subtle, visual signs. Soon you will know more than other fishers who have not kept their eyes wide open. And you may know more than the so-called experts. (Once I met a fish checker from the Department of Wildlife who asked me how I knew the steelhead in front of us was a ripe male. To me it was so obvious, so fundamental, that I inquired about his credentials. "I wrote my thesis on shellfish," he explained and went on to add that he had received little instruction in salmonids. I would have thought that all fisheries biology students would be grounded in the basics of salmonid identification, but this wasn't the case.)

In time, with more experience, he would learn what river fishermen know early. The ripe male steelhead has a kip, a big red stripe down his lateral line, and a deep green-gray cast to his flanks. The rest of him is muddy, though his belly may be a dark cream. A female steelhead resembles less a male steelhead than she does a female salmon. She is brighter, slenderer, sleeker, and has a smaller head. This holds true for all the salmonids.

Scientists rely on what they call meristic characteristics for identification. These are numeric and fall within various frequency ranges.

From sheer numbers, within specific areas of measurement, one species can be told from another. But in the field you aren't going to bother with counting rays or performing a hasty autopsy. It is your eye that will tell you what you need to know and confirm what you are looking for.

I am indebted to Pat Trotter again and his book on cutthroat trout for much of the following. Pat writes simply and coherently about complicated subjects, including scientific ones. He cites Webster's definition of meristic as "characterized by or involving modification in number or in geometrical arrangement of body parts." Salmonid identification characteristics include gillraker count, pyloric caeca count (these are intestinal appendages), and number of scales, starting to measure diagonally just above the lateral line and going up to the dorsal. These are the primary ID checks. Other, or secondary, ones are from branchiostegal rays, number of vertebrae, and ray counts on other fins. These are genetically determined and not subject to environmental alteration (except over eons).

Trotter says that computers today quickly analyze such data and produce readouts in the form of a Hubbs and Hubbs diagram. There is an example on page 16 of his book and he states that a diagram is useful in determining sub-species (in which cutthroat abound) and in identifying hybridization among rainbows and cutthroats. Karotyping is also used. This is a chromosomal approach and counts pairs (including the presence of fused pairs) within a genotype. Phenotypical and genotypical differences are simply those caused by environment and those that exist among species. They often can be told by the trained eye. The more you look, the more you see; and the more you see, the more you know. This is the great satisfaction in learning how to observe more closely.

Trotter is interested in problems of hybridization because cutthroats are easily dominated by and bred with rainbows. There are degrees of hybridization within each of these species, since hybrids are usually not sterile and dominant characteristics will change from generation to generation. This is not so likely in rainbow or steelhead (or seems not to be, though further research might prove otherwise) and it is necessary only to note at this point that Trotter's discussion of Binns' scale of hybridization might be useful in classifying native, wild, and hatchery steelhead strains and their "degrees of purity." The scale runs A through F, with A being pure and F an obvious mix.

Totter's description of electrophoresis is masterful. In simple English he outlines the process of biochemical protein identification so that even a person with little scientific training such as myself can understand the physical traits used in determining unmistakable sub-species identification. Listen to him:

"Take a slurry of tissue from the muscle or liver of a fish and place it on a cell composed of a starch gel. Now place an electric field across the cell so that the negative electrode is at the same end of the cell as the tissue slurry. While the field is operating, the proteins in the fish tissue move through the starch toward the positive electrode. After a time, shut off the electric field and spray the starch gel with chemical reagents to render the proteins visible. You will notice that the proteins have separated from one another as they migrated through the gel. This is because each protein has a different rate of movement, or electrophoretic mobility, in the electric field, caused by different electrical charges on the surface of each molecule. By mapping a fish's proteins in this way and comparing the 'map' with one from known specimens, fishery scientists can often determine the subspecies or race of the individual and tell whether or not it is a hybrid."

They can often tell from this data which components of a river are wild and which of hatchery origin, since their protein maps will vary considerably. And within wild populations (which include second and third, etc., generations of hatchery fish born in the "wild," though not "native" fish) they can identify various electrophoretical characteristics. Two polymorphic loci, LD-4 and T0, were used to spot the coastal and inland strains of steelhead. These are lactate dehydrogenase and tetrasolium oxidase (also called superoxide dismutase-SOD). A host of protein systems is identifiable through this process.

Complicated and complete as it sounds the science is in its infancy. Further research may lead to the identification of other subspecies and subsets of subspecies of the various salmonids. It is good for us amateurs to know in general about the types of identification used by scientists so we can recognize them when they are referred to in the literature. The confusion among scientists in regard to complex genetic matters should make us feel less alone in the bewilderment we often experience in the field trying to determine if wild is truly wild, that is, "native," and whether our fish had a life in the river and ocean, and not in a hatchery and rearing pond, before entering the ocean.

Often problems in the field and problems in applied science are semantic and have primarily a vocabulary difference. Science helps us see and learn from what we observe. To know of the confusion that abounds in trying to distinguishing native, wild, and hatchery stocks from each other enables us to look more intelligently at what we experience in the so-called wild along a river.

To tell the different species of salmonids apart is knowledge that must come first; to distinguish the various components of a given species is next in importance. Finally there is the need to know the differences among individuals within a species. They vary widely, as they do in people. Each fish is an individual. And circumstances can make a big difference in a fish's appearance. A nine-pound male fish, for example, may look very different in saltwater, upon entering his natal river, as he approaches spawning, when he pairs and spawns (and perhaps pairs again and spawns again, the following year), and after he grows wasted and drifts back to sea. But all the while he is the same fish.

A winter run of the same sex and weight will look different from a summer run fish and both males will look unlike a bright, slender female of the same approximate weight. But even one individual of the same subspecies, year-class, weight, and maturity will have small differences that the experienced (note I don't say trained) eye will observe—a difference in color and spotting above and below the lateral line, for instance, or a secondary pink stripe along the belly, or the tendency toward developing a "wrist" at the tail, the breadth and quantity of spots on the tail, or caudal fin, and the amount of kip formed in the snout and the lower jaw.

In time you will begin to think that you can detect by eye alone whether or not the fish you behold has spawned *previously*. There are clues. For example, a previously spawned fish is not necessarily larger. The fish may have lost much of its original weight in the earlier spawning effort and hardly have had time, in less than a year, to gain it back from sea-feeding. A fish of the same age that didn't spawn—say, a fish that has been three years away from his smolting migration—will be much bigger than a previously spawned fish, for his feeding will not have been interrupted by time in the river. Of course scale analysis will show a dark, jagged ring from spawning, indicating that the fish has gone without feeding. In the case of a summer run it will abstain from food for up to a full year; with a winter run only for a month or so. It isn't often I take scale samples or read them or have them looked at professionally, so I have to make my best guess in the field. It is this judgment that determines what we should do, such as deciding to release a fish that might otherwise be killed unwisely.

Work in the field is not always exact. The situation is often unclear. A previously spawned fish may reveal its condition by a certain vague look. I suppose the look can be objectified and the many small changes recorded and written down. But nobody does this. It is more important that the angler learn to look closely, bringing past experiences and book knowledge to bear on what is in front of him. If a fish appears healthy, and you think you can do it carefully without hurting the fish or risking infection, take a few scales with your pocket knife from two rows above the lateral line. This is at the shoulder, just in back of the dorsal fin. Put them in an envelope and take them home. Keep them moist, so they don't curl up and become brittle and useless for examination purposes. A tiny Ziplock bag, out of which all the air can be squeezed, is useful. Flatten down the scale while soft and find a way to project it onto a screen. (There are books that tell you how to do this or you can come up with a way of your own. A photographic slide projector works, but there may be a focusing problem. If the local librarian will let you, look at your scales through a microfiche reader. I like this best and a copy can often be made on the spot.)

Look at your scales, look at others. Study pictures of scales in a book. (Mallock, Taverner, *et al.*) Get familiar with them and their characteristics. Scales are the fish's fingerprints and they look much like tree rings, too. If you are uncertain as to what you see, you will be advancing in the learning process, for science is never as neat as we'd like it to be and uncertainty is a fact of life. However, more has been learned about salmonids in the past 10 or 15 years than in all the previous decades. Knowledge of substance about steelhead is coming together. Its sum is impressive.

Now is a good time to be alive and learning something new. Who knows but one of us amateurs may make an important discovery, adding to the sum of knowledge that is the science of fish biology today.

19

Big Yellow Rock

THE ELBOW HOLE IS ONE OF TWO GREAT POOLS on the North Fork. The other is the Deer Creek Riffle, along with the pool immediately below it, the Manure Spreader Hole, both of which are in continuous flow some years.

The Elbow was made famous by Enos Bradner in his book, *Northwest Angling* (1950), in which he carefully diagrammed it, but in keeping with the closed-mouth tradition of this river slightly disguised its configuration and hid its name. Of course many recognized it and laughed. It is much changed from Bradner's time, and from my boyhood, and the dry line of rocks you see on shore today at the edge of the beach used to be out in the middle of the river. You stood in deep water, balanced on the balls of your feet, and cast impossibly long distances towards them. Now they are ever at your back.

The river has moved North since then, as this river is ever doing, alternating cutbanks the length of its course. Over the years floods have done extensive damage. On the North side are cabins routinely in need of protection in the form of riprap. Repaired but for a little while the bank is presently being attacked by the river from the East. The huge, silty floodplain there is being steadily eroded. The land upstream, where there is no riprap to protect it, annually experiences wide-spread flooding miseries. Several times each winter the river rages and people who have built homes and summer cabins too near are punished for their temerity. Riprap provides no simple solution and often causes greater problems above and below where it is installed.

The old Elbow Hole was a demon to wade even in August, when the bottom drops out. The rocks you stood on were big and packed closely together, and the slickest thing this side of an ice-skating rink. While the river elsewhere received its usual green and brown algae components the Elbow grew a coat of grease on its rocks. Good waders all we kept falling in and getting soaked. The white-water chute at the head was especially dangerous.

Once Walt Johnson plucked Ken Ohnemus out by his wader suspenders as he floated by—face down—in the fast current. It was probably August, when people take more chances because the river is low, the water warm.

"Walt saved my life," Ken told me many years later. He was not prone to exaggerate.

On about one out of every three visits I used to ship water or fall down, and didn't think much about it, for the weather was mild, usually until October. Once, fishing with Ed Weinstein, he went downstream to investigate another hole, promising to return. In the interval I took a tumble and was spun roughly down the river through a line of boulders for about twenty feet before I was able to gain my footing. In the process I banged my elbow. (No, this isn't how the pool got its name, but thanks for asking.) And my knee received a bad whack. I had gone completely under. Even my hat was soaked, while my glasses streamed water. Ed, approaching, remained his old preoccupied self.

Finally I asked him, "Notice anything different about me, Ed?"

He looked me up and down. "What is it?" he finally said.

"I am thoroughly soaked. Look at me. Every bit of me is wet, even my wallet."

"Oh," he replied, "did you fall in?"

Yes, you might say that I did. Next it was Ed's turn. There was a place where the main pool spilled over into a nice little slot along the far side that ended at the old Stump Hole. Fish would hold in the slick along the far bank, but it was a difficult cast, very long, and to make it humanly possible you waded up to your armpits and stood on a boulder. The boulder was slick and shaped like the head of a ring-necked duck. Even then the cast was almost out of reach, and you had to mend slack line immediately to hold the fly on the far side and keep it from being swept away from where the fish lay.

Ed was a first-class caster and left-handed to boot, which helped greatly here. He cast and mended and a fish took his fly hard. The pull was enough to upset his delicate balance, even before the reel started to run. Down he went, into a deep fast gut. When he rose, sputtering, the fish had broken off. It was your average daily performance for this pool and Ed couldn't be faulted. I offered him about the same modicum of sympathy he had given me a week earlier.

Twenty years have passed and the Elbow, along with each of us, has

Ed Weinstein

been considerably tamed. It is easy wading now. Then I disdained a wading staff and occasionally paid the price for my folly. Today I have no need for one even in high water. There is a sandy path winding easily among the tops of the big boulders; the lower portions of these rocks are buried in sand. Even in heavy water I can pick my way easily and safely along the route. It isn't nearly so deep as it looks, either. The amount of holding water has been reduced by about 90 percent. This portends poorly for this great pool and for the future of the river.

The Stump Hole just downstream used to be a fine, difficult pool. It remains tricky and hard to fish because of its back eddies and conflicting currents. It is a ghost of itself and nobody knows it by this name. It was Walt Johnson's favorite spot and he fished it with great success, year after year. I didn't do too badly myself. Today about 50 feet of holding water remain. Yearly it seems to shrink. I can cover most of it from two or three wading stations, none more than a yard or two apart. It holds a few fish in season and is a good signal pool, telling me a great deal about the strength of the native run. It is a favorite resting place for salmon, too, and an indicator of the relative abundance of their various species in the river.

The Elbow begins where the river rounds the upstream bend, gently coming down from the Pocket and making a left-angled turn at Steve Raymond's Camp Bucktail. That corner takes a lot of abuse at flood stage and is giving up its bank by the cubic yard. There is a riffle at the top of the run, but it is too swift and shallow to hold fish well, and can't be expected to put out more than the odd steelhead except perhaps at dead-low water when it is a little better.

Where the river slows marks the start of the Elbow. Anglers coming long distances to fish it do not recognize it because there is no elbow today, only a straight shot. (Anything resembling an elbow lies high above it and is undistinguished.) To reach the so-called Elbow it is necessary to cross the riffle at the bottom of the Pocket. (The Pocket was destroyed by the great flood of 1990.) This is a broad flat, mostly sand, and can be easily negotiated, often even in winter. In Bradner's time the crossing was hairy even in August and so I remember it as a boy.

The top portion hasn't changed so much, but no longer holds fish the way it used to because its bottom is different. Rather than lie where the boulders look best to the angler the steelhead tend to collect as individuals at the small tailout. This is about the only place where the swing of the fly covers them well. If you fish down much farther with a sunk fly you will lose it in the stones. But with a floating line, and the fly riding in the surface film, you can cover the water carefully and not risk a hang-up.

When there were a lot of native summer runs they would sometimes occupy this water because all the better lies were taken, sometimes by salmon. They would invariably strike hard and the take was followed by a long, slashing run that usually meant a lost fish. Such a fish was landed about one time out of three. The losses were instructive and memorable.

The second pool (which carries no special name, the whole reach being imprecisely called the Elbow) is lovely, and I fish it each time and often with pleasure and high expectation. I'm usually not rewarded for my affection. But occasionally when I reach the very bottom, where the river slows and shallows and spills over into the vestiges of the old pool, I will hook a fish. It is not called the Stump Hole by anybody but Walt and me and Bob Bettzig, who remember it from its better days. Whatever you call it it remains an intriguing spot. Early in the year it is good wet-fly water and in August and September, when the river has receded, it is ideal for the floating fly.

I call it floating and not dry because how it is fished varies considerably, but the common characteristic among anglers is to use a floating line. I like to riffle or wake a fly here and believe it gives me more strikes, but Walt often fishes in classic dead-drift style, and makes it produce for him. Consequently we can sometimes fish the pool together (though we both would prefer not to) and not get in each other's way too badly. This is possible because of our great difference in styles.

He has a patience and quietude that is found only in the best trout fishers and is not common in steelheaders unless they are trouters at heart. Walt is. He will fish upstream whenever he can, with a light rod and line, and present his small dry fly time after time to the same place, if he knows or suspects from past years that a fish might be lying there. There are three or four places in this tiny run that meet LaBranche's criteria for "Sacred-Inch Fishing," and Walt will work each one and never seem to tire. I—younger, less calm—grow impatient with fishing so precisely. I know this is a major fault and each year strive to slow down, but fear I am constitutionally incapable. So I fish a riffled or waking fly, but stop expectantly whenever I near the Sacred-Inch Water and try to give my fly more time to do its seductive work. And often I start fishing it on an upstream dead drift like Walt does. Sometimes being a copycat pays off.

When waking a fly I like it to work quietly, with varying speeds, now slowing down and almost stopping, now starting up again, now leaving a wake, now not. And I will cover the same lie repeatedly, even while I know I am most likely to get a strike my first time through untouched water. The immediacy of this type of fishing is what makes it so exciting, so much fun. The strike is often a followback or comes with a slash. Sometimes there is a swirl on the surface or else you spot the fish's wake behind the fly and what follows is violent. Suddenly the sliding river is full of foam and the air with explosive energy. The fish is either on the surface or such a short distance beneath it that the effect is the same. When the battle slows often you will see the fish flash long and slender and green; the green is the cast produced by the water, of course. The fish tires and drifts along with the current, looking spent, but comes to life again and is off on another long run. This repeats until you either land or lose it.

The take of the surface fly is more exciting than that of a wet fly, which rides a foot or more deep. This is because you can see everything that happens. Fishing on top continues good until something changes the conditions. A small, mid-summer freshet will do it. Then wet-fly fishing becomes tops again. I fish with great excitement and hope on a newly risen river. While it is high the flow is more straightforward and there is no back eddy to impede a good drift. Some fishers continue to do well fishing dry now, but not me.

On the far side, where the no-name pool ends and the leftover Stump Hole begins, is a huge yellow boulder. It is submerged until August, but you can make out the vee-slick it creates in the current much earlier in the year. Fishermen and fishing writers characterize boulders by certain standards of comparison: this one is smaller than a Volkswagen, but bigger than a bathtub. It is golden yellow when emerged; when the river is high it is pale, lemony. (I describe it so you'll know it when you see it and go away.) To identify it from all the other rocks in the river means you have reached the start of the best water. I always take heart here, no matter how barren the day has been.

If a strike is not forthcoming I move downstream in small increments, continuing to cast as far across the river as I can and letting my fly swing and work in the current. I draw abreast of the big yellow rock. As August advances and the rock emerges the back eddy worsens and line has to be mended continuously to avoid a huge, dragging belly. In the middle of the river I can see sunken rocks, stretches of smooth cobbles, and recently sand—lots of sand. I see fish, too. Less desirable species include suckers and whitefish, and they sometimes strike a wet fly or are inadvertently snagged, as are salmon. In fact, dark salmon are a big problem here. Chinook will break you off quickly, but humpies, in an odd-numbered year, can be a plague. When they are abundant you have to be careful not to strike when the wet fly pauses in its drift or when you think you might have a steelhead strike; steelhead usually take more solidly, even in slow water. When you feel a touch you should feed line instead of tightening. Often the humpies will strike a sunk fly hard. Even if you slip line you will probably hook some as their numbers mount. It is a good argument for fishing only with the floating line and surface fly so late in the season.

As you work your way through the water that lies below the big yellow rock the pool broadens and deepens. It also becomes sandier and less interesting. Along the far bank are target rocks, as I think of them. They remain more or less constant from year to year. They serve as markers—points where you can relocate yourself after you've hooked a fish and moved downstream with it. They are places to return to and concentrate on, on future trips. There is, for instance, a triangular rock on the far side, just out from the bank, rising from about two feet of water. Your fly will catch on it if you cast to the upstream side of the bank in very low water. So you must cast just below and begin the first of several mends to make the belly in the line disappear. (This never works for me but must be tried before you give up and accept the drag.)

Often a fish will take after a two-count or perhaps a three. Rarely will it grab in mid-channel. This is a great place for searun cutthroat, too, but you must fish differently for them. A wet fly needs to be worked in a short, rapid manner. A dry fly may interest both cutthroat and steelhead. It is the best of both possible worlds and increases your chances of hooking a worthwhile fish by several degrees of magnitude.

In this pool you may encounter steelhead, cutts, Dolly Varden, jack salmon, and adult chinooks and coho. I like fishing both wet and dry, alternating methods, and find that on different days one may be more effective than another. If I have time, and nobody is waiting for the hole, I'll fish it twice, once each way. Dry goes first is the rule of thumb. To wet is accorded sloppy seconds.

The pool ends disappointingly. It just . . . dies out. The sandy bottom comes to dominate. The water deepens and slows, the rocky bottom disappears, and the pool becomes one big yawn. I fish my way through the lower part systematically once or twice a season, but seldom am rewarded with a take. Salmon show here frequently and on a dark day it may be excellent for cutthroat.

Walt surprises me sometimes by fishing sunk fly late into the year, some years well into August. But when he goes over to the dry line it is

Walt Johnson

for the rest of the season. I, an inferior fisher, vacillate between the two methods. I can't quite make up my mind that dry is always best.

On a given evening in August, when we must share the water, it goes something like this: just after the dinner hour we arrive separately at the pool. One night he is first, another I am. (It is possible, I suspect, for each of us to arrive earlier each night and always be the first, but neither of us tries to beat out the other.) He will start in low, in the unattractive slack water at the bottom of the Stump Hole, casting upstream and mending just a little. He may be fishing for cutthroat with a floating line or he may be after steelhead. It's hard to tell. If he strips in line in a certain way, rather than gathering it back in preparation for the next cast, I know he is after cutthroat, which usually take just under the surface. But if he casts more across and down, and mends to get a drag-free drift for most of his fly's course, I know he is fishing primarily for steelhead. As he nears the big yellow rock he slows down; this is what I do, too, for it is a point of high expectancy.

I am at the top of the Elbow proper, about a hundred yards above him, fishing a riffled fly that doesn't float too high and rides along in the surface film, half-submerged. This is called damp fly. I fish it downstream mostly, quartering my casts across the pool, and either mending right away or else taking the slack out of the line and fishing the fly tight so that it wakes. I can cover a lot of water fast this way, but soon grow bored when no strike is coming. So I start working through the upper water faster than Walt would like me to, I suspect, and find myself in danger of bearing down on him. I try to hold off and slow down, but it's hard.

Generally I quit at the bottom of the no-name pool and am guilty only of a little long-lining to get my fly into the very top of what we both acknowledge is the best water. Then I make myself back off, returning to where I started or else bypassing the part Walt has fished and all the dull water below it. All the while he knows I want my crack at the water that lies out from the big yellow rock.

Sometimes after he has covered it methodically for a while (to me it seems like hours and to him it must be only a minute or two) he will invite me to fish through it, for he is a generous man. I know this means to riffle my fly fast, and then get out and give it back to him. I am grateful—for fast is more my style. So I wake my fly hurriedly, wading deeper in the run than I should like to cover it quickly and risking scaring some fish in the process. I hurry, for the light is beginning to fail.

One such night not long ago Walt hooked a fine big steelhead on a dry fly, one that raced all over the pool and finally shot upstream and to the far side of the river, coming to rest just above the big yellow rock. I settled back to watch a good fight between skilled opponents. But the fish soon fouled Walt's long leader on the big yellow rock and he could neither wade to free it nor cross the river to reach it from the other side. Nor could I. He was forced to break it off. Marilyn Stone, who lives on the other side, and often comes down to watch us fish on a summer's evening said, "What a shame." We lowered our heads in mourning.

Walt was not as unhappy as I might have been; he had worked that fish over for more than an hour and finally it had come up to his dry fly. It was a satisfying accomplishment and the fight was only what comes afterwards. By now it was too late for any more fishing, so we said goodnight and went our separate ways.

On another night, if there is even a little light left, I will fish on. I will go back to the top of the Elbow, switch my dry to a sinktip line, and cover the hole one more time, fishing very fast, a cast to each step, each step a wide one, as the dark settles down. Sometimes I will hook a fish when it is so late, so dark, that I can't see it and must play it by feel. Or else—fishless—my fly catches on a rock and hangs up solidly. A lost fly or broken tippet means the end of the fishing, for I can't see to tie on another. Walt usually has the good sense to quit earlier than I. He'll be satisfied to watch me fish, seeming to pull for me, and then we will walk out together the short distance before our routes fork.

Having but ten minutes left in which to hook a fish is exciting to me. I like the challenge of compressed time and the narrow window of opportunity provided by the rush of night. My concentration is twice what it ordinarily is—though never approaching Walt's normal fishing intensity. And if I am lucky and I hook a steelhead I will play it as though my life depended on it, even if it is to be released. September is drawing near and the fishing for the wild fish will end when a freshet moves them up Deer Creek. Each fish may be my last of the season. If so I want to remember it in detail for the long nights—and perhaps the years—ahead.

20

Dry Fly Dream

THE GREAT HOPE OF THOSE OF US who cast flies for anadromous fish, especially steelhead, is to take our fish on the surface, preferably on a floating fly. The use of the shortest, lightest rod possible allows the fish to perform at its best and provides the maximum sport. It calls for all the skill and knowledge you hope you possess. If something goes wrong and you fail to raise the fish, or lose it after you do, there is always the prospect of a better day.

Lee Wulff did it first and best, and afterwards wrote about it. Reading him is to the benefit of all of us who wish to become more accomplished fishers. He set the standards for capturing big fish on small tackle. Many people have repeated his feats, but few have topped them. We are mere mimics. All the same something can be learned from going through the Lee-Wulff motions. At the least it will lead to a greater appreciation of the difficulty of what he's done.

The use of a midge rod and dry fly is one such feat. Each year fishers try to emulate him. This is how it goes: In your right hand you have a flyrod measuring six feet in length and weighing under two ounces. You have a reel to match—say, a Hardy LRH or its equivalent. You tie a light tippet on your leader (four- or six-pound-test) and a suitable dry fly, and off you go on your vision quest: a dry-fly steelhead. If you hook one and land it you must promise to release it. This is part of the code.

I took my first midge-rod, dry-fly steelhead over 25 years ago and have not forgotten it. I did something difficult and unusual. It marked a milestone in my life as a flyfisher. But the local fishermen were not impressed. What I did was merely queer. A trout-sized rod and reel for catching steelhead was not considered manly. Fishers used long, stout rods and brought their fish under muscular control. Not I. I was so proud of my accomplishment, I kept the small fish. It was at a time when nobody ever put one back. Ed Weinstein took my picture on

Kodachrome A slide film. I still have the print on my wall up at the river. I am a clean-shaven young man without a streak of gray in my dark hair. I appear cocky, while at the same time blasé. My manner says I accomplish similar feats every day. My nose is burned to bacon from daily trying on an August vacation.

Ed took two pictures that day. In the first I am holding the fish by the chin and looking off into the middle distance. In the other the fish lies laid out on a short weathered plank, my little Hardy rod and reel stretched out alongside, a Rat-faced McDougall lodged squarely in the fish's snout. The deer-hair fly looks like a bristly mustache.

In the mid-60s the river contained a lot of wild steelhead. They were small and trouty, weighing four to six pounds, a few bigger, and most were fools for the dry fly. This was not widely known and had to be discovered for one's self. Once learned it was knowledge not to be shared. In August the wet-fly fishers might take a fish at first light, but afterwards the fishing went dead. The steelhead were disdainful of any fly fished beneath the surface once the sun hit the water. Anybody trying for them with a dry fly might be met by a huge surprise. Few did, however.

Lee Wulff had set the stage for this kind of fishing more than a decade earlier. You had to read books to know about it and how it was done. Most steelheaders then read little, if at all, and those that did believed the techniques wouldn't work for our fish. Wulff wrote about Atlantic salmon fishing in Labrador and New Brunswick, not steelhead in the Western U.S. Our fish were different. Or were they? I and a few others began to wonder. Walt Johnson, Ken McLeod, Louis Marsh, Wes Drain, and a few pioneers had experimented with dry-fly techniques. They were alone. Most steelheaders didn't want to change their style. A fly fished on the surface was frivolous. Everybody knew so. It was the deeply sunk wet fly that caught fish. These were the same people who fished only bait in winter.

Roderick Haig-Brown believed otherwise. Steelhead in winter could be caught on flies, he said, but only after Ralph Wahl had convinced him by example that it was so. And in summer they could be taken greased-line style like Atlantic salmon or—better yet—on floating flies. In other words, Lee Wulff's techniques worked here.

I first read Wulff as a young man and believed everything he said. I still do. What he accomplished I wanted to do. A dry-fly midge-rod steelhead was high on my list. Other things he said and did impressed me, too. For instance a right-hander ought to hold his rod in his strong hand—his right—and reel with his weaker hand—his left—which was exactly the opposite of what everybody else was doing. Of course: I saw at once he was right. So I switched over. I remember the day. It was midwinter and cold. Something went wrong with my reel, however. The line now came in over the top of the spool and when I stripped off some—preparatory to making a cast—I found I had no drag; the drag worked only when I reeled in. Its sole possible setting caused the reel to fight against me, not any potential fish.

Fortunately I hooked none that morning or it would have been a disaster. After lunch I reversed the line on the spool. To do so I ran out the reel's full complement of backing along the beach, all 200 yards, until the spool was bare. Then I cranked it in the other way so that the line spooled up from the bottom the way it was supposed to. But the drag worked against me still.

Before the reel would work right I had to find a special part that would permit the reel to crank left-handedly. When I did the cam cost much more than I thought it should. Five dollars. I think it was about a third the cost of the reel. A few years later the reel's manufacturer bought the patent and made the cam reversible. There was no need to buy the special part. By then, however, I was fishing Hardys.

I continued reading Wulff. His book, *The Atlantic Salmon*, was the bible for myself and a few others. There were one or two counterpart books on steelhead, but they usually only had one chapter on flyfishing and it was pretty general. The rest was on gear and bait fishing. I studied Wulff's words and—even more—his pictures. A midge rod, yes—but a camera, too? The camera hung at the ready round his neck. It was an early Leica with a knob film advance. Evidently he played the fish with one hand (it would have to be his left, for the moment) while he snapped away with his right. Okay. I would do it, too.

I bought an old bayonet-mount Leica and taught myself how to operate it with one hand. I learned about hyperfocal-zone focusing, that is, using a wide-angle lens and small aperture to get the maximum depth of field, for there is no time to focus while your fish is in the air. Then I discovered that, if your release of the shutter was not timed perfectly, all you got was a picture of the ring on the water. With a little more luck you got the great bathtub swirl from a fish that had just disappeared back into the depths. I took a lot of pictures of an empty river before I quit, the first time.

One day I was lucky. I caught a man's fish at the apex of its leap. I rushed the film to my basement darkroom and developed it. I squinted at the tiny wet negative. There hung the fish in the sky, looking like a nail paring. How proud I was. I printed it up on a test strip. Seeing the print come up in the developing tray gave me gooseflesh. I tracked the man down and gave him the test strip. He looked at the new moon rising. "Is that my fish?" he asked. I nodded. Never was I able to do it again and I soon gave up trying.

I read more Lee Wulff and tried to think as he did. I saved my money and bought a Hardy midge rod (fiberglass) and a small reel of the lightweight type that balanced it. It was a large expenditure, and what did I have afterwards but a rod and a reel that looked like a toy. I took it afield only when I was sure nobody was looking. It seemed fatuous. One hot afternoon my milestone steelhead came to the surface and spiked my fly. I was triumphant. The other fishermen mocked my feat, but not Ed, who was also a Wulff reader. I caught a few more this way, then put the outfit aside. I felt silly, always having to explain myself to people. No, I was not fishing for trout, a full-grown man like me, on a great steelhead river.

I dry-fly fished with my longer rods while the little rod gathered dust on its tube. A seven-and-a-half footer was as short as I would descend. Mostly I used a manly eight and one-half footer or a light nine. They worked plenty good and kept my backcast high, the line away from my ears. With a little rod there are always casting problems. And I found it tough switching back and forth between a midge and an ordinary wet-fly rod. You nearly have to learn to cast anew each time.

Some seasons were terrific. Once in the early 1980s there were numerous fish in the river and I started taking them up on top as the river got smaller and the wet fly stopped producing. In mid-August there was a streak of cloudy days, the weather humid and close. It was perfect for the steelhead dry fly. Most anglers were waiting for rain to arrive and make the fish take wet again. The river was deserted, dead low, with fish piled into every little riffle that had a bouldery-bottom. In the big deep pool where people fished each morning at daybreak there was nary a fish to be found. Still people kept pounding it with wet flies. Up in the riffles where the fish were the wet fly did not fish well, for both fly and line got quickly swept away. If you fished deeper the fly hung up in the rocks and was lost.

It was hard water to wade and cover fish in, too. The rocks near shore were slick and too large to provide footholds. People made a few casts wet and moved on. This was a big mistake. There were plenty of fish available. They wanted a dry, something buggy and natural looking. They were not particular about what it was and presentation wasn't a problem. A dark fly worked well, but so did a bright one like a Royal Wulff. A neutral fly produced sometimes—a pattern like the Elk-Hair Caddis. If you liked floating the fly naturally the fish did, too. But if you'd rather drag it across the current this made them angry and they chased after it. The take was often violent and came in the form of a slashing rise. Such a fish might break you off immediately.

I much preferred the soft slurp with which they took a fly drifting without drag; it gave me a moment in which to tighten before the fish exploded. But I would take a rise, and a fish, anyway I could get it. At such times dry-fly fishing is the easiest way to catch fish in the world. There's nothing mysterious about it. You throw the fly out there, try to relax, and let nature take its course. You can see everything that is going to happen.

Usually nothing much does. It is blistering out. The day is quiet, the river purling. Not a fish is to be seen rising. Oh, a parr may swat at your fly every so often, so you feed slack to avoid hooking the little guy. When a steelhead goes for your fly it is something different, though the rise might be equally small and deceptive. Your rod comes back with a solid weight on it and you have a hook-up. Your reflexes send a message to your brain, "Please, God, don't let anything go wrong."

Such a moment has been known to alter a fisher's life. You're experiencing life at its fullest. You know at once that what the fishing writers have said, in all their amassed hyperbole, is true. Surface steelheading is wonderful. It's great. What's more this super event is happening to *you*. It's not vicarious. It's not on TV, Saturday morning. Men adjudged to be sane in all other respects will abandon jobs and families, and devote the remainder of their lives to searching for a repeat performance. It is a worse case than hard drugs.

I remember a special time less than a decade ago. Ken McLeod is still alive, though in his mid-'80s, and no longer spry. He and I both know about the wild fish locked into the Manure Spreader Hole. Without discussing it we have agreed to keep the information to ourselves. Rarely will a fish break the surface and reveal his presence. Then it may be mistaken for a salmon. An hour or so will go by without another fish showing. But they are there, finning quietly in water that is not very deep. Though we work over them hard we do not get frequent rises. The fish seem uninterested in what we have to offer, most of the time.

Why a steelhead breaks the surface in the first place is anybody's guess. He may be feeding on a terrestrial—a bee, perhaps, or a caddis fly. Or he may be splashing around for the sheer joy of movement. He

Ken McLeod

has left his known element, water, for the strange world of air and has taken a taste, however briefly, of what we experience daily. He does this mostly early and late in the day. When the morning fishers see him splash they get angry because they are unable to catch him with their wet flies. They turn sour and hope to have better luck the following day, when they will be back on the river even earlier—perhaps while it is still dark. This type of reasoning doesn't produce many fish. Having the crowds appear early, and then be gone, is much to my liking, for late morning and all through a sunny afternoon are the times I like best. And anytime, any day, the skies are cloudy.

These are the dog days, with no mercy from the sky. The river bottom is visible, rock for rock, except in the riffles where there are boulders and broken water flowing over them in a blur. Can there be fish in water so clear and fast? You'd better believe it. If you can't see them they probably can't see you, which is to your benefit. A bit of bushy bank cover helps.

You go to the head of the riffle and begin casting with a bristly, well-greased fly. You immediately discover that you can't see it. The few times you can make it out it seems to be behaving unnaturally. This isn't so bad as it sounds, for these are not selective trout. A dragging fly may be just what they are waiting for.

The problem is, how do you strike a steelhead when you can't see your fly eighty percent of the time? How do you spot the rise and know when to hit back? A fly often needs to have white in it to be seen—not by the fish but by you. Hence all the white-winged dry flies, the Wulffs, the Bivisibles, the ones with the matched white duck wings that are designed to be visible in fast water, flecked with foam and full of tiny white freckles. I suspect the reason Walt Johnson often ties in some bit of fluorescent color—cerise, pink, hot orange—is so *he* can see the fly better. If the flash of bright color appeals to the fish, so much the better.

For the steelhead sees all, even in off-color water. I am convinced of this. It is the premise we must operate under. He is aware of everything going on in his watery environment and in much that extends into ours. If he chooses not to strike our fly it is for a myriad of reasons, but surely not because he is unable to see it.

Even if your fly is visible it may soon sink and not float again until dried thoroughly and regreased. Flies tied with hollow deer hair or elk float best. All flies get sucked under the surface on a tight line when captured by the current, but the good ones bob to the surface as soon as tension is slackened. They will shuck off their moisture and keep floating. (When a fly loses its ability to shed water chances are a parr has been caught and some fish slime has rubbed off on the hackles. It is time for a fresh one.)

A well-tied fly will float for a long time. The bad thing about such a fly is that it is most likely overdressed and may push itself away from the fish's mouth on the strike or, worse, look so unnatural—turning and twisting on its tippet—that it won't arouse a strike. It may scare fish away, too. Many of today's steelhead dries are designed to ride low in the water; they may not float so well, but they attract the fish better and when they aren't floating naturally wake provocatively. This brings strikes that will not otherwise be forthcoming.

Once you have found a fly you can see (and you may have to try out a few first, depending on the particular light-on-water effects that day) fishing it well is a matter of presentation. That means keeping it behaving naturally. This is done through line control and is slowly acquired with experience. Walt Johnson fishes carefully and deliberately, as if for selectively feeding trout, and moves upstream slowly, presenting his fly as drag-free as he can get it. He fairly pussy-foots. But other times he will cause his fly to riffle as he fishes downstream and across. Ken McLeod's style was to try for a drag-free drift, but he liked to make it very long, the fly matching the speed of the current and the drag minimal, since drag really is unavoidable and always present. Yet his fly dragged noticeably sometimes and the effect must have been intentional.

So both men fished for steelhead at different times in different ways. Ken always used a stripping basket, which helped him control his fly's drift. His son George and George's son, Ken Jr., fish very much as he did. The basket-style can be effective. The fly is false cast and laid on the water lightly—either upstream, directly across, or slightly down. When the fly nears its drag-point line is allowed to run freely out of the basket. Often the line is fed out of the basket with the free hand, a few feet at a time. This enables the fly to continue on its bumpy ride many yards farther. From too great a distance the angler loses control of his fly, even with careful mends and lifts of his rod tip. It is hard to set the hook when a fish takes the fly on a long line, though often you can feed line and hook a short-taking fish. It is a good trick to try at a time that is apt to be maddening.

I've fished with a basket and had success with it. Frankly, I don't find it pleasant. Let's say I respect it, but use it rarely. Holding line in large coils in my left hand is more natural. True, it shortens my drift, but I gain tighter control. The fingertips of my left hand can respond quickly to the strike. I can pull back softly, hard, or not at all. Sometimes a return strike needs to be done without deliberation. That is, it has to be made instinctively and not according to forethought. For me coiled line and the hands work best.

It was a great pleasure to watch Ken fish. He knew this water perhaps better than anybody, fished it earlier, and caught many fish from it. I stood nearby, chatting with him, my eyes fixed on his fly, often forgetting to cast out my own. Surface fishing doesn't always require great concentration, I've found, for the fly works away out in the current, doing its job even if vaguely attended. At the end of the drift Ken would allow it to bounce around, riffling and sputtering. I'm sure he picked up many fish this way. He did not hurry to make another cast, but let the fly hang below him. Often he used a bucktail Royal Coachman. It fishes a little different from a Royal Wulff, because it has a conventional, dense, wet-fly wing. Such a fly can be fished on a sinking line as well.

I sometimes try to imagine myself a steelhead lying in a shallow, bouldery run, watching everything going on about me, just as I did as a fry and parr, missing naught, able to swim with a total economy of motion and no need to feed. What will induce me to strike today? It will take something unusual to trigger my aggressive instincts, perhaps the same impulse that led me to feed voraciously as a fingerling and again while ranging the sea. Some bit of provoked savageness? But I can only speculate, for the fish is not telling.

A steelhead watches—that is what he does—all day long and perhaps into the night. He sees my fly on every cast, but does nothing about it. Yet on one cast that seems no different from all the others he rises eagerly and inhales my fly Why? What made this cast different? I shall never know.

Occasionally I am aware of having done something right—something out of the ordinary. Perhaps the cast was a little longer or the mend one that permitted the fly to float a foot or two farther and behave a bit more naturally on its downriver course. But often it is nothing special. It is a cast just like the others and I am left with my head buzzing with theories.

Ken always wore hip boots for his dry fly fishing. They were mainly for comfort and ease in setting out for the river. But they also served to remind himself not to wade too deep. Wet-fly fishermen stride to the tops of their waders, even when it is unnecessary. Ken was short and a little loft was useful to him in wet-fly fishing. But in low water wading deep spooked fish, so he stayed well back, often casting from shore. If nobody was in the water below him chances are a fish might be lying near the beach. So he would cast short at first. Then he lengthened out his casts. The long, slow drift was his mainstay. It was the water directly downstream and across where he sought his fish. His style differed greatly from Walt's. Under no circumstances would you mistake the one for the other, even at a great distance. I stole a page from the book of each in order to forge my own hybrid style and I'll vary my technique considerably if I think the day requires it.

I don't know the particulars of Ken's success that year. I fished only a few evenings over two weeks. I know he killed enough fish to fire up his smokehouse. He never put a steelhead back, wild or hatchery. It was against his principles. The fish were all wild and most of them small—three to seven pounds. I rose 15, landed six, and killed none. The 15 rises I remember well, even though they varied greatly. (I made notes the same evening.) One fish broke me off immediately, when I set the hook too hard in fast water. It was an easy mistake to make and I do not fault myself entirely for it—though I would do it differently, given a second chance. (You never get one, though.) Other rises are those categorized in the trout fisher's handbook. Yes, they rose much like trout do. But I had a couple of rises no respectable trout would ever make.

Several times I saw a fish glide beneath my fly, but never touch it. I called these ghost rises. The fish appeared under my fly, drifted along with it, maintained an interval of an inch or so, then turned away. I've fished lakes from the shore where trout will follow a stripped fly on nearly every cast, but turn away just as the shore rises to meet them or when I lift the fly preparatory to making the next cast. The steelhead behaved very much like that. When a steelhead drifts along with your fly, but refuses to take it, it is exciting but frustrating. The fish is so close, yet so far away. What does it want from you? It leaves you chewing on your lip.

When a slashing, violent strike takes place to a fly that has just begun to drag I suspect it is from a fish that has been following the fly. The fish drifts along with the fly, having nothing better to do with his day—no appointments to keep, no luncheon meetings—then decides the fly is not something he wants, thank you. He turns away. Then the fly starts to whip across the surface, heading for China. Now he wants it badly. He must decide—make up his pea-brained mind, all in a nanosecond—whether to intercept it or let it get away. Pugnacious since the day he came out of the gravel he attacks. And while such a strike sometimes produces a breakage surprisingly often the fish hooks itself and the leader holds. Wonder of wonders, the fish proves pinned in the hinge of the jaw.

I began to notice something unusual that summer. Fishing a certain "Sacred Inch" of water I knew held fish, and casting time and again to the same spot, after a long while I would see a long silvery flash at the bottom directly beneath my fly's path. Now flashes along the bottom of the river occur fairly often. The quick, short ones are salmonid parr or whitefish; the big golden ones are suckers. In the odd-numbered years humpies flash a little like suckers, at least in their coloration.

The long bright flashes I saw were different. I was sure they were steelhead. On the cast immediately following the flash I invariably got a solid strike. Why was this? I concluded that my earlier casts had made the fish nervous. Ordinarily a nervous fish might leave the pool. Not this time. Unless I flubbed the next cast the fish would take. It happened to me enough times that year and others that I decided to ask Walt Johnson about it. He was the authority. Had I uncovered some new and funda-

Bob Taylor

mental principle of steelhead behavior?

"Tell me," I asked him, "in all your years of fishing, have you ever experienced anything like it—the flash and then the take?"

"No."

So much for uncovering new truths. My experiences were atypical, I guess.

One day Bob Taylor and I were fishing the Deer Creek Riffle from opposite sides of the river. We stood ankle-deep and cast into water directly in front of each other. Some time passed. We grew bored. It was a hot, stifling day and we'd had no strikes. We began lengthening our casts. I suspect we were trying to hook each other's boots, for lack of anything better to do. I waded a bit deeper and made a fairly long cast (long for my midge rod, anyway) in order to cover some different water. I saw one of those bright flashes near to where Bob stood. I hurried my next cast and made it as much like the one before it as I could. This is like trout fishing. I think I said something to Bob about what I saw. The fish rose at once, took the fly solidly, and threw water all over Bob. I enjoyed his getting soaked almost as much as fighting the fish. It was firmly hooked along the gumline and the little Wilson hook cut an inch-long gash, but didn't let go, bless it.

If I attempt to analyze all the different rises from that year I find no intelligent pattern. Each was different and spectacular. But a few can be categorized. There is the quiet *sup* that takes place in mid-drift, the fly about as drag-free as I can make it. There is the noisy take in about the same location, with a big splash and a fair volume of water thrown into the air. There is the take when the fish has covered more than six feet of water, obviously chasing the fly, and is not going to let it get away—though the cast is, so nearly as I can tell, exactly like all the ones that preceded it and, after the battle is over, all the ones that will follow it.

Often a fish will hit at the moment the fly goes under the surface. The fly swings around at the end of its drift, forms a straight line, tightens, and drag submerges it. This is precisely the way the fish wants it that day and no other trick will do. The fish rises and takes the fly quietly and deliberately. It always proves well-hooked. There is also the take the moment the fly first begins its cross-stream sputter—when the fly swings around and begins its hesitant bob-and-weave that is always the goal, but rarely gets produced when I most want it. Doubtlessly the steelhead has been eyeing the fly all the while and thinks it isn't worth going after, not until drag makes it dance. The take is deliberate, solid, and proves determined. Again the fish is well hooked.

There is yet another rise that I can't describe simply because I've never seen it. It happens when I am looking away. An instant later I behold the ring widening in the water and my fly is gone. I've missed the rise entirely. What happened? For an instant I am befuddled. I lift my rod tip experimentally, expecting a slack line. It is exactly the right thing to do. A delayed strike is produced. The fish is hooked by the soft action of the lift.

What is most interesting about the delayed strike is that I generally see my fish return to the bottom and resume its holding position. There it flashes. The flash is identical to the pre-rise flash of the steelhead that takes on the next cast. Again it seems merely a restless movement, as if the fish has rocked sideways in its place. The motion permits its silvery side to heliograph. On a bright day it is like a mirror held up to the sky; on a dull day it is muted, appearing white rather than silvery, but unmistakable all the same.

Upon the fish's turning I tighten reflexively and the fish surges off on his first run. Usually it is long and spectacular, terminating in a jump. The leap places the fish over my head, it is so high. (I enjoy looking up at my steelhead as a sign of respect.)

In shallow water, in a run lined with boulders, there is a calming effect that comes from knowing your fish is hooked on a floating line, for it has little chance of snagging the leader on a rock while you are playing it. Walt's big Elbow Hole fish was an exception. Most fish go crazy, but are at a loss to know what to do to fight free; often they rush about desperately, running every which way, and shallow water is where they usually stop to catch their breath. Deeper water is where they choose to fight it out, however. It is a good place for you, too, for less can go wrong there.

A floating line in a bouldery run proves no problem most of the time. If the fish goes around a rock the line can be mended away from the rock or lifted over it. However the line may cling just long enough for the fish to break a light tippet or else the fly loosens in a skin hold. Sometimes the fish makes a long run and will not swim back to you. Here a long rod, holding a length of line extended in the current, acts as a safety device to protect against quick moves and a subsequent breakage.

A midge rod is disadvantageous in playing a fish. It is so strong and exerts so much leverage that there is a constant threat of breaking the leader. Nonetheless I soon came to enjoy fishing the midge again. I grew less concerned about the locals disparaging my wand. Let them laugh; I am catching fish. When I play a fish on the midge I try to leave as much line out in the current as I can, for it reduces the chance of breakage when a fish moves off briskly without notice. When it comes time to beach my fish I maintain a long line, too. The added length acts as an extension to the rod and makes for safer handling of the fish in close. But it is not very gainly.

In midge-rod casting there are two immediate problems. The first is to refrain from hooking yourself in the ear or some other part of your rearward anatomy. The other is overcoming the casting problems that result from trying to correct the first problem. Once I've started casting an effective distance with the midge, I am unable to cast well with a longer rod, so I stick with the short rod. Using barbless hooks helps a lot in overcoming the first problem; you can pluck the point out easily—if you can reach it. (What's a little blood to a flyfisher?) In a few minutes you'll find your cast straightening out nicely and achieving your relatively short distance again.

Mid-week evenings around the dinner hour is the time I like to go dry-fly fishing most. Often I find the river deserted. One August afternoon I strung up the Hardy midge for the first time that season. How pretty it was in its reduced configuration, as though designed as a practical joke on some small person. I went to the Manure Spreader Hole, a good one in low water. I had a positive feeling about the pool that night. I tied on a Gray Wulff (for it was a gray day) and tiptoed to the water's edge. I began at the head of the riffle and started laying out a short line. It was difficult to cast the little rod. (In fact it was an abomination.) A fat fly made matters worse. A fish took immediately and ran the width of the river and jumped next to the far bank. It was hooked in the hinge of the jaw and soon I landed and released it, after a fine fight. It weighed about six pounds. It was probably a female; with fish this small and so far off from spawning sexual characteristics are indistinct.

Fifteen minutes later I hooked a second fish. It was on the same fly—why take it off if it had worked once? The fish was about a pound heavier, ran farther, but jumped only twice—unusual for a Deer Creek fish, which is often out of the water most of the time. It had a rosy cast to its sides, so it no doubt was a male. Quickly I released it. Straightening up, I felt my heart pounding. Two fish in half an hour—that was phenomenal. And on the small rod, too. It was a perfect day; it was impossible to improve on it. So I quit. I snipped off the fly and reeled in.

My friend Merlin Stidham came striding down the beach. He saw me standing there and noticed that my rod was not strung up.

"Nothing going on?" he asked. "You quitting?"

Then he saw my happy grin. It meant I had hit fish. You can't fake such a grin. It can only be produced naturally. I burbled out what had happened. His eyes brightened.

Merlin—dead now more than a year—tied a beautiful fly and was an excellent fisher. Without glancing at mine he put on a dry fly almost exactly the same color and size. I knew he would do well. Later I learned that his first fish had hit when I was barely out of sight. He hollered, but I hadn't heard him over the roar of the riffle. He got a second fish, too, I remember hearing. We were lucky. But I suspect that anybody coming down to the pool that night would have hooked the fish we did. Still, I'm glad it was us.

21

Drowning In Air

ONCE I ASKED CURT KRAEMER HOW LONG a fish can live out of water.

"About as long as you can live *under* water," he replied with a grin.

I remember his words and they continue to flash into mind whenever I watch anglers handling fish they intend to release. Often they keep the fish out of the water way too long. There are several reasons, but none is good enough. The mania for catch-and-release fishing makes people reluctant to say goodbye to a fine fish. And there is the need for pictures to prove that it really happened. Back when everybody killed his fish it didn't matter so much how long the fish was kept out of water before it was killed. Survival was not the issue. Today, maintaining wild fish stocks is crucial.

Many waters have catch-and-release regulations during their best seasons, the ones for wild or native steelhead. Anglers no longer cart home corporeal evidence of their success. Instead they depend on photographic testimony and often the fish are trophy-sized. Guides are dependent on clients for their livelihood and must give their charges something for their money—often considerable—other than nice scenery, a boat ride, and a sunburn. This may be a color print of the client cradling his fish like a newborn baby, a beatific smile on his face.

This bothers me. The horizontal fish picture has replaced the vertical one, true enough. The fish lives, or will if all goes right. The picture today isn't always a color slide from which a print can be made. Guides often carry camcorders in their boats —a camera that produces a video tape of the day's action that brings the experience back to life long after it's been paid for and faded away. The first I heard of taking video pictures of fish was when Jerry Wintle took me for a boat ride on the Skagit a day or two before the season ended in a recent year. He is not a guide, but the consummate flyfisher, who has cast over about every good piece of water in the West. He had a new hole he wanted to share with me, but not tell me about, and offered to guide me to it since it could only be reached by boat. It offered me a new experience, traveling in a boat under power on a river, and I was anxious to see what it would be like, for I had been critical of boats on rivers in the past. It was raining hard and a strong wind had come up. The boat provided access to some splendid water in a remote, near-wilderness setting I should not have visited otherwise.

Thanks to Jerry I soon hooked and began to play a good-sized fish during the worst of the storm. The wind was howling and flapping my parka hood. Jerry started back to the boat for his camcorder, which was in a water-tight compartment, in order to record the happy event. I gathered it was routine. I soon lost the fish, so the camera wasn't necessary, but I've vainly wondered since what it would be like to see myself playing a fish . . . on television. I would probably love it like everybody else does —at least the first time I saw myself doing it. But it would put the fish to poor use.

The following year Trey Combs invited me to fish with him and B.J. Meigs for a week in April. Again this was on the Skagit. I was able to get away for only three days. Fishing was slow. Again cameras and picture-taking were the order of the day. The acceptable picture was of a spent fish lying on its side in the shallows, the beaming angler clasping it paternally by the wrist of the tail prior to letting it go.

For a while it seemed we were fishing entirely for the pictures, pictures Trey needed for his wonderful book on steelhead flyfishing. This put a weird emphasis on the day. The idea was to hook a fish and hurry it in for the photo opportunity; without a picture or two the day seemed wasted. Soon Trey hooked a small fish, but disdained a picture because of its size. It was gently put back without ceremony. When I hooked one a day later, a fish of sufficient size, B.J. and the cameras were one-hundred yards away in the boat. While she ran for the Nikon I set the hook a second time, then fed the fish slack, hoping it would settle down on the edge of the current and remain calm until she returned. She hurried. I waded ashore. Talking to Trey, with my back to the fish, I felt the line grow taut. Unseen by me the fish had jumped.

"I think you lost your fish," he said.

I reeled in. True enough.

"I actually saw it spit out the fly," he added.

Funny but in the summer, while fishing alone, this trick always worked, and sometimes I had even returned to a short distance to my car for a camera while the fish waited patiently in eight inches of water next to shore. Of course the hook was smaller and had a barb. The barb probably made all the difference.

The following year, again fishing alone (alone now meant without Sam and all the attendant problems), I needed some pictures for an article. I carried a self-focusing camera loaded with a flash and slide film, for it is what editors require for color separations. I began hooking fish. About 70 percent reached the beach. But I did not enjoy fishing for the camera, even when *I* was wielding it. It changed the nature of the day and made it frenetic. Hooking a fish, I got anxious about the picture and found myself horsing the fish to the beach. After a few pictures I gave up fishing this way. I stopped carrying a camera, too. Now my vest is two pounds or so lighter.

Not much was sacrificed, however. I already have a drawer full of pictures of dead fish from back when we regularly killed our catch. Some of the fish are big. All look very dead. Some are in stiff and unnatural poses from rigor mortis.

I've seen boats on the Sauk net a large fish, pull ashore, disembark, take the fish out of the net, carry it to the water's edge (where I presume it is more photogenic), fetch the camera, check the exposure, arrange the fisherman and his fish artfully, back up, move in close, recheck the camera settings, repose the fish and the fisherman, tell the fisher to remember to smile, and trip the shutter. Then comes the "insurance shot"—the one you take in case something happens to the first. Finally the fish is returned to the river, lowered gently into the slack, and taught how to swim again. The process takes up to five minutes.

I've wondered (but not for long) how I would react if held under water for five minutes. Not well, I think. After two minutes I would stop struggling and quiet down, just as the fish does. I'd become docile because the struggle is not getting me anywhere. I'd struggle because I'm drowning, of course. Soon I'd be dead. After I'd been returned to my air supply I'd gasp gratefully, but my lungs wouldn't work because they're full of water. Unless somebody helped me empty them out and get me breathing again I'm a goner.

The fish that we thoughtfully resuscitate—after two to six minutes in the air—is doing the best he can to survive. Sometimes it isn't good enough. We grow impatient and pump him back and forth in the current, trying to speed his recovery. Slowly his gill plates open and close, like a yawn, but he remains still, barely able to hold himself upright. His swim bladder isn't working yet. We move him faster in the current. We are impatient and wish he'd "get well soon." Then we begin to panic. We say, "Don't die on me, big guy." The fish begins to weave and fight against our gentle hand restraint. It's a good sign. We sigh with relief. When he heads for the deep we ourselves begin to breathe naturally again.

There is something just awful about this. The fish needn't have been taken out of the water in the first place. If he is, whatever the reason (and it had better be a good one), he ought to be put back immediately. There should be no dallying around. I can remember what it's like to have a snoot full of water and be coughing my lungs out.

I don't bother with a tape measurement usually. I carry one, rolled up tight in my vest pocket, but rarely unfurl it. Let my fish's length and girth remain a mystery; I can guess close enough. (I've never underestimated my fish's size, by the way.) I have a measure from the butt of my rod to the stripping guide, besides. One glance tells me about how long my fish is. I've placed a piece of tape at the 30-inch mark and on another rod a wrap of thread in the same spot. Close enough for daily matters. But you can put a mark at 40 inches, if it is trophies that you seek.

I've never taken a girth measurement of a fish. I suppose I should, if I ever want to know my fish's weight without subjecting it to the torture of a scale. But it requires too much man-handling to be healthy for the fish. A fish will beat itself senseless on the beach before it will submit to being circumscribed with a cloth band. Forget it. Your fish was big and fought well; that's what counts. Besides fishers are such liars nobody is going to believe you anyway.

A big fish is a highly personal matter. It's strictly between you and the river. You might consider forgoing the picture, too. Fish look much alike—I'm sorry to say. The light is bad, most of the time the fishing is good. Let there be an end to fish pictures. Let our quarry and our achievement become mysterious to us, unknown to others. Let the mind take the picture and file it away in its vault.

Surely there is a better way to gain immortality? When we stop posing our fish we have to deal with the treacherous stuff of memory. We must learn to use our eyes—instead of our cameras—to record what is happening around us. It is a common experience to miss the event because we are looking for the picture.

I used to have to take a lot of photographs for my job as editor of a magazine. I loved it—the cameras and lenses, the darkroom work, the ultimate product in the form of the picture printed on glossy stock. And I cherished the mounted print on the wall. But I wonder. If you take away the photographer's camera do you render him blind? Can he see only when his eye is at the viewfinder? I enjoy a fine photograph, as well as the next guy, and like to travel around inside the frame, observing the fine details. But much of life needs to be experienced directly to have meaning. This might be called seeing life without filters. Filters are reductive, you know. They take away light. If there is anything outstanding about your fish, commit it to memory. You will be the richer for it.

And the fish will appreciate your consideration—as it speeds out to deep water like a little motorboat, without so much as a backward look at the photographer.

22

Wet-Fly Tactics: Low Water

DRY-FLY FISHING IS EVERYBODY'S FAVORITE SPORT—when it works. Many places that's a small part of the year. Mostly steelhead flyfishers fish wet. Wet is more difficult, even though you don't have to watch what the fly is doing at every moment. In fact whether or not you can see your fly and its behavior might be considered the criterion by which wet-fly fishing can be distinguished from the various forms of dry and we can do away with such confusing terms as damp fly, waking fly, riffled fly, dead-drift dry fly, etc. If you can follow your fly's course throughout its drift you are fishing dry or something so close to it that the difference doesn't matter. And if you can't—even though your line is floating and your fly riding high in the water column—you are wet-fly fishing.

This may not be important except for purposes of discussion, for the angler out on the river is casting his fly into the current and letting it do what he wants it to do, if he is fishing it right. The cast is laid close to where he intends it to go and he manipulates his line—generally by back mending portions of it—to help the fly do its work. The fly may be asked to sink deeply, sink some, or sink hardly at all, depending on conditions. And it is at these three levels or depths that we may formulate the ways of fishing wet.

September is a slack month, with dead-low water mostly and fish that have become dour. A floating line is generally in order. Bill McMillan, along with others who love to use these, vary how they fish different rivers, depending on conditions. Fish entering rivers on the East Slope of the Cascades and in many Canadian rivers are more inclined to come to the surface for a fly. This is not my theory, but is based on biological differences observed by scientists. There are two major races of summer-run steelhead. Protein electrophoresis, a genetic identification process, confirms that they differ from each other. A race of coastal steelhead extends from Alaska far South and used to reach all the way to the Baja Peninsula. These fish are not known to come eagerly to the surface. The other race is found inland and is confined to the Upper Columbia and Snake River basins and the Fraser and Skeena River drainages in Canada. They will readily rise to the top, even after the water has cooled considerably.

While these protein characteristics are minutely physiological they are supported by the fish's behavior. This race of fish is summer-run whose spawning is a long ways off. In practical terms it is a waste of time to fish for coastal winter steelhead on the surface in cold water. (Under such conditions McMillan will stick to his floating line, but will use flies on big or heavy (or big *and* heavy) hooks that get to the bottom fast.) Not so for the inland fish. One needn't put away the floating line when the water gets cold, for they will continue to come up on top. But they will take under the surface as well. When the water temperature gets below 43 degrees F. I generally fish only deep, for the fish are less likely to move for the fly.

Royal Wulff Dry Fly

When I talk about surface fishing or shallow wet-fly fishing most of the time I am talking about inland rivers such as the Wenatchee, Grand Ronde, and Methow or else Canadian rivers such as the Thompson, Bulkley, Morice, etc. There a floating line and a fly either waking on the surface or sunk in the first few inches will bring more strikes than a deeply sinking one. And a period of transition exists between warm and cold weather when both methods work well. Then you are doubly blessed and it's a tossup which method will be the most effective. It may pay to try first one, then the other, on a given day.

On coastal rivers such as the North Fork my experience has been that continued use of the floating line and sunk fly is wasted once the river rises or cools much in fall. Fish on the surface or fish deep, but not in between, and gradually go over to the deep-sunk fly. A few fish are caught each year by anglers fishing by the method that is so deadly inland, that is, on or near the top, but nowhere near so many as could be caught close to the bottom. Occasionally during the hot summer I find anglers fishing sunk fly on a floating line; I consider them handicapping themselves. I will usually get the fish, if there is one around. I'll either get it dry or, more likely, catch it on a deeply sunk wet, even though the river is low.

In Eastern Washington my experience has been the opposite and by sticking to a method that has worked well for me on West Slope streams out of stubbornness, I've missed out on some good fishing. Which is to say anglers around me caught fish while I didn't. Though painful it was a "meaningful learning experience," as they say facetiously about such things.

I had been badly outfished on the Grand Ronde the previous fall; that is, I didn't catch my share of fish. It bothered me all through the following winter. What was I doing wrong? The next year I began the fall season on the Wenatchee, where the floating line was king. It outproduced the sunk line greatly. It was hard for me to accept this because I'd fished West Slope streams so much. But gradually I was won over to the floating method. I began catching most of my fish on top, too. The day I made the transition I remember well, for I had trouble fitting my long, thick, double-taper eight-weight line on my biggest reel, a Hardy St. John. I had to discard a hundred feet of backing to make room for it all. The backing ended up in a nightmare tangle on the grass and because I was in a hurry to depart I cut out the snarl, tied a knot in the backing, and threw the snarl away. Then I headed for the Ronde.

It was a long drive and I arrived in Clarkston too late for any fishing. My first morning on the Ronde I took one fish and lost another on a sinktip line. Why didn't I use the floating line? Force of habit I guess— the old bugaboo. I stuck with what had worked best for me in the past. This was based on West Slope experience and a different race of fish. It was foolish. I knew there were fish in the river, but wasn't hooking many. The next day, no wiser, I fished as I had the day before. Some people are slow to get the message. By noon, after a late start, I had touched one fish and missed it.

I made myself go ashore. Instead of eating lunch I changed lines and returned to the river with the big St. John loaded with the thick dry line. I waded out in the current where the rocky ledges were most treacherous. It was so slippery it was all I could do to stay on my feet and I balanced there delicately. I tied on a dark fly similar to one I'd fished all morning and stripped off some line in preparation for making my first cast. A steelhead seized the buggy fly, now drifting along on top, and was off on its maiden run. I had good fishing for the rest of the day.

I tried to puzzle this out. There was food on the bottom as well as on the surface. But there were no fly hatches and I saw no fish feeding. Only once did I see fish break water and I assumed these were fish just entering the river from the Snake; they were jumping out of sheer exuberance, happy to be moving again. Even if they were not taking surface food they remained surface-oriented. The Ronde was many degrees cooler than the Snake because of recent rain in the mountains and cool nights. The fish were on the move and were eager takers. This was so different from what I had experienced on the West slope. The nearest thing to it was the spring run of hatchery fish. Those all took near the bottom. Here cool water might have called for a sunk fly but it didn't.

Effective methods of fishing for steelhead have developed largely through trial-and-error. They differ slightly, river to river. When lots of fish are running anyone can catch them most any way. But when there are a few fish trickling in—say, under thermal-block conditions—the fishing turns dismally slow, and there is time to experiment with tactics and techniques. A floating line is best for this. An angler can sink a fly fairly deeply on a long leader by casting upstream and mending line. McMillan has a nice trick of rolling a big loop of line directly at the fly, letting the hook sink on its long leader.

Conversely, a floating line can also be held tight and the fly worked in the surface film. In water that slows on your side the fly can be speeded up through the British method of "pulling through." This means mending line to your side of the river and tightening or drawing some back in so the fly will hurry along its course and not swing dead and inert. And a fly can be made to wake or sputter on a tight floating line.

Note: *any* fly can be made to wake or sputter. It can be a conventional dry fly or a large wet fly, one intended to be sunk; it doesn't much matter except for the niceties. Books mention but two types of riffling hitches, but there are more. Like many good things riffling goes back to

Lee Wulff. He and his friends developed the Portland hitch for moving dour Atlantic salmon under the worst of low-water conditions, when the water was very warm. Wulff did it by appealing to the fish's aggressive instincts. The rapidly moving fly looks nothing like a real struggling insect, not even a drowning one. Yet a sputtering or fluttering fly accounts for many fish and is deadly. It must be doing something right.

The fishing classics describe a fly hitched to riffle from the right and from the left. After the conventional knot—say, a jam knot—is tied, a half-hitch is thrown over the head of the fly and snugged up. (Some use two overhand knots, but usually I don't; it may be slow to release and return to a straight-line pull.) Please note this is not an overhand knot. The hitch is designed to slip off when the line is tightened with a strike and will let the leader pull normally on the knot.

If you are fishing from the right bank (looking downstream from where you stand, when you have waded in from the right side it is the right bank you are fishing from) the half-hitch ought to have its knot on the left side of the eye of the hook, when you are looking at it head-on. If you are on the left bank the knot goes to the right. It takes about three seconds to make the loop and throw it over the head of the fly and nestle it up into the correct position. Every so often you ought to check it, for it tends to slip off during false-casting, especially if the leader is substantial and not drawn up very tight. You'll know almost immediately when it has, for the fly will stop or slow its motion.

There is a third way to riffle a fly, which I learned from George Johnson of Pullman, Washington. He puts the knot formed by the hitch directly under the eye of the fly—neither to the right nor the left. It is always in the middle. What could be simpler? You don't have to worry about which bank of the river you're on or which side of the fly to position the hitch. But care must be taken not to have the hitch knot press up against the knot which fastens the fly to the leader. Two knots coming together is always bad news and reduces the breaking strength of your leader considerably.

George's knot-position gives the fly a strange appearance, for the standoff of leader-to-fly is exaggerated and produces a decided drop. This keeps the fly moving ahead of the leader and if a floating fly is used causes it to ride high in the water. He often uses the hitch with a conventional wet fly. The wet fly behaves crazily, unlike anything found in nature. It's a good trick to have in your bag for that day when nothing works and you feel you have little to lose by experimenting. And it's fun to see your fly darting around on top as though possessed by a demon or else chased by one. It may provide your only strike of the day.

Some fly patterns are tied with a hump in front that works like a wiggling disc on a lure. On these the butts of the bucktail wing are left on and are often given additional stiffness by the application of lacquer so that the butts protrude and hold firm above the fly's head and eye at about a 30-degree angle. The fly cannot help but plane on its nose, all the while the line and leader are kept taut in any water that moves at all. On a slack line the fly behaves like any other dry fly and may be fished dead-drift without any unnaturalness. Harry Lemire's Greased Liner is a good example of this type of fly. The Bulkley Mouse is another. And the various Muddlers, with their conical heads of trimmed deer or elk hair, are older members of the family and fish much the same way. Spade or a fly like it will riffle too.

Generic Spade Design

The great joy of fishing with a floating line is that you can see what is going on at all times and cover every bit of available water without fear of hangups or producing excessive drag, for drag is precisely what you are after, most of the time. It is basically dry-fly fishing, but you can switch to wet without a change of lines or leaders. Often the same water can be fished either way, or both. And if another angler is standing nearby watching you he probably won't observe any difference in what you are doing even though the way the fly fishes is new. While it is not so effective on West Slope streams, wet-fly fishing with a floating line can be conducted nearly all year long on East Slope streams.

Finding fish is always the big problem in anadromous rivers. Searching for them with a wet fly on a floating line is a pleasant way to spend a day, going quickly from pool to pool, looking for the stray fish that can be enticed into taking. It works well on stale or potted fish, too. You will cover most of the water in a pool—all of it, if you don't mind your fly whipping peculiarly in fast, narrow runs such as are found at the heads of pools and aren't fished well, either wet or dry.

Jerry Wintle says he likes wet-fly fishing on a dry line because he is lazy and doesn't want to keep watching his fly. I suspect he also likes it because he can feel the tension of the fly on the line—when it is either slack or taut—and make minute hand-line adjustments to vary its action. It is the kind of fishing at which he excels. I find it often brings a strike without much effort.

A word on mending. Most anglers mend excessively. There is a man I know who fishes the Wenatchee and catches, by his own account, a great number of fish. He puts his fly on the water and throws out upstream loops of line continuously. This allows the fly to drift without drag and keep sinking. He wants the fly to come to the fish as it is descending on a slack line. This is the secret of his presentation. Often he'll lose a half dozen or more flies on the bottom in the course of a morning while fishing dry line. He might as well be fishing a sinking line, I think. He would have to mend it less and find it less tiring. Excessive mending is a waste of energy. It is tiresome to watch as well as to do. Oughtn't fishing be graceful and done with an economy of motion?

Bill Ewing, a good fisher from the West Side, will cast a floating line almost straight downstream from a position to which he has waded well above where he thinks a fish must be, after skillfully reading the water. Then he too mends, but only an occasional hoop and sometimes he throws it ahead of him so there is no bow of line in the current. This allows the fly to sink a little. Better yet it permits the fly to drift along naturally as though unattached to a leader or line. Both anglers fish the same stretch of water two very different ways. I enjoy watching them and observe the drift closely, as though it were *my* fly. And both men catch fish frequently. But if I had to bet on who would get the fish on a given day, my money would ride on Bill.

And how do I fish this run, which is one of my favorites? Every which way and then some. I try to vary my techniques and mix them up. I don't like the multiple-mending method, but have resorted to it on occasion so know at first-hand what displeases me about it and in what specific ways. Most of the time I fish it much like Bill does. But now and then I try a tight-line swing of the fly instead and sometimes it produces. And I will throw out some downstream loops, which Trey Combs calls back-mending, and lead the fly around the last few feet of the drift, the fishing of which would be ineffective otherwise. Once on the Wenatchee's Turkey Shoot doing this brought a 13-pound male up for a surface take. It was exciting to see the rise of a fish so big. Another time on the Orchard Drift I caught a frisky seven pounder that I'm sure wouldn't have taken, fished over any other way.

I will often fish through pools on this river in sunk-fly fashion exactly as though it were a West Slope stream. It works, though few fishers try it. The fish like dull, buggy patterns, but will go for marabous in red, purple, orange, and black just as they do on my home river. I don't suppose I am revealing any great secret by stating this. I'm sure others have discovered it for themselves. As the water cools and rises at the end of the irrigation season, and the diversion stops, I tend to revert to West Slope practices. However Bill McMillan continues to fish this river on top and reports much surface activity to his fly. It is because in a transitional stage both methods work nicely.

On the North Fork, even in low water, if the fish aren't holed up, a wet fly fished slowly and just off the bottom, but high enough so that you aren't always losing flies, is most effective. And when the fish are ganged into a hole it works, too, but requires patience to keep on casting until the fish hit. At this time of the year some people use floating lines and weighted flies. They cast upstream to let the fly drift down to the fish. As I recall, Bill Stinson was among the first to do this successfully, back when he had a home on the North Fork and fished it regularly.

Instead, I prefer the classic downstream-and-across presentation, varying the degree of the angle to the distance across to the far bank and the speed of the current; the faster it goes, the more nearly straight across I'll cast. In slow water I'll cast almost directly downstream and add or mend no line at all. A fly fished this way in certain kinds of water will drift into the face of every steelhead in the river. The fish then has to decide whether to take it or move out of its way. The right fish in the right place will take the fly immediately. If he doesn't, after two or three drifts through his resting place, he will usually vacate the area.

There are a number of lines that make fishing this way productive. It used to be that all suitable fly lines were shooting heads or tapers and were manufactured a uniform thirty feet in length. This is still the industry's standard for lines whose weight is determined in sufficient grains to make a rod flex fully and cast efficiently. I recently tried a new Orvis head, 38 feet long, but couldn't keep it all up in the air before the shoot and soon cut it down to manageable size.

Rods are classified by their ability to load and cast the first 30 feet of line. But this length is often impractical to fish. Many streams are too narrow to cast a 30-foot head across and fish it without a huge belly forming and dragging the fly around in an unnatural sweep. So shorter sinking sections were developed, with floating line spliced behind them, enabling the fly to be snaked through a narrow channel or gut. Thus the old 30-foot standard fell into obsolescence. Lines today come in sinking lengths of 10, 13, 20, and 24-feet, or you can make up your own by splicing together pieces cut from longer sections. Most good fishers assemble their own. Both of Combs's books describe in detail how to do this. An Epoxy splice bonds the sections in a nearly seamless fashion.

Scientific Angler–3M makes a Wet Cel (IV) Hi-Speed Super-Fast Sinking line that has become a favorite of West Coast steelheaders. Only nobody likes it just as it comes off the spool, 30-feet long, so we modify it by cutting and splicing it to other lines, generally ones that float. Dan Rife has developed a line that I like and use much of the time. (Naturally I've made my own modifications to it.) Dan buys a weight-forward floater, usually a Cortland 444, then cuts 16 feet off the forward end. (The hardest part is to slash into a line that has cost you 30 or 40 dollars. After you've chopped up a few you learn to take a deep breath and think no more about it.) He Epoxy-splices 16 feet of Hi-Speed Super-Fast line to the front end. The two lines should be of approximately the same weight or size, eg. WF8, WF9, etc. Or the forward sinker can be one size heavier.

A floating 16-foot forward dry taper is left over and also a corresponding section of sinker. I don't know what Dan does with his, but I've found a good use for mine. I cut 24 feet off the tip end, instead of 16, since the line has a taper of about 42 feet in front before the level back line begins. This is plenty to keep up in the air. With the leftover piece I make a second line, turning the floating portion around and fastening to its butt the left-over piece of sinking line, which is 14 feet long. This produces a second line a little lighter in weight than the first and is good for water that doesn't have to be fished so deeply or that is dropping to its summer low. Behind this short shooting head I attach a piece of long running line such as SA's .029 or Cortland's .031. Instead of using the Epoxy splice I whip on short loops with which to connect them. Thus I can easily join heads of other lengths and weights and densities to the same floating back-portion even in mid-river. The original floating line can be put back together whenever I need it and continues to cast well. And I use the Cortland 333 lines because they cost half as much as the 444, seem to have the same tapers, and last about as long.

Loops are made by stripping the finish off the ends of the lines with acetone (fingernail polish remover will do as well) and doubling back their Dacron cores to form loops. The loop is whipped tight with flytying thread, using a whirling bobbin to keep the many whips snug and tight. I treat the wraps with several thin coats of Pliobond, allowing each to dry for several hours before putting on the next. (This method was taught me by Ken McLeod, nearly 30 years ago, so you can see I'm not offering anything radically new.)

Other modern bonding materials will work just as well, I suspect. Anglers often use Super Glue. Care must be taken to keep the wrap semi-flexible so it won't crack and weaken the joint. The two loops interlock easily and if you wrap them correctly are very strong. After a few good-sized fish have been landed on them you will come to trust them. Of course everything breaks if you pull hard enough. Even the Epoxy splice will break above or below the bond if you subject it to a monstrous pull.

Variations and proportions of lines and their weights are nearly infinite. One man I know cuts his 30-foot Super-Fast head twice, making sections of 15, 10, and five feet. (Stan Young.) I have no use for a five-foot head, but he fishes slower water than I and catches fish in a pool I'll pass by because it is not to my liking. Many other combinations cut from one line are possible—18 and 12, 17 and 13, 15 and 15 (but, remember, the equal lengths won't weigh the same or sink at a similar rate because of the slender forward taper).

A popular combination is 20 and 10. Mike Kinney uses this one and markets it commercially. It serves him and others well, the lighter portion for summer, the heavier one for winter and spring runoff. Twenty-two and eight is another possibility, but I know of nobody who uses it. (Note: To avoid waste of this expensive material, all cut sections should add up to 30 feet.)

These lines cast fairly well and form the core for most West Slope fishing. Factory-made lines perform well, too, but they may be more awkward to cast. (And a few are a genuine abomination; I won't name these, for some fishers may be fond of them, but I have a hunch they will soon go out of production from word-of-mouth complaints.) Most of today's graphite rods will cast lines of several different weights if you are careful not to jump up more than two line sizes. So a weight-forward eight dry line, and sections from nine or ten fast-sinkers, will fish nicely together, but are not so pleasantly as a nine spliced to a nine or a ten to a ten. Go up too heavy and the line casts like a rock and is tiring to fish with. And you have to be careful not to hit yourself on the head with a too heavy line. Too light, however, and it won't load the rod and will shoot only a child's distance.

You can use slower sinking shooting tapers for your forward sections, too. These are lines of less density (lower specific gravity) and carry a lower rating number. Extra-Fast Sinking (Wet Cel III, or Hi-Density) is a favorite of mine and has accounted for many fish, when the Super-Fast Hi-Density hangs up and loses flies. The material used in making this line wears well if you don't pull on it too hard when it is fastened to the bottom. This stretches it, and core and finishes have different rates of elasticity, so the surface develops cracks. One line of mine is over ten years old and shows little deterioration. And Fast Sinking (Wet Cel II) is useful when the river has undergone its big seasonal drop. Each line has its right time and place. When and where to use them is what fishing is all about.

One last word on this subject: Never throw away a line, or a piece of line, unless it has rotted. If you splice your own you'll soon find a use for it.

23

Wet-Fly Tactics: Mid-Water

RARELY DO ANY OF MY RIVERS RISE and stay high for long during September and early October. Instead, there comes a day or two of rain and the dry weather returns, along with the sun, and the river begins to fall back into shape. More and more now there are leaves littering the beach. On odd-numbered years carcasses of humpies pile up in the shallows and begin to stink. Gulls and crows are everywhere; without them the litter and stench would be prolonged. The dead salmon provide what little nutrients the river receives, so the process is vital. (Breathe through your mouth; it helps.)

I now see chinooks finning in the riffles, white patches of fungus on their heads and shoulders. A pale, slender female of about 15 pounds appears on the beach above the Elbow Hole. She is dead and looks spawned out. A few days later I spot the gummy corpse of a male that must weigh 30 pounds. His head is a gargoyle.

While the river is running high I return to mid-water wet-fly tactics. They are not awfully different from low-water ones. A little heavier line is called for, perhaps a 15-foot tip, and a few more mends of line are thrown into the current. Also a fly that is a size or two larger—#2 or 4— and it ought to be bright if the water is tea-colored as it often is. With leaves in the river I shun yellow (although—oddly—cutthroat fishers often do well on it now). My hook frequently comes back with a huge black cottonwood leaf on it. The bigleaf maples are about the same golden color and take with the lunge of a salmon.

A steelhead is what I'm after today. (Aren't I always?) Summer runs have been in the river since May, along with ones that have trickled in later. These are fish that have hung out in the lower river but not moved upstream until the rains motivated them. And there are some fish fresh in from the bay. These too are intensely colored. Steelhead at this time of the year have acquired much the same coloration as rainbow trout in spring, the time the trout are spawning. The females have lost their silvery sheen and have acquired spots below the median line, some with the same rosy band as the males. The males have elongated heads, green/gray sides, and bright red stripes running down their sides. Their bellies are as gray as stones in the rain.

Different rivers produce fish with somewhat different characteristics. Often fishermen report catching a steelhead "fresh from the sea," which turns out to be a female that's been in the river for quite some time. She is bright only in comparison with the males. Fishermen prize silvery steelhead and put inordinate value on them just because of their color. September fish are not bright nor are they fresh. Many times they don't fight well. It is probably because of warm water and confined habitat. A narrow river reduces the fish's mobility and usually the quality of its fight. As the water cools and the river swells the fish perform better.

A dark September fish is nonetheless pretty, beauty being in the eye of the beholder. You should accept that color as natural, the inevitable course of all living things. Sexual maturity of the species is necessary for its replenishment. It would be wrong for a fish to mature and not take on its special coloring. Brightness is not the measure of a fish's worth, anyhow. Fishermen set themselves up for disappointment if they expect a bright fish in the fall of the year.

I have before me a four-color brochure produced by the Steelhead Society of British Columbia, an honorable and respected group of anglers. Many are flyfishers and my friends. Four big steelhead are pictured. All are mint bright. This impression flies in the face of reality and indicates careful editorial selection. As a matter of fact most B.C. steelhead are dark. They enter the river in the fall and ascend a long distance to their redds. It is a dark time of the year, as well, and the fish are suitably colored, if not for spawning, for protection from predators. Now I love a bright fish as much as the next guy, but September isn't going to be when I find one. They just aren't around.

I remember a beautiful male fish of about 12 pounds from Blue Slough. I took its picture. He lay in among some chinooks that were spawning and seized my fly, the black Woolly Worm you can make out in his jaw. The fish is typical, dark, the way a brawny male should look by mid-September. I've come to admire the splendid colorfulness of fall fish. It does not lessen them any. Mine was caught under mid-water conditions by the traditional wet-fly methods in use at the time. I fished a full 30-foot sinking shooting head with floating line of small diameter behind it. It was hard to fish in such a narrow pool. Today shorter heads are available that work better, making it possible to place the fly closer to the fish and to mend less. Improved fishing techniques are largely the result of synthetic materials used in the manufacture of flylines.

You can use a section of the same length but of greater weight, say, a nine- or a ten-weight instead of a seven or an eight, in a line of the same density such as Super-Fast or you can go to longer lengths of a line of the same weight, such as an eight or nine, or you can choose a line of higher density, say, Deep Water Express or Kerboom. If you go up in line weight you will probably have to switch to a more powerful rod or else overline your regular rod and risk aggravating your tennis elbow. (I presume you have one by now if you fish much; it's from rearing back too hard, too often, on a graphite rod. It may be more slender than you or I, but it is much stronger.)

Often you can keep using the same rod/line combination that you've fished all season, and love so, by lengthening the forward section of your line, say, from 12 feet to 18 or 20. This will give you a longer line to keep up in the air and make you delay your forward cast, accordingly, but if you are in decent shape you can slow your casting rhythm and get away with it. Your line pick-up off the water will be shorter, of necessity, but the line will work out through the guides more quickly. You will be casting a line that sinks faster and deeper, which is what you are after.

The freshened pools are longer and deeper, too. I like the seasonal change immensely, for I prefer a big river, one with lengthy runs that flow swiftly and deep. I will head for them and bypass good, smaller pools that I know hold fish. It takes more hard rain than September usually brings to produce my desired conditions, though.

One time on the Elbow Hole the river didn't have to rise for conditions to change and provide excellent fishing for me. The river only had to color up briefly. It hadn't rained at all, as a matter of fact, so I had no idea where all the color was coming from. At odd hours of the day the river suddenly turned gray-brown. It was the color of fresh soil and I thought some road-building project upstream was causing it. Summer is when most road-repairs are made in the country, and often the earthmovers work right to the edge of the stream channel and push their loads into it. The discoloration lasts but a few hours and does no real harm to the fish or the substrate. But this seemed different.

At mid-afternoon in a year that had been unexceptional I found a couple of hours to fish. I hurried down to the river's edge and was surprised at what I spotted. The water above the Elbow contained only a few inches of visibility. It was full of mud. I almost left but decided to give it a try since I had nothing better to do this beautiful September day. I sat down on a rock and waited to see if the river would clear. Sure enough, in a few minutes the visibility began to return, first a foot of it, then two. I crossed the riffle to reach the main pool. By the time I got there the river carried only a modest amount of color. My fly was purple, a marabou.

I hooked a fine fish at once. It jumped and jumped, and ranged the length of the pool. I guessed its weight at seven pounds and released it. A second fish took half a dozen casts later in nearly the same location. The fly was the same, reknotted to the leader. The water had now achieved three feet of visibility. Where had all the color come from and why had it cleared so quickly? It was most peculiar. A third fish took, fought hard, and was landed. It weighed about nine pounds and was beautifully proportioned, the best fighter of the lot. All were native Deer Creek fish, runners and jumpers, slow to come to the beach. The river was now as clear as it would ever get and as low as always.

It would be a crime to continue fishing, so I left. As I crossed the riffle above I saw a section of bank had come loose and was sloughing off into the river in huge chunks. This was directly down from Raymond's Camp Bucktail. The current gradually ate them away. Each time it happened the river colored up until the clot was gone. This took an hour or more. I should have recognized the situation at once, but I was too eager to go fishing to use my eyes.

Today the sloughing had been a godsend, for it caused the steelhead to disregard their normal caution and take flies recklessly, under conditions that put them off their guard and obstructed their vision only slightly.

That evening I returned to the river to watch the others fish. I wanted to see how they did on a day when I had had such good luck. Now that the river was clear again, would the fish still be hitting? Was my luck a fluke? There was Walt, there the Byrnes boys. I watched until deep twilight. Nobody touched a fish. I concluded that the colored water was all important and had accounted fully for my success.

Often we take credit for skill when we are only lucky. It is a mistake. The slumping bank and the timing of my arrival produced a set of circumstances leading to an afternoon's outstanding fishing. It had lasted a short length of time. At such times a wet fly generally works best.

An off-colored river can be approached boldly, with little fear of scaring the fish, as one can also do on a newly risen river. Both types of water have regained their mystery. Their depths are hidden. They need to be probed, explored. The fly may be presented quartering upstream, directly across, or slightly downstream, line mended and the cast lengthened out to permit the fly to sink and fish slowly. The fish will be lying near the bottom. Black or purple are good colors now and show up well in dirty water. They will continue to be effective whenever the river rises slightly or colors up. (They aren't bad, either, when the river is clear, the day dark. Or as a change-of-pace fly on a bright day.)

Marabou Spey Wet

Many fishers now use the standard bright colors including cerise, hot orange, red, pink, and chartreuse. These are the colors of winter flies. Steelheaders have great faith in them at all times of the year. To the fish color probably doesn't make much difference. Besides all these they will take white, which has been a sleeper as of late.

It is pleasant to fish in the days of reduced heat—with evenings that require a warm shirt, for there is a decided coolness at dusk. To fish a sunk fly on a river flowing strongly and known to be harboring fish is exciting. A strike can come at any time and, though I think I am prepared for it, it always comes as a surprise. I've never gotten over my sense of wonder that a steelhead will take a fly in the first place. If I anticipate a soft take, a mere stopping of the fly in mid-drift, I am met with a fish that hits hard and is immediately off and running.

But sometimes—as I anticipate—the line simply stops and I know nothing until I tighten cautiously. Then the fish starts to move away slowly, with strength instead of suddenness, often in an upstream direction. I don't know it's a steelhead for sure until it goes into its steelhead act. The jigging and shaking are unmistakable signs it's not a salmon.

A river flowing at medium height once more offers hope, expectation, and challenge. You can mend an extra loop or two of line and not risk losing your fly on the bottom. That extra mend will permit the line to sink further and straighten out better. It will also allow you to continue your slack-line drift for another few yards, which may put the fly in the face of a steelhead lying directly downstream. Steelhead love to lie in water the same depth at which you wade. Sometimes the strike is so fierce it will snap off the tippet if you are a bit careless or unprepared. I've landed big males that drove the hook right through their upper jaw, but the leader held. Other fish give the fly a couple of light raps to announce their presence, as though knocking on your door of opportunity. When you answer with a return knock the fish explodes. It leaves you marveling at the speed and strength of these newly awakened autumn fish.

Such fish are said to have "freshened." The river has freshened, too. It is a beautiful phrase. It means both river and fish have responded to a change in conditions—perhaps in seasons, too. It is a teasing form of knowledge, though, for you know the river will not rise and remain high for another month, at which time more fish from the sea will be arriving daily.

24

Wet-Fly Tactics: High Water

MOST EVERYBODY HAS GONE SOMEWHERE, for October is here and it is the favorite month to be away. The Skeena system's famed Kispiox puts out its best fishing now, along with the Bulkley, Morice, Sustut, and Babine. I generally stay home and fish the rivers nearby. Two of my favorites are the Grand Ronde and the Wenatchee. They lie on the East Slope of the Cascades. But practically all the rivers are good now. The North Fork often enjoys some of its best fishing when the water rises in October. To the South the Kalama, Klickitat, Wind, Lewis, and Oregon's Deschutes are rejuvenated with fresh runs of steelhead entering their lower reaches and rapidly moving upstream.

Hard rains have a lot to do with the abundance. At home swollen rivers call for a sudden change in tactics. High-water techniques work well on East Slope rivers now, too. I welcome the change, for I love high-water fishing. Some years the rivers to the East remain low well into October, because of the lack of rain and continuing irrigation withdrawals. Other years the rivers naturally rise and stay bank-high until the first strong freeze. This effectively ends the fly fishing season.

Even though the number of fish returning to the North Fork is not as great as to the streams that lie East of the Cascades, there still are plenty of steelhead to be found. West Slope rivers rise and fall from heavy rains and often start coming into shape just short of being bank-high. This calls for heavy lines and rods capable of casting them far. Special fast-sinking lines have been developed for just these conditions. Traditional deep-sunk-fly methods are the order of the day. They will be in widespread use until the drought of February. After it ends they will be needed again periodically until the early days of summer. Many places, and for most of the year, high-water, sunk-fly technique is mandatory.

Traditional Bucktail Wet

For sustained high-water fishing there are two schools of thought about flies and their effectiveness. One groups sticks to dark flies, black or purple, and maintains that they show up best under all water conditions—low, mid, and high. They are good in clear water, too, this group maintains. The other group insists that bright colors are what is called for now and fluorescent ones are most effective. A fly can't be too bright to suit them nor can it be too large. This school thinks brightness helps steelhead find the fly, especially in badly colored water. They don't realize steelhead can see well. I agree with them only in the sense that I think steelhead like bright colors. I attribute this to their saltwater diet of shrimp and elvers, and to the roe they find drifting free in rivers at certain salmon-spawning times of the year. But they see all colors well under most conditions and will take them.

Both groups agree that fast-sinking lines are necessary. They want their fly to get down to the bottom fast. They believe that fish no longer will move more than a few feet to intercept a fly and this notion holds up well, though there are exceptions. Fast-sinking lines were created in response to the demands of high-water anglers. They were technology-driven applications. By this I mean new materials had to evolve before lines could be made to do what fishers wanted of them. This often involved a long wait. I know it did for me.

Leon Martuch of Scientific Anglers deserves the most credit for the lines of today. He was a friendly, accessible man who liked to hear from active fly fishers. I wrote him once and received a long letter back. From then on we corresponded irregularly up to his death. I know this was the case with many of us. I was always after him to come up with a line that sank in front, but floated behind. He wrote of the difficulty of manufacturing such a line. He would make it when he could, he said. He meant he had to wait for the materials to be developed in the laboratory. At the time he had no way to bond dissimilar materials to the same core. (Cores at first were braided nylon, which stretched and soon destroyed the line's finish; Dacron lines helped solve this problem and additionally provided a superior backing line.) Meanwhile we waited. We used what was at hand. Often this was plastic-coated, lead-core trolling line. Syd Glasso devised some of the best early ones and we copied them, when he told us how. When pressed he would share what he knew about materials and section lengths.

As the revolution in plastics and space-age materials made new compounds available lines were manufactured that sunk better and faster. They had higher and higher densities. Previously our sinking lines were silk floating ones that were left untreated with floatant so they would absorb water and sink. As they became water-logged they got heavy and hard to cast, but they sank and caught fish—if you didn't break your arm trying to cast them.

In the '60s Martuch marketed the first Wet Cel II lines, with a braided nylon core and a finish of polyvinyl chloride. Ken and George McLeod helped Martuch so much in developing these lines that he put their family name on the box. These lines were fine for summer, but they didn't sink fast enough for winter. Again we had to wait for the materials to evolve. Wet Cel III was developed to fill this need. It came on the market a few years later. This stuff sank about twice as fast and was named Hi-Density. It was available at first only in a weight-forward taper as a full line, so inventive anglers (always dissatisfied) cut theirs off at 29-33 feet and made shooting heads out of them. These they spliced to thin running line or heavy monofil to increase their casting distance. The lines shot far and sank better than anything previously available. And they caught fish. Soon shooting tapers (only 30 feet long) were manufactured out of the Hi-Density material. We snapped them up.

The Cortland Line Company began producing and marketing competitive products. Their fast-sinking lines contained a special cobalt finish, they proclaimed. Anglers liked the supple finishes better than SA's and arguments ensued over whose lines sunk faster. Other line companies got into the act—Gladding, Newton, Sunset, among others—but the two original companies dominated the market. They do so still today. Competition between them and the unceasing demand of finicky flyfishers inspired the companies to develop more flylines, some highly specialized and of interest to only a few. Probably many more lines are manufactured today than is necessary from a good business standpoint or for our diverse fishing needs, and the two companies are in the unenviable position of having to match each other, line for line, or lose their market share—even if they must compete at a loss. All the while fly fishers benefitted. Yet they remained ever dissatisfied, always on the prowl for whatever was new and might give them an advantage.

What they were after was a slender, flexible line that would cast like a dream and sink like an anchor. Scientific Anglers introduced their new High-Speed, Hi-Density line with a sink-rate of 3.75 to 6.50 inches per second—depending on the line's weight. We soon began chopping these up, of course, to make our own versions. Cortland countered with one whose sink-rate was 4.25-5.0 inches per second. It was followed by Kerboom from Cortland and SA's Deep Water Express, with sink-rates of 7-8, 8-9, and 9-10 inches per second. It won't end there, believe me.

Ultra-fast sinking lines are difficult to use under normal circumstances. They settle to the bottom and lie among the rocks. If you aren't careful you can lose a fly every cast. Or a section of expensive line. And—I'm sorry to say—some of the new lines are impossible to cast. Many an accomplished angler has hit himself on the back of the head with one and vowed never to use it again. But it is an idle boast. The time will come when only that line will get down fast enough to catch a fish in heavy water and the damned thing will get put on a reel spool again to prove its utility.

I won't stop trying to improve on what the factory produces, nor will most other long-time steelheaders. My own lines are looped together with tightly wrapped connections, which I make. I like to be able to change them as the need arises. With them I use a very short leader. For this I am indebted again to Bill Stinson, who first pointed out that they catch more fish than long ones. Regularly I use ones that vary from four feet in length to perhaps only ten inches. They keep the fly and leader from drifting upward—contrary to what the line is doing. (Of course with surface flies and floating lines this tendency is exactly what you want, so leaders are kept long.) High water and fast-sinking lines and short leaders equal more fish hooked and brought to the beach.

Anglers have developed a catch-and-release mentality partly in response to the abundance of fish. But there is no good biological reason to release a hatchery steelhead, especially in autumn. It is a good time to keep one if you want it. Steelhead are great eating. In spite of their dark coloration fall fish are far from spawning and their flesh is pink and firm, with a thick layer of ocean fat. People often smoke these fish because of their color. They think of them as they do spawners. This is a mistake.

Norma bakes ours in foil at 350 degrees. After about forty-five minutes she tests the flesh with a fork for doneness. If it's not quite cooked, but close to it, she'll let the steam inside the wrap continue to cook the fish a few minutes longer. (Lately she microwaves it in plastic wrap. Note: If you microwave it for 45 minutes—yuk!) A day or two afterwards she serves the fish cold for lunch. She'll make it into a sandwich with mayonnaise or serve it plain with salad and bread alongside.

Ed Weinstein makes a big production out of cooking his steelhead. He poaches it and serves it in a sauce made from its own juices. This is called *court bouillon*. It is how Atlantic salmon is prepared for royalty. Gourmets and fine restaurants serve it poached, too. I can understand Ed's reasoning. Steelheaders believe their fish—Alec Jackson's Prince of Wales—is no less deserving of royal treatment.

25

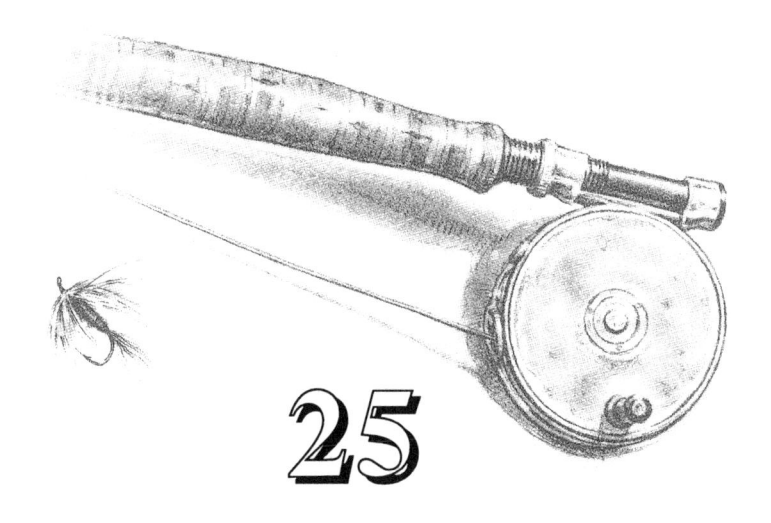

This Year's Fly, Last Year's Rod, A Reel of Antiquity

THIS YEAR'S FLY HAS NO BODY. It doesn't have a tail, either. But it catches fish. [Since I wrote this, my flies have changed again. They have bodies—often fat, tapered ones. Its tails and wings I'm doing without. But I have a hunch it isn't going to stay this way.]

This makes me think that many parts of a fly are redundant. I mean, you may need a body on a fly, okay, but do you also need a wing, a hackle? Maybe you need *either* a wing *or* a hackle, but not both. And a tail—unless it is red or is thickly extended to act as a horizontal stabilizer, as it does on my low-water Spade—may be unnecessary. After thinking this way for a year or more an ordinary steelhead fly starts to look badly overdressed.

Last year's fly was one of a series of marabous, a few of which had tails (tails in general should be red, I believe) and all of them bodies. My bodies were invariably medium chenille and ribbed with flat silver tinsel. But a few springs ago I began fishing with Bob Aid/Joe Butorac/John Farrar-style "wrapped" marabou streamers, and they looked great in the water and caught fish. So when summer rolled round and I went out after the first of the fresh fish, I stuck with these bodiless flies. They produced well.

As the river dropped (the British say "fell in" and I like the phrase) I reduced the size of my hook and the length of my marabou wing. Then in late summer I tired of tying marabou flies and went over to bucktail and calf wings. (Actually this urge began to overtake me in March, but I fought it off until August.) Now I'm fishing a debarbed fly with a short, bright wing of marabou or hair and a forward hackle wrapped Cosseboom style. On the smallest of these flies I don't bother to wrap the hackle, but tear off a chunk and lash it down over the wing, making a short secondary wing. This is a beard-style hackle, only it's tied on top. It pleases my eye, looks good in the water, and steelhead take it as well as any fly.

Ralph Wahl once told me steelhead will take *anything*. His implication was that we tie flies in order to please ourselves—to fulfill our sense of beauty, design, and function. Well, what's wrong with that? The fish couldn't care less. This year's colors—for what they're worth—are red and yellow. Because I use the combination of red wing and golden yellow hackle so often it is what I catch most my fish on. (If I used something else I'd catch them on that color combination; it only holds to reason.) But everybody has his favorite flies and it is because they work well for him. The possible color combinations are nearly infinite.

Yet certain colors prove themselves year after year. Ken and George McLeod's bright/dark/neutral threesome of Skykomish Sunrise, McLeod's Ugly, and Purple Peril are about as good a selection as can be found. Walt Johnson fishes Spey flies with similar colors successfully. So all you need is one bright fly (red/orange), a dark fly (black), and a neutral one (purple, always) and you are in business. I could probably fish Skykomish Sunrise and a dark fly, say, the black Woolly Worm, happily the rest of my days with no loss of effectiveness. But this would take away all the fun of developing new patterns and learning which ones work best.

Flies from yesteryear that I've abandoned, but took enough fish in their time to prove their worth, jam my fly-storage boxes and I dig a few out annually and fish them in order to see if they still will catch fish. They do. There is a whole family of Spade derivatives, for instance. They were developed for fishing the North Fork. They are effective on East Slope rivers, too, where steelhead readily come to the surface and are so trouty.

For a number of years I fished mainly double-winged marabou streamers. These are tied with separate wings of the same color placed above and below the shank of the hook so that the body shows through. I developed a family of them and they all were successful. Names are not important or necessary for these flies. Call them by their colors. Successful combinations include: red body/purple wing; dark blue body/red wing; black body/hot orange wing; purple body/cerise wing; yellow body/orange wing; red body/black wing. I've fished these flies extensively, beginning in 1978. They've accounted for hundreds of steelhead, winter and summer.

Two named patterns, however, have endured and I use them regularly. They are dependable flies. They will produce most any time. One is Deer Creek: tail, red hackle fibers; body, flat silver tinsel (preferably metal, for mylar breaks easily and ruins the fly); rib, oval silver; wing purple marabou, tied fore and aft in two separate clumps about the same size; hackle, silver doctor blue or Laxa blue, depending on what's handy. The other is Royal Flush: tail, none; body, navy blue chenille, wool, or dubbing; rib, flat silver tinsel; wing, bright red marabou fore and aft, tied in two bunches; hackle, none. (Recently, I've started using pearlescent tinsel in place of silver. It works fine, but it breaks easily, thereby ruining the fly.)

From 25 years ago there remains, Garth: tail, red hackle fibers; body, red or fluorescent orange medium chenille; hackle, light grizzly, palmered; wing, moose mane—on smaller flies, I use moose body hair even though it is darker; head, either red or black, depending on my mood, Warlock: tail, red hackle fibers; body, fluorescent orange chenille; hackle, hot orange saddle, palmered, with a second, webby hot orange feather wound in at the head; wing, darkest moose, Timm: tail, red hackle fibers; body, black chenille; rib, flat silver tinsel; hackle, hot orange, bent down or tied beard; wing, dark moose again. Timm is a pretty fly and a little like a hair-winged version of the Atlantic salmon pattern, Orange Charm.

These are good bright/neutral/dark combinations and fish well. Eventually I switched over to marabou wings, but I reckon they have lost none of their effectiveness. Steelhead remain the same in their tastes.

The reason to change fly patterns is simply because you want to tie something different or new. Steelhead respond to certain classes or types of flies and so as long as you stick to the basics and to proven colors you won't go wrong. New materials demand to be tried and given a chance to show their value, often when added to traditional dressings. Flashabou arrived and was soon available in fluorescent, luminous, and sparkling colors. Next came Crystal Flash. It is good for tails and as an additive to wings and can be purchased as a ribbing tinsel for the body. In the water it does astounding things with light.

I find I don't always want astounding things to happen, however. In clear water there can be such a thing as too much sparkle or flash. I save it for adverse conditions and use it sparingly even then. It is hard to buy flies today that don't make use of these new, miracle materials. Many tiers use them to excess, I think. It is the erroneous idea that if a little something is good a whole lot is even better. Well, they are wrong.

In heavily fished waters the new materials may provide the difference that brings the only strike of the day. I once caught a spring steelhead in water with only three inches of visibility on a fluorescent cerise Flashabou fly. I doubt whether the fish would have hit anything else that day. Yet I rarely use the stuff. I simply don't like the looks of it. (Good reason?)

Similarly a fly that stores its visual energy and emits it luminously will take fish at dusk or even later. I used it a lot years ago and it extended my fishing day by a full half hour. Even when quite dark out and to my eye the material had lost its glow it would bring strikes. I remember catching fish on it when it was too late to see them in the water and having to play them by feel. (This is not as much fun as it sounds.) Now I don't fish so late, so I use the stuff seldom. But I respect it.

My tailless flies—the ones without bodies, also—look good to me. And they behave naturally in the current, I use them winter and summer. I tied up some dry flies without bodies this year and caught trout on them, but no steelhead. I don't think I gave them a fair chance. Maybe next year.

Come to think of it a bodiless fly *has* a body of sorts: The hook shank provides it. The hook is black and black is one of the easiest colors for fish to see, since it reflects no light and is opaque. The marabou on my flies obscures the body and tail of my flies so badly that I'm not sacrificing much by leaving these parts out. Actually I'm saving materials. But one day soon I'll grow restless and want to try something new. My flies will develop a different look. I have no idea what it will be.

Steelheaders love to buy rods and probably accumulate more than they will use in several lifetimes. Catching your first fish on a new rod is always a challenge. It's called, "Breaking in the new rod." Sometimes if you aren't lucky you may go a long time without a fish and you will begin to think the rod is jinxed. You may want to shun it, steelheaders being superstitious to a fault. Though its main job is casting hour after hour the satisfactory playing of big fish is important in a rod. Until it's proven its value a new rod can't be trusted. (Afterwards it is probably trusted inordinately up until the time it breaks.)

So many books have addressed the subject of rods—picking out the right one for you or building a custom one from a kit—that I needn't repeat their advice. At a certain point you simply make your choice of a blank and hope it is a good one. If you follow the ads in the fishing magazines you'll go crazy. You can't completely ignore the hype, though, for some of it is true. But I wonder whether this year's Sage is any better than the one they tried to sell me last year. True, the proprietary name of the graphite material has changed and the price has gone up. Rods by Fenwick and Loomis and Orvis are marketed exactly the same way. When I waggle one it doesn't feel much different from past rods of theirs—certainly not enough for me to shell out all that money.

Over the decades there's been a steady evolution of materials. When it came along fiberglass was recognized as superior—that is, lighter, stronger, than bamboo. And graphite is stronger, lighter, thinner, and more powerful than fiberglass. Graphite is in its umpteenth generation. It's great stuff. And there is boron, but something bad happened to it along the way. It was supposed to replace graphite. It has practically disappeared (except in tarpon rods), while graphite has endured. Some graphite rods now contain a low percentage of boron.

The solitary boron rod I own is too stiff to be much fun to fish with and casts a bow so tight it nearly braids itself in the air. I have to make a major adjustment in my casting technique. But it is noticeably more slender and stronger than graphite. On a windy day it slices through the wind like a blade. Yet I rarely take it out with me to the river. Perhaps it is possible to invent a material too strong, too dynamic, to be any fun to fish with.

Anybody who has used graphite (and everybody has, I think, unless he's been in prison for twenty years) loves its light airy feel, its inherent power. It makes possible the use of very long rods without accompanying fatigue. These rods permit easy mending and other methods (such as lifting over) of controlling the line on the water. You can also Spey cast one-handedly with them—at least you can perform the single Spey. Consequently I rarely use a short rod anymore. Before graphite came along long rods were man-killers. They wore us down and sent us to the showers early. Today I regularly use rods of 10 1/2 and 11 1/2 feet without fatigue. The longer one is a tad stiffer than I'd like, but I can still fish a long day with it even in the wind. The shorter one is a dream and I can fish seemingly forever. However the longer one will outcast it by ten or 15 feet. If I slow down my backcast and don't fight the rod's power the longer one will fish more satisfactorily, even badly overlined for heavy water. And though both are rated for eight-weight lines the longer one can be pressed into service for short heads up to ten-weight. This gives it the edge for year-round fishing.

My old friend, Ed Weinstein, is master of the double-haul. Once he borrowed a Hardy Salmon Deluxe bamboo rod from George Keough and took it out for a day's fishing. It was 10 1/2 feet long, but in bamboo that is heavy. I came across Ed two hours later, sitting on a rock by the water's edge, wondering if he'd caught the flu. It was only the effect of the heavy rod, worked as hard as he works the smaller ones. It had unstarched him in minutes. This is not such a problem today. Graphite rods are so light that even a skilled distance caster like Ed can double-haul line all day and not become exhausted. Still you have to be careful or you'll hurt your arm from forcing the rod to work so hard.

A man will own and love a variety of rods in a lifetime, but over the years he will put most of them aside and buy new ones. There is always the promise of a better one on the horizon. This gives rod makers assurance. It seems to me that rod materials are what make the difference, not the minor variations in how that material is used by various rod makers. Nearly all of today's graphite rods cast well. But it is lines that have made us the casters that we are.

So many fishers like a custom-finished rod that I wonder why anybody buys the ready-made ones. I guess they like the status that comes with the brand name proudly displayed above the grip. To me this is nonsense. There is so much variety in rod handles, reel seats, fittings, colors of wraps and trims, etc., that I would think most fishers would want to pick out their own and have a rod made up just for them. I know I do. *I* make the choices, thank you. The rod blanks, however, are from reputable companies, ones that know there is a secondary market for fishers like me. Often I'll buy a reject, a blank with some slight imperfection. So will my friends. We don't want to look like the herd, but we demand high quality products and—above all—performance.

Knowledge of how to assemble a rod is available in many books. Bill Stinson has written a good one. Know-how can be acquired by following the step-by-step instructions. However, applying the Epoxy finish over the wraps is tricky and requires a rotisserie, a knowledge of finishes, and skill in applying the material, which bonds so quickly to the rod that no mistakes are allowed. A smooth, handsome finish is not easy to come by. I'm dissatisfied with my past performance and have not finished enough rods lately to be good at it, so I pay Bob Ferber to do mine. He is a fine craftsman and is reasonable. *Our* product is a rod that is as solidly, dependably put together as the top brand-named rods for sale in the stores. Often it is a little better finished.

Until you know what you are doing, or are willing to take a big risk, it might be best to buy factory-finished rods and to arrange with a store to try out several in the line sizes you think you will be using. Most good tackle stores will let you take the rod and line out in the parking lot and practice casting with it on cement or asphalt. (This won't cause the lines much damage if you don't do it for long.) While not in any way approximating river-fishing conditions it is better than no opportunity to try it out before buying an expensive rod or line.

It is difficult to judge the action of a rod blank when it is unfinished, without the guides wrapped on and a reel on the seat and a cork grip in your hand, and afterwards it is too late to select another blank. You and your money are committed. If you can't learn to love a rod that is a mistake try selling it to someone who is not a good friend. This is not quite the dirty trick it seems, for it may be just what that person is looking for.

Lines matter most. I've said this before, but it bears repeating. Casting well is vital. When compound forward tapers came on the market people such as myself, who didn't cast well, overnight found themselves to be fairly good casters. We could suddenly throw a fly a long distance. How wonderful this was to experience. It made all the difference between fishing being fun and an ordeal. Soon everybody began benefitting from the new lines. They were modeled after the tapers developed by Marvin Hedge in silk lines decades earlier. But they were much cheaper and more easily available, thanks to mass-production.

That rods take credit for what is made possible by the advance in lines is not commonly understood or acknowledged. Surely rod manufacturers won't tell you. They want to take all the credit and—sell you another rod next year. Even today's cheapest rods are pretty good. An average caster can pick up an unfamiliar rod and cast a variety of lines with it, right from the start, varying his technique only a little from rod to rod. If the line is way too light it needs to be lengthened out considerably before it will load up the rod; conversely a too heavy line requires shortening up or choking, as with a baseball bat.

To make fishing pleasant and endurable a rod ought to cast with minimum effort. Most rods will do this with a wide range of line sizes, that is, line weights. Rod makers even recommend the use of more than one size line with a given rod. It is harder to go wrong in buying the right weight line for a rod than at any time in the past. This is good news for everybody and not just for beginners.

"This year's rod is the best and I shall never need another." How many times have I said it? I have a heap of rods, most stuffed in tubes stacked in the closet and apt to spill out each time I open the door. I have loved each in turn, as I shall all the beauties to come. As you grow older you become the prisoner of your past; you are the sum of many different experiences with tackle that is ever being replaced. When you take down an old rod tube and assemble its sections you are flooded with memories of great, good times. That dirty, well-worn cork handle is a genie's lamp that with a stroke of your fingers brings back every fish you've hooked and played on it.

Reels are a great joy. Perhaps they are valued more because of their mechanics and (I hope) their fine tolerances. Sometimes I'll write an article and sell it and eventually get paid, and I will buy a rod blank and fittings with the money. Or else I'll buy a reel, but probably only if it is on sale, for they are expensive—now as always. A good rod requires a commensurate reel. I prefer a Hardy, either new or used. A Hardy is my big weakness. It is the weakness of many.

Dr. Nate Smith is a flyfisher who will accept no money, but only a gratuity, for surgery performed on a colleague or a member of the colleague's family. It is invariably a Hardy reel. Over the years he has acquired quite a collection. They are mostly vintage reels. Well, he is vintage himself. Hardy reels have long set the standard of excellence and are impossible to displace. After all the English royalty used them and also rods by Hardy. Ernest Hemingway fished them. The list of testaments goes on. Yet there are many fine reels on the market, probably more than at any other time in history. I suspect some of them are better than Hardys. But I will always love Hardys best.

Until recently I have owned and used only Hardys—that is, after my Initial Pfleuger Medalist Experience. Hardys have their flaws and faults, but they seem minor in comparison with reels by most others. Tolerances are not all that good and the finish doesn't hold up. Call it "patina," it is still the sign of early wear. Hardy feels no need to change their ways. They remain staunch and staid.

Soon somebody will come along and make a better reel. It may have already happened. It will not be cheap. The designers will start out by keeping the best of what Hardy offers. They'll keep the pawl-and-rachet drag system, for instance. They will improve the tolerances and finish, perhaps anodizing the reel. And they'll improve the range of drag settings. (The new Hardy Sovereign does some of these things, but in the process the price has shot up to $400, which is way too much, unless you are a prince.)

One good reel is made in Argentina and marketed under the name of STH. It is anodized and has extremely close tolerances. Its gears are of naval brass. The reels are carried by L.L. Bean and Orvis, among others. I've used one for two seasons, taken fish on it, and find its performance flawless. The drag system offers a greater range of settings than a Hardy, with a light coming-in click and a strong out-going check that is nicely audible. In fact there are dual out-going drags, one light, one heavy, and they can be combined. Understandably the reel is not cheap.

Each of the old Hardys has its charm and distinct "song"—as it is called—when a fish is running. Art Smith and I used to play a game. We taped the sound of different Hardys under simulated fish-running conditions and then played them back to each other, trying to identify the different models while we drank beer in the evening. (One or the other of us would grab the end of the line and run off down the road, while the other clung to the reel frame. Meanwhile the recorder ran.) All the reels were sufficiently alike that we soon became confused about what we heard. We drank some more beer—then abandoned the project. We began to argue about something else. Who was the better composer, Mozart or Beethoven?

The Hardy Perfect in any one of its many incarnations is a great reel, arguably the best of the lot. You either love a Perfect or else you hate it. The first one was made in 1891 and they were kept in more or less steady production until 1967 when they were discontinued. In the early

'80s the model was slightly redesigned and reintroduced. (Some say it was degraded.) Several of the earlier sizes and models were discontinued. Those who love Perfects quickly bought the new ones. A few were disappointed with the product. They expected, well, Perfection.

Those Perfects made prior to 1921 are called Mark I; those manufactured until 1967, Mark II. My father gave me a Mark II, 3-7/8 inch Perfect in the early '50s, and I have fished it and caught steelhead on it every year since. It cost $20—a whole lot then. I had it customized to left-hand crank a few years later, after reading Lee Wulff on the subject. The work cost $5, Hardy being most cooperative and reasonable about repairs and modifications. I did not understand about the value of patina and stripped off the finish once it became scratched and pitted. It was what my Canadian friends did and I thought it cool. Overnight my reel became as shiny as an aluminum pot. Regularly I must buff it up. It now shows corrosion I can't get rid of. I probably devalued it by hundreds of dollars. I don't much care, for I don't intend to sell it. (If you want one, too, you have to find somebody who will sell you his, but nobody will. They only turn up in estate sales.)

Perfects today are manufactured in 3-1/8, 3-3/8, and 3-5/8-inch models, with either right or left-hand crank. I bought a 3-5/8 inch model in left-hand crank through the mail from England when they became available again. The pound stood at $1.07. It cost about $50. It is a good reel, but—make no mistake—it is not as solid as the older ones. I'd like to see Hardy put the 3-7/8-inch model back into production for the many American steelhead and salmon fishers who long for one.

It is hard to put ones's finger on what is so great about a Perfect. It is easier to make a case for what is not. The widely advertised "nearly frictionless" ball-bearings prove to be thrust bearings and do not effect the drag system at all. The check work is the familiar spring-and-pawl arrangement, with the compensating cam that all Hardys have. Each reel has a narrow range of drag settings that is barely adequate at both the top and the bottom end of the scale, yet Hardy never extends them. (There is one exception, the Mark I St. John, that can be cranked down to near a stout leader's breaking capacity, but will lighten up to just about the right tension. The reel is too big and heavy for most people's uses, however.)

Fishermen today demand better tolerances and finishes, and are getting them from other manufacturers. Nonetheless I admire the old Hardys, warts and all, and recently bought a used narrow-drum 3-5/8 Mark I model. A natural left-hand crank model, its appeal was irresistable. It was broken in several places, but the shaft was tight and the bearings good. Hardy repaired it and refinished it for $20 again, proving their continued dedication to low-cost maintenance of their products. It is really a trout reel, though I had to go out and catch steelhead on it, of course. The check work is too light for big fish. Yet I will keep bringing it out and using it. When a fish is running it has a wonderful song.

What is so great about Perfects is the velvety feel of the gears releasing line when a fish takes off. The reel housing, which serves as an audio baffle, is more deep-throated and sonorous than the other Hardys, I think. The narrow-drum 3-7/8 size is just right for steelhead, holding 100 yards of backing and retrieving it more quickly than smaller diameter reels can when a fish suddenly reverses course. It is big, solid, utterly dependable and kept lightly oiled and free of sand it will never let you down. Mine is an old friend who has seen me through the steelhead wars. With it locked on the reel seat of practically any rod I feel capable of taking on the world. At least the world of freshwater fishes.

26

Big Round River

MY FIRST VIEW OF THE GRAND RONDE RIVER was from color slides brought back by Ed Weinstein in the early '60s. I thought it the most beautiful river I'd ever seen. I credited Ed with being a terrific photographer. Now I've learned that nearly anybody can take great pictures of the Ronde. It is the river that is spectacular, not the camera or the photographer. Not to discredit Ed, but I have my own slides to prove it.

The fishing was poor then. The river was suffering its long decline. My friends were fishing a spirit river, one inhabited by ghost steelhead. I couldn't be bothered driving 300 miles to a river that had no fish in it, no matter how lovely. The beauty would make the loss even sadder, I reckoned. Instead, for the next 15 years I stayed home in October. Then I learned that the Columbia River salmon and steelhead runs were on an uptick. Maybe the fishing would be worth the long drive.

In early October Arnold Timm and I planned our first trip. With advice from Marc Bale we pointed our cars at Beamer's Lodge and the popular reach that lies a mile or so upstream from where the Ronde empties into the mighty Snake. We fished the mouth area primarily, though we made a one-day diversion to Bogan's Oasis near the Oregon border. There the river is even prettier if that is possible.

We who fish West Slope rivers with their vast floodplain and thickets of trees and brush looming behind us are astonished and delighted at what we encounter in the desert East—the camelbacked mountains and dung-colored canyons that angle away in their slanted topography for as far as the eye can follow them. Their image gets engraved on our retina and keeps drawing us back about the time the nights turn cold and apple boughs bend low. And when the season ends, and I reluctantly head home across the green Cascades, those brown hills will haul me back as assuredly as I know anything. The annual pilgrimage East has become important in my life.

Arnold Timm on the Grande Ronde

Many anglers commute daily to the Ronde from Clarkston over 30 miles of road that is equally divided between good blacktop and a graveled corduroy terror. Clarkston has a number of passable motels and restaurants; its big sister, Lewiston, is just across the Snake. If you can't find what you want in Clarkston cross over the bridge into Idaho and it's yours.

Clarkston is where the big Clearwater meets the bigger Snake, which you will follow to the mouth of the Ronde. As you head upstream you find no guardrail between you and the river, and it roars and churns forty feet below. In the dark, or during one of the frequent dusklike dust storms, your first mistake will be your last. Each year I hear fresh horror stories about drivers who've plunged to their deaths in new, original ways. These echo in my head and keep my sleepy eyes open when I drive back after a long day's fishing.

The latest version goes like this: A man decided to drive his four-wheeled vehicle across what seemed a shallow channel in order to reach an island a few yards out in the Snake. Perhaps the lure was better fishing. Nobody knows. The water was deeper and swifter than it looked. His vehicle got swept into the cauldron below. His body and truck were never found. The tale plays into our deep reservoir of fear and is plausible. The Snake is awesome even now at its summer's low.

Beamer's rises to greet you just when you begin to think, "There is no such place." It is a restaurant with tiny, thin-walled cabins on the rise opposite you that were built for the convenience of overnighting customers who are taking the jetboat excursion to Hell's Canyon early the next morning. Beamer's is a long way from anywhere. Sometimes the owners can be persuaded to rent a fisherman a cabin. This we arranged by phone. Beamers's may stay open for dinner if the season is not too advanced. The food is plain, but good, and expensive as might be expected. Just about the time the fishing gets good Beamer's shuts down for the year. The weather turns cold—bleak and inhospitable. You will have to provide your own food and accommodations, if you aren't content to be a day-tripper. Many fishers bring RVs. You can park them most anywhere, for this is rangeland. But if the fishing is good the campsites will be jammed.

The section of river from the mouth to the Tin Bridge (now a concrete one) a couple of miles upstream was formerly catch-and-release water. Recently the regulation was changed to wild-fish release. Hatchery fish can now be killed. This may prove a big mistake. If not every fish is released the easy-going character of the river will disappear and a fierce competition to catch and kill a fish will replace it. Dedicated flyfishers will abandon their favorite river rather than see it change.

As it turned out Timm and I were the only overnight guests. We found our water shut off. After taking our money the restaurant closed for the night. No dinner available, we had to make do with some hard scrabble from a package. In the night we woke up shivering under our light summer blankets. We went on a mad search for more. Fortunately our simple key fitted the lock of the cabin next door. We stripped its beds of additional thin blankets. Warmer now, we slept fitfully. In the morning we found Beamer's open. They served us a good breakfast. Patrons were hunters camped down the road. The excursion business was about over for the year. Air and water were too cold for most people.

Lingering over coffee we watched mule deer grazing on the slopes of Idaho two miles away across the Snake. With the aid of a hunter's spotting scope we recognized the dim, brown specks. Occasionally one of them moved. In response we oohed and aahed. The restaurant began to fill up. People descended at mid-morning for a cup of coffee and to exchange tales of the morning hunt. Too cold by the weekend there probably would be no breakfasts, either, for the place shut down in stages.

Steelhead were in the river now, fish that had traveled hundreds of miles up the Columbia and Snake, transcending eight dams. Two hours later I caught my first Round River steelhead. It had a tall unnotched dorsal, which meant it was wild. As a smolt it had traveled downstream past all the dams, avoiding the turbines, flumes, and the nitrogen supersaturation problem that meant death to 80 percent of the smolts. A steelhead from here would spend only one year feeding in the ocean. Almost all Columbia River steelhead are maiden spawners and none will live to come back again.

Sometimes a river will give you a fish right off the bat, then make you pay for it dearly, so it is best not to compliment yourself too early on your skills. My first fish so soon delighted me. It was a typical female, slender and pretty, trouty in appearance and behavior, not very big. It had rosy gill plates and a small neat head. After jumping several times it ran a short distance into the backing. This it did twice more. I can't say its fight was spectacular, though.

A few moments later Timm hooked a scrappy fish that was not a steelhead. It took no line off the reel, but splashed around considerably. It turned out to be a small-mouth bass. I'd never seen one before and was envious. A new species, how I would have loved to have caught it. Small mouths are common in the Snake system, I've since learned, and there are anglers who fish exclusively for them just as we do for steelhead. They consider their fish superior to ours. They have their own brand of fanaticism.

My second Ronde fish was caught two pools later the same day; it fought like a wet rolled-up newspaper. It was a dark, seven-pound male. I examined it for signs of illness, but could find none. I had heard that upper Columbia fish were poor fighters. Why? Did they burn up all their energy with their long swim up the Columbia and Snake? Past all those dams? It seemed an unlikely explanation.

That year the crowds had not yet materialized and we had the pools pretty much to ourselves. Each was beautiful, with a deep gut running down its center, a bedrock bottom, and slippery boulders where you had to wade; the rocks were coated with a greasy brown algae that made me feel like I was on skates. Most Columbia River streams are like this and have great slabs of tilted rock right where you must wade. Cleats are mandatory. A wading staff is, too.

We soon met Jake, the old Man of the River. Every river has such a person. He is a fixture, normally in residence. He showed us the tungsten-carbide studs he wore on his boots. He had them shot into conveyor belting, which he then glued to the soles of his wading shoes. He could go where we could not. On his hip, in a leather holster, he carried the first collapsible wading staff I'd seen. Its several sections were held together with elastic shockcord. The staff could be whipped out of its holster in a difficult situation and flipped into a quick extension that would unfailingly support him. A good wader, who knew his river well, he didn't need to use it often. Like the six-gun in its holster it resembled he used it as a last resort.

He knew every rock and ledge along the bottom of the Ronde—at least in its lower reaches. He carried a small notebook in which he recorded every fish he raised, hooked, lost, or landed, along with pertinent data on air and stream temperature, fly pattern, hook size, pool name, water height and color, and probably whether or not there were clouds in the sky. Jake was thorough, his notebook an art form.

Jake was on the river through September and October, his competition primarily himself. There was also Howie, who (Jake-like) kept a data sheet and scorecard. Howie was a fine fisherman in his own right. Jake beat him out in the stats most days. To be outfished by Jake was no disgrace. But sometimes Howie won the day; it happened just often enough to keep him enthusiastic.

They began fishing at daybreak. Each took a long pause at mid-day, then continued without pause until early dark. They were on the honor system. It looked to me like an 18-hour day. Week followed week without respite. What happened when one of them got sick, I wondered? Was the competition called off until he was well again? I doubt it. They gave each other no quarter. The sick one simply forfeited his day's catch in the season's grand sum. While I admired their persistence I was glad not to be part of the rat race. It would take all the fun out of fishing for me.

I found Jake both friendly and reticent; he talked a lot, but he didn't really tell us anything useful. He sent us off in a number of different directions, but I had the feeling some of them were wild-goose chases. Was he keeping the best pools to himself and Howie? It is what steelheaders do.

There were few fish in the river yet, the bulk of the run holding out in the Snake, where the water in the deep reservoirs was cooler by at least ten degrees. Hooking one fish per day in the Ronde was considered good. It took a lot of hard work to do it. Jake and Howie were doing better than that, but keeping their particulars to themselves. But I doubt whether they could hide much from each other.

During the middle part of the afternoon we lay sprawled in lawnchairs around Jake's makeshift table, fashioned out of an old cable spool. We exchanged the usual lies. He had a self-contained trailer complete with TV mast. Timm and I listened greedily to what he said, and what he didn't, for we needed to learn all we could, but what he told us was rife with ambiguity and contradiction. It was up to us to sort it out.

Jake had a long dedication to this river. Most of the year he worked as a telephone lineman in the northern panhandle of Idaho. In September and October he escaped on his fishing vacation. This was vital to him. Like other manias it was tolerated because he was a good worker. As with many of us fishing kept him out of the asylum, I suppose you could say.

He and Howie practiced catch and release long before it was common or required. They took it for granted that nobody would kill a Ronde-River steelhead. But catching many of them was a point of pride. Timm and I were in solid agreement. The pool in which I caught my first Ronde fish was properly named the Shadow Pool, because the sunlight never strikes its surface. Timm and I called it the Black Rock Pool (not knowing any better) because of the dark boulder that marks the early good part of the run. (Actually the best water starts about one-hundred feet higher up.) The next day we had to share the pool with two other anglers. We didn't touch a fish nor did they. In fact, we fished a number of excellent pools the second day with no luck. Late in the afternoon we drove back to Clarkston perplexed. A golden twilight hung over the road. It was dust from the car in front of us. Below us ran the fuming Snake. It lay in wait.

Over burgers in a fast-food restaurant we discussed the opportunities for tomorrow. We decided to head for Bogan's Oasis far upstream, leaving early in the morning. The name, "Oasis," was appealing, hinting of the French Foreign Legion and a past crammed with mystery and intrigue. The place proved otherwise.

Leaving Asotin we climbed steep switchbacks that led to a huge palouse—a broad high-altitude plateau dedicated to wheat farming. The road became arrow-straight. The harvest over, a thick brown stubble clung to the fields and when the wind raced over it it rippled. The effect was like that of the sea. The road wore fresh blacktop, for it was a major highway leading into Oregon. Ahead was Anatone, a flyspeck on our map. It proved to be a long-closed cafe that faced old-fashioned gasoline pumps that hadn't seen service for a decade. Time had erased Anatone, but not from the maps. Soon we began a steep descent, dropping down to the valley of the upper Ronde. This was the famed Rattlesnake Grade. We were glad to see sturdy cable barriers on the outside of the worst turns. I kept popping my ears for the relief that it brought. Dropoffs of hundreds of feet appeared. We dangled on the edge of the known world.

After about ten slow miles of this the road lost its steepness and straightened out onto a low flat. Ahead we saw the bridge that marked the site of Bogan's Oasis. Soon we'd know what it was like. The Ronde was a different river here, more gentle and tamed, flowing from right to left. We crossed the bridge, stopping in the middle of it as fishermen do and peering into its depths, searching for fish. We saw none. But it was green and beautiful. Different terrain causes a river to change its characteristics. The Ronde came out of a true mountain range and flowed through a narrow farming valley. As if undecided as to what it was it alternated personalities, now flowing quietly over rocky ledges, next tumbling noisily into riffles that poured into small canyons.

Bogan's was a fusty old place with glass-fronted counters loaded with merchandise from years ago, some so old as to be quaint, and overstuffed chairs out in the middle of the room along with a sofa, all arranged in an empty circle of hospitality. We sat up at the lunch counter and waited for somebody to appear in response to the little bell that had tinkled our arrival. Finally a woman appeared from behind a curtained opening to the rear. She looked as old as the store itself and wore a gingham dress whose tiny pattern stretched across her ample frame and strained to cover it. The dress dragged on the floor. Boots she wore. She sighed as a form of greeting. She seemed about as glad to see us as a flat tire on a hot day.

We ordered sandwiches and coffee. She put them together in a cluttered work area that looked filthy. Flies circled noisily. We ate in a hurry, for we were eager to get out of there and fish. The bill came to twice what it should have been. We paid without a murmur and departed. Outside we saw some dilapidated cabins for rent. They looked uninhabitable.

A pleasant campground appeared less than a mile upstream. It was empty. The Ronde purled and plashed alongside a large parking area with a tin outhouse. A man stood on some rocks, casting bait into the hole. This was illegal. No car was in sight, so he must have walked here from his home nearby. Probably it was his usual fishing hole. He would keep anything he caught. This too was illegal. So far from civilization and law enforcement these people had a code that didn't include releasing wild fish.

In the course of a day only a few cars passed along the road. This was sparsely occupied rangeland and farming country. Every half mile or so a farmhouse appeared alongside the only tree in the neighborhood. The river stuck to the road, or vice versa. It was beautiful. Aside from the poacher we had it to ourselves.

We stopped at the first pool and took off in opposite directions. With so much river there was no need to share a pool, not unless we wanted to. We agreed to meet back at the car late in the day and compare notes. How time flies on a new river. We did poorly. Perhaps it was too early in the season to expect fish up so high in the watershed and they hadn't had time to shoot up from the mouth.

The pools were deep and green and clearly defined, each with a riffle spilling into it. It was a pleasure to be here, never mind the chance of fish. We drove upstream and went through a pool together, for Timm had spotted one he had liked and wanted to share it with me, it was so beautiful. He was right. It lay at the foot of a steep canyon whose wall of soft soil we descended at a diagonal trot, it was so unstable. We could not believe the pool would not give up a fish, so we went through it a second time. Not even a bump. The sun was now low and it was time to start back if we wanted to climb the Rattlesnake while there was light, which we did. We reached Clarkston in an hour. Pooped, we ate junk food and went early to bed.

The next day we returned to the pools at the mouth. We knew there were fish. This was our last day. We each took a fish and they were good fighters. It was a satisfying trip and we had done fairly well, considering that there were few fish in the river and we were unfamiliar with its pools and runs. It is important to catch a fish in a new river, for unless you do you will remain a stranger to it and it will not belong to you in any meaningful sense. Next year, we vowed, we would come earlier and stay longer. We would make a meal of the Ronde.

It was not to be. Timm was 70. He had retired only a year ago, for he needed the money regular work brought in. At the end of November—a month after our return—we talked on the telephone one night about a trip to the North Fork, which would soon give up its fly-only status for the year. We wanted to fish it one more time. We said goodnight. Timm put down the phone and walked into the bathroom. There he collapsed and died from a massive stroke.

Since then my trips to the Ronde have been solitary excursions. One year Sam went with me, but he doesn't like motel life and I don't blame him any. The river was crowded and we left early. I thought of Timm and how he enjoyed the river and looked forward to experiencing more of it.

When the fishing was good, and steelhead came eagerly to my fly, I thought of how some of them properly belonged to Timm. I wasn't exactly catching his fish, because it doesn't work out that way, and nobody thinks like that, but sometimes there were more steelhead than I deserved and I felt a little guilty. It would have been good to have had him along, for he was good company. This is never a gloomy or depressing thought and it does not occupy my mind for long.

Several times I've made the 600-mile-plus roundtrip and been skunked. But I've had great times, too. Once I drove to Clarkston on the heels of autumn's first storm. The river rose overnight from rain and fresh fish started ascending in the morning. I had the Ronde all to myself for hours. I rose fish after fish, in a wild, dream-like sequence that left me breathless and wondering back in my motel room that night whether it had truly happened. I hooked six fine fish in about four hours and landed them all. They were fresh and strong. One measured 34 inches—large for the Ronde. All the evidence I had of my good luck was a sore arm.

Another time I drove to the Ronde in a storm that had no rain in it. I was on the river for two days and didn't touch a fish. The third day I headed out again. The wind increased to a gale. Broadleaf maples—sturdy as houses—bent Westward like ballet dancers. The air filled with huge golden leaves and dust of about the same color. Leaves scudded across the road as though chased by dogs. Then they shot into the air and did a parachute descent. The Snake reservoir was laced with whitecaps. I drove more slowly, studying the effects of the wind and trying to make up my mind what to do next. Suddenly I realized I wouldn't be able to cast 30 feet, for the wind wasn't going to abate today. I whirled the car around and headed for Seattle a day early.

Once in another October, on a day with a fierce sun in it, I got a taste of what summer must be like in the great desert country. In the shade of the Shadow Pool I could see my frosty breath, so I pulled on my down jacket. Soon I grew uncomfortable. Piece by piece I discarded my clothing on the bank until I was down to a T-shirt. Did I have a tropical fever? No, it was merely an abnormally warm day at the end of October. The temperature soared past seventy. When I hooked a fish it made me hotter still. Finally I crept off the river in a lather. It was too hot to fish anymore. Out of the shadows the heat became worse. I cranked down the car windows and turned the heater up to cool, the fan on to high, and drove away.

On one trip I found my favorite pools occupied with anglers, so I decided to fish the bar at the mouth (which is the Snake) largely because it had nobody in it. But after a few minutes a camper with Oregon plates drove up and two men leaped out, strung up flyrods, raced to the water's edge, and began casting both above and below me. I felt caught in a sandwich. I moved downstream between casts and soon drew abreast of the lower angler. He did not budge; maybe it was a favorite spot of his, though the Snake is vast and most places look much the same.

We struck up a conversation, the lower man and I. He told me he was from British Columbia—the Campbell River. This was Roderick Haig-Brown territory. Haig-Brown had died recently. Had he known the great man, I asked? Indeed he had. He'd been around a lot, according to his own account. He had lived in Eugene and before that in Everett. My ears went up. This was *my* turf. If he was bluffing, as many fishers do, he wouldn't be able to fool me here.

Had he ever fished the North Fork of the Stilly? I asked. Yes, yes, many times. He knew the river well and its fishermen. Did he know Art Smith, I asked? (Art was a North Fork fishing bum, who had camped on the river each summer for many years. He was dead a decade.)

He knew Art well and mentioned several things about him most people wouldn't know. I was convinced—this man was for real. We were talking in code. I dropped some names and he picked them up quickly. He pitched me some and I caught them. Finally I asked his name. It was Bill Nelson. I had heard of him. He went way, way back. He was now a guide in British Columbia, he said.

Just then a steelhead struck and went racing down the Snake, cartwheeling far out in the current. Line disappeared from the spool of my commodious St. John. I scrambled ashore and ran after the fish. As I passed Bill Nelson I told him my name and we shook hands. A moment later I lost the fish. As I reeled in we resumed our conversation. We talked for a long while, then headed off in different directions to fish, but I kept running into him and his partner, Marty, all afternoon. Each time our conversation resumed at the point where we'd left it.

He told me how he'd founded the Federation of Fly Fishers—right on this spot. He pointed to the ground. I looked down in a manner I hoped might appear reverential. I held his claim in abeyance until I got back to Seattle, where I verified it. This chance meeting led to my joining the FFF and becoming its first Northwest steelhead chairman.

Bill fished the Ronde in the early '60s at the same time as Art Smith, Martin Tolley, Bob Taylor, George Keough, and Ed Weinstein. That sounds like a lot of people to be on a river, all at once, but there weren't many more. The Ronde was known to have terrible fishing, its runs ruined. Bill knew my friends. He said they fished catch and release because there were so few fish left in the river that it only made sense.

There, at the mouth of the Ronde, where its smooth flow merges with the awesome Snake, Wes Drain almost lost his life, Bill told me. Later Wes confirmed the details. Nelson and Lew Bell were fishing from a driftboat, while Wes, Rick Miller, and a big, raw-boned Swede known only as Dave were in a second boat. Dave's boat was new and he was inexperienced at handling it. He said he'd give them a ride they wouldn't forget. He pointed the boat out into the chop where the rip from the Ronde meets the Snake. The boat upset. Everybody went overboard. Wes was wearing no life jacket and had his Exacta camera slung round his neck. Suddenly he found himself at the bottom of the river, being tumbling along the rocks.

"At least I've saved my camera," he thought, unaware that it was a millstone. He bounced up from the bottom, gasped some air, and sank back to the stones. About 150 feet from shore he surfaced a second time, sputtering. Bill spotted him and tossed him a lifejacket. Wes tucked it under his chin, hung on, and began to paddle towards shore with his free arm.

"Bill saved my life," Wes told me years later, when I interviewed him for an article and I brought the episode up for verification. All their gear was lost, including Wes's six leafed Wheatley flyboxes with clips holding 238 flies each. Wes tied a beautiful fly and the loss was huge.

Back in the '60s diehard steelheaders from all over the West came to surface-fish for the handful of steelhead that was left in the Ronde. They gathered round the campfire at night and told hero stories. Some belonged to flyfishing clubs in British Columbia, Washington, Idaho, and Oregon. It was Nelson's idea for them to form a single organization—a "federation" of clubs and individuals. Bill belonged to a club in Eugene, but retained membership in his old Everett gang, the Evergreen Fly Club. Soon he and others organized a meeting that brought together flyfishers from all over the country. It was held in Eugene and, a year later, another was held at Ocean Shores in Washington State. Though a national organization the FFF always has had a strong Northwest component. The Grande Ronde—the Big Round River, as I think of it—flows right through the heart of the Federation and has, ever since its inception.

Each year friendships are renewed on the banks of the Ronde. Its extraordinary fishing is returning. Not all of its steelhead are from hatcheries. Some wild ones survive. Today's race is apt to be a mix of hatchery and wild stocks, inextricably interbred and genetically jumbled as they are throughout the Columbia system. But the numbers of returning fish indicate a recovering fishery and a promising future for the Ronde.

# 27

Wenatchee Mornings

MY FIRST FEW VISITS TO THE WENATCHEE were stopovers on my way to the Ronde. I pulled the car over to the shoulder and fished for an hour or two in the vicinity of Cashmere or Monitor, then hurried on my way. I caught nothing—oh, a big trout once, but that was all. My route took me many miles off my course. I arrived at my motel in Clarkston long after dark. The next morning I drove out to the Ronde, but it was often crowded and my mind kept returning to visions of the Wenatchee. I recalled how it swept round a bend, then dipped in a rush to form the next pool. Perhaps it wasn't as beautiful as the Ronde, but it had its own charms. Gradually—through these stopovers—I came to know and love the Wenatchee. I even enjoyed the long climb over Stevens Pass, which usually took place in a hard rainstorm. On the other side the sky opened up and greeted me with burning gold aspens and flaming vine maples stacked along the highway's edge. Cold nights put a snap to the air and produced tremendous clarity.

Orchardists that I've gotten to know near Cashmere are proud that I find them and their countryside so interesting, for it's known I'm from the city and we are supposed to be sophisticated. What they have they feel is superior to what's on "The Coast"—which is what they call Puget Sound's urban sprawl. I'm inclined to agree in some ways. Chelan county is beautiful, with its pears and apples, its craggy dun vistas, its river twisting and roaring through rugged Tumwater Canyon. Fall's catch-and-release season is to my liking, but not so much to theirs. They think fish, like fruit, ought to be plucked from the river and taken home to be eaten. It's a valid point.

The special season draws a different type of angler. He is not your usual fish killer. Often he is a city dude like me. Catch and release begins in early summer, when only a few fish have entered the river, and lasts until the end of October, when it is normally full of them. Recently regulations have changed and fin-clipped hatchery steelhead may now be kept. Overnight the character of the fishing has changed. Anglers leave the river with a hatchery fish dangling from their fingertips, a grin on their faces. According to the Wildlife Department the river is sufficiently seeded with wild and hatchery fish to permit a consumptive fishery targeted on the hatchery fish. I disagree. I think we need the hatchery fish to spawn, too.

By November first snow has arrived, sometimes closing the passes (besides Stevens, there is a beautiful alternate route over Blewett and Swauk, which is just as fast) and making driving adventuresome. Not many fishers from the West Side come over anymore. You are apt to be met by a "Pass Closed" sign, the results of drifting snow. Those who make it across will find motels cheaper. A week or two ago they were dear because of the tourist trade in precious Leavenworth. Now there is a general shutting down. The stucco-and-half-timbered shops mandated by the business community of Leavenworth will reopen for the Christmas Lights Festival and future lavish promotions sprinkled across the winter.

That is a long time off. It is late September, hot and dry. The pears are usually picked by the time of my arrival, but not the apples. Red and gold, the massively ladened boughs are propped up with sticks for fear they'll otherwise break and spill their cargo to the ground, where it will rot. The sight is of trees leaning on crutches. In Wenatchee—Cashmere, actually—I've gotten to know farmers, tradesmen, migrant workers, bartenders, checkout-stand employees, waitresses, fruit pickers and packers. There is a friendliness lacking on the West Side, which seems cold and secretive in comparison. I am very much a part of it, I know. At first I was broadly tolerated here, an evident foreigner, but now I've been accepted by degrees.

"Wondered if you'd be back for another season," I'm greeted each fall. "Just try and keep me away," I respond. Soon my first name is included in the greeting. With each passing year my list of friends grows.

Everywhere I am met with apples. They form the pride of the place, comprise its copious commodity. And provide such waste. Much fruit falls to the ground early. There it feeds the field mice, which in turn attract the coyotes. Elk, bear, and a cougar or two often show up. When the pears on the ground ferment, the bears begin to reel around in the orchards, or so I am told.

The big Alar scare is over and red-apple prices are now subject solely to market conditions. Recently there have been record years, which drag prices down. If it isn't one thing it is another. Orchardists grumble that their crop isn't worth harvesting, the price is so low. But they love their trees and will bring in the crop even if it means at a loss. Overhead I hear helicopters beating their blades on noisy sweeps to spray a dubious chemical called No-Drop. It supposedly enables fruit to cling to the bough long enough to redden handsomely and appeal to people who may still be afraid to buy it. A crazy economics is at work here, where Meryl Streep remains a dirty word.

Trees unburden themselves to the ground because the rain washes away No-Drop or a wind comes up just before picking. Fruit on the ground is lost money. This year these fallen apples aren't worth a trip to the juicer. I, a fisher, with nothing of the farmer in my bones, wonder why an apple tree doesn't die when it's done bearing, like a salmon does? But it is such a silly question, from so different a world, that I dare not speak my thoughts.

There are salmon in the river as well as steelhead—the famed upriver bright chinooks. But they are darkening fast as spawning spots them with white fungus, the sign of impending death. Evenings they boom in the same pools I fish for steelhead. They attract snaggers—sly, nefarious men with treble hooks and stout spinning gear. Chinooks are so powerful that hooked anywhere except in the mouth they will break free and take part of the fisher's tackle with them. It is illegal to fish for salmon or to molest them, and nobody but a fool would try to eat such a fish, but the attraction is irresistible to the immature. Snagging is the sport of the morally destitute.

I was a long time coming to fish this fine river. Bob Strobel first alerted me to its prospects. "Why aren't you on the Wenatchee?" he would ask me every fall, while I flogged my home river, which was shy of steelhead. Doggedly I stuck it out. Others asked me what was wrong—didn't I know a good deal when I was told of one? Merlin Stidham generously drew me a map of the best pools. Still I held off. Tom Crawford told me about his exceptional luck, and offered to drive me over and put me on the best water. No thanks. If I tired of the North Fork I had the Ronde to console me, didn't I?

The first pool I fished on the Wenatchee was the Orchard Drift. (That's not its real name, but if you know the river even a little you will recognize it.) Merlin gave it to me as a gift. It lies near the hamlet of Monitor. To reach it you take a pleasant stroll between rows of golden delicious trees, while dodging sprinklers that try to soak you in their arcs.

Two anglers were already in the water, casting lines. I should have paid attention to the car parked on the orchard's edge, as I've since learned to do. The men looked familiar. They were Bob Aid and Alec Jackson from Seattle. I called out a greeting to the nearest one, Bob. Alec, who I knew better, was so intent on his fishing that he was unapproachable.

"Who told you about this pool?" I sputtered.

"Who told *you*?" Bob replied. "We've fished it for years. Where have you been?"

It was a good question. "Merlin told me," I said quietly.

"It figures," said Bob.

Merlin was famous for his generosity with information that others routinely kept secret. I asked Bob, as I prepared to leave, "Tell me about some good water nearby. I've only got an hour to kill before I must move on to the Ronde."

"Why go to the Ronde? Lots of fish here."

"I've made plans," I said vaguely, for the Ronde was uppermost in my mind. I was booked into a motel that night and had given them my charge-card number to pay for it.

Bob directed me to the upper Monitor bridge, where he'd caught fish before. So had Merlin, I remembered. It was in plain sight just upstream. I waved goodbye. Later I learned they had been hooking fish all afternoon. It was a good year, one of Wenatchee's best, but I only managed to catch a 14-inch rainbow—the darkest trout I had ever seen—before driving on to Clarkston. The Ronde proved a disappointment. My favorite pools were clogged with people whipping flies through the air. Meanwhile the Wenatchee's many unoccupied pools were carving a niche in my mind. Home again, I could see the two runs at Monitor and the unfished Orchard Drift.

A year passed. I returned to the Ronde again by way of Cashmere. It was a scorching day and I did not linger. As I wound my way out of town my route took me past the fruit-packers, the sawmill, the entrance to the fair grounds, the Chevron Station at the intersection up from the blinking light, where you were given a free right turn but everybody else had to stop. They formed an unmistakable tableau, one that has remained with me.

Cashmere is a small town literally dying for new business. Many storefronts have the look of desperately seeking tenants who will stay more than a year. Yet the town has a particular appeal. I can't explain it. Perhaps everybody needs a small town to haunt his life.

Sam loves Cashmere. He has a separate doggy life. New sights and smells and dogs occupy his mind. He gets all worked up as we reach the outskirts, and begins to fidget and bark. By the time we reach the river he is wild with expectation. When I release him from the car he's off on a half-mile sprint of sheer exuberance. He races off down the dusty road, then reverses his course at the end of his trajectory and runs the full distance back, his tongue lolling crazily, his hips a little off kilter, the way male Labs do. He stands panting happily, goofily, waiting for me to get suited up. Much more dignified, I contain my enthusiasm as I pull on my waders and mislace my boots. If I find the Orchard Drift unoccupied I am ecstatic. But if there are fishers in it I will sigh and go away and perhaps come back later. Often it gives me a fish then.

Sam's and my first overnight trip was a disaster. We were new to each other and to the river. We camped out. I slept in a puptent, while the pup got the back of the stationwagon, where it is warmer. It was a brisk October night. The temperature quickly plunged below freezing. I lay on an overinflated air mattress—which is a mound—unable to sleep. I opened my eyes to a thick hoar frost that looked like a brush of snow. Finally I pulled on my stiff clothes and shoes that were half-frozen. It was very early.

Going fishing, I reasoned, might make me a little warmer. I made a quick pass through the closest pool. Nothing, and I was just as cold. I drove to the nearest restaurant and ordered a huge breakfast. It made me queasy and I couldn't finish it. I checked us into a motel and took a quick nap. By evening I felt well enough restored to put on my waders, but caught nothing.

The next day I took my first Wenatchee River steelhead. A typical dark male, it fought like a pile of leaves and skidded to the beach early. I released it with disdain. Sam and I returned to Seattle, less than enthused about the river. Fresh snow in the passes made it easy not to return for the last days of the put-back season.

The camping-out experience had gotten us off to a poor start, yet the Wenatchee had an uncanny hold on me. That winter I bought a tent trailer. It was more with the Sauk in mind than the Wenatchee. I took it on its maiden voyage to the Skagit at Rockport, one day in raw March. That night I slept like granite. I grew comfortable with it in all kinds of weather. Sam's homey bed was the passenger seat of the stationwagon. We had good fishing.

When fall arrived I looked for a place to camp near the Wenatchee. I wanted to be as close to the river as it was physically possible to be without drowning. Everybody had a clever way of saying no to me. The public campground was out because dogs had to be restrained and this was no way to treat a young Lab. So I drove to a pool that I thought was on State land and boldly set up my trailer a few yards away from the river. The land belonged to the Cashmere Gun Club. The president drove up the next day and ordered me off with an angry wave of his hand. Disheartened I almost gave up on the Wenatchee. If it didn't want me I didn't want it.

Orchardist Lawrence Peterson came to my rescue. He owned the land next to the gun club and had donated a long strip of it to the Department of Wildlife for a public access. No camping was allowed. However Lawrence said I could set up my trailer for the night at the edge of his pear orchard. I thanked him profusely. Here was a man not inhospitable to fishers from the West Side. Later I learned that he was a professional wildlife biologist who had gone into the family pear and apple business after World War II. He understood the problems of fishermen and hunters and their need for access to the public resource. Maybe Cashmere and its people weren't so bad.

"Haul your rig over here," he told me, pointing to an area next to some trees that had already given up their pears. "It'll be dry, for I'm done sprinkling for the year."

Lawrence cocked his head and grinned at me in the winning way he has. We soon became friends. Too busy at the harvest time to fish himself he took an insider's interest in my luck. He liked to hear that his guest had caught a fish. I tried to oblige. His many kindnesses, and those of his son, Larry, largely determined how I was to think of the river and its environs in the future.

In response I developed an openness unusual for me and began to encounter friendliness all over Cashmere. Why couldn't the whole world be like this? I camped alongside Lawrence's pear trees for the remainder of the season. The following year he suggested I set up my camp across from the hired man's house, a hundred feet closer to the river. A stone's throw away was the Wildlife Department's public-access pit toilet and the fisherman's trail that led down to the river. What could be handier? I found myself only a stroll away from an exceptional pool.

All night long I could hear the river's purl without straining my ears. It was wonderfully soothing and conducive to sleep. And Lawrence's pear trees provided a shady retreat in the heat of the day. If that wasn't cool enough I could duck down to the river for a quick dip. I even got used to the roar of the Burlington Northern freight train that broke the silence of the night with its shuddering approach and shook the ground and made Sam growl a warning. Then I briefly returned to consciousness, smiled into the darkness, and drifted back to sleep, for I had worked for the railroad during college and loved trains. Hearing the long wail ahead I knew the locomotive had slowed for Cashmere crossing, after which it would regain speed. A couple of years later BN replaced the rails and put down a new bed of crushed rock for the crossties. Crossings are quieter now and not so romantic.

After that first poorly performing steelhead I caught more of the same and began to think all the Wenatchee fish were dogs. None went more than a few yards into the backing, not even the 13-pound male that was my top fish for the year. Still, I never thought of abandoning the river and going elsewhere in the fall. Sam and I loved the look and feel of the place, and had made friends. His was Larry's young Lab-Weimaraner mix, a yellow female named Tug. She and Sam had grown inseparable.

I'd heard stories about Wenatchee River "smokers"—fish that burned your reel bearings and left you with blisters on your fingertips—but I chalked them up to the hyperactive imaginations of fishers who had not caught many steelhead. Then I hooked one myself—a fish that hit like a rocket and was into the backing in seconds. It jumped and jumped, each time clearing the water fully and falling back in a shower of spray. This was a fish every bit as good as one from the West Side.

It takes years to get to know a river well and its pools. It is pleasant knowledge to gather. Good fishable water can be found from the U.S. Highway 2 bridge at Wenatchee, where the Columbia lies in plain sight, up to and past Leavenworth, 20 miles to the West. This is not far as rivers go, but almost all is prime water and holds fish throughout the fall and winter. Steelhead lie in the easy reaches for a short time before proceeding upstream into less accessible areas. Because it is a big river, the fish have much protection. There are many places a fisher can't wade to or cover with a long cast. Unfortunately boat fishing reduces the sanctuary water necessary for wild fish. Eventually limits may have to be placed on the number of boats permitted, if they continue to proliferate.

Most flyfishers reach their pools by car and walk a short distance to a wadable stretch. The river is nicely fished this way. If you start at Dryden and walk upstream from behind the fruit packers' warehouse you will find a series of gorgeous pools that are seldom touched. People believe it is private water, which it is not. And there are good runs alongside the highway between Dryden and Cashmere, most of them in sight of a passing car. If it looks good it probably is. Trucks often honk a greeting when they see a fisher; it means they are fishers themselves. I always wave back.

There are many fine pools in this stretch and all are worthy of investigation. Put your fly where the water deepens and slows, but don't forget to cover the riffles, too. Access is often complicated, so most fishers drive by while heading for water that is easier to reach. It is worth the effort to get to know the dirt backroads that wind off through pretty orchards along the river. Generally farmers are friendly and the sight of a man in waders gives them a chance to stop work for a moment and chat with a stranger. Always ask permission to trespass. It is usually cheerfully given.

As the month of October wears on there are signs that winter is near. Rain arrives sparsely and the river begins its annual temperature drop into the mid-40s. Nights grow nippy. The season is ending, the easy fishing about over. To me it seems the year ends when October does and a new one begins in November. It is a natural division that falls between seasons both here and at home. A feeling of completeness hangs in the air. There is snow in the mountains. It is time to break camp and head for Seattle. There is work waiting to be done and the pressing obligation mounts.

As I write these words another October has come round. I am back in the city, working instead of fishing, for the crowded weekend has arrived. Cashmere vistas continue to invade my consciousness and I don't want them. I have a razor-sharp memory for the details, besides. Everything is as I left it, I'm certain; I'm seeing Cashmere as it exists at the very moment, though I am more than a 100 miles away, bent over my word processor, working on a book—this one. It is weird, but I'm getting used to such visions.

In my mind I drive out of Cashmere and head West. I take the Turkey Shoot Road turnoff, with its quick narrow plunge, its sharp jog to the right, its straight drop after Duncan's farm. A black steer crops grass on a short tether. Now the road branches to the right, just past the railroad tracks. I see the dust cloud from the previous car and the standing puddle from last week's rain, barely a shower. It is held in a dry basin. Off to the side is the big rock on which Bill Lombard busted a tire, driving out in the dark in his big Bronco.

Lawrence's pears take dominion here and occupy both sides of the road. They are mostly d'Anjous, with some Asians mixed in, down by the river. His are the healthiest, most abundant pears around for miles—just ask anyone. They're the envy of the other orchardists. Ahead I see where I camped beside my car, that terrible night, years ago. What a long way I've come, thanks to the generosity of my new friends.

I reach the public-access parking lot. My pulse quickens. Each year this pool gives me fish. No other run on this or any other river has been so consistently kind to its visitor from the West. I shall never forget the sight of a 13-pound male—taking all the time in his wet world—coming to the surface for my dry fly. But there is a better memory—one of a smaller fish at the end of a difficult day and season.

Once in the fall I lost four fish in a row while fishing downstream; I lost them every which way you can. Yet I had done nothing explicitly wrong. I hadn't broken a leader on any. I returned to camp at twilight, raging with frustration. I decided to make one last pass through the home pool. I did not want the season to end on such a sour note.

As the light faded I hurled one desperate cast after another into a black river. I reached the bottom of the run where a clutch of rocks stood seventy feet out in the current. Suddenly my rod tip went down and a fish leaped. My reel began running hard. Back and forth the battle went. I fought the fish on a long line until the last light fled from the sky and overhead emerged the full darkness brought on only by a clear sky. The fish would not give up and neither would I. A Wenatchee River smoker—it seemed impossible to land and now there was this enveloping darkness.

Then a wondrous thing happened. The sky brightened. A great golden moon tipped out from behind a hogbacked hill. The sky flooded with thin amber light. It increased until I could see the tops of every rock at the tailout. The river turned silver and black, oily looking. I gained a bit of line on the fish, then lost it as the fish ran away with the current again. It refused to be conquered, but was tiring. The length of line in the water grew short and I saw the fish's dorsal fin weaving toward me, 40 feet out. Its back became visible. The moon rose higher and its light turned toward the white end of the spectrum. As the fish snaked in through the dark rocks, each one became a mountain top. The fish hesitated, then went over on its side, helpless. I had won. A female of about nine pounds, I slipped the hook from her lip and righted her. Holding Sam off with one hand, I watched her swim into the inkblot depths where the river devoured her.

The episode happened years ago. At my computer now the river and the fish remain as sharp and distinct as they were that magical night. I watch as the beaten fish cruises off, then submerges. I return to camp—only a few yards off—and do a little victory dance in my heavy waders. The moon beams down in a cone of golden light. It is Halloween, the moon a pumpkin. Tonight I will sleep the sleep of the victorious. Forgotten are those four lost fish and my near despair. In the morning I will crank down the tent trailer, hitch up, and drive home—probably through a snowstorm at the top of the pass.

And there it ends, this book about rivers and one in particular, the North Fork. All rivers are one. They flow through a single mind (ours, collectively) and merge into the universal flow of men and ideas. Rivers and men are much alike. And we fishers do not differ so much from each other as we think we do, for our quarrels are generally over small things. We are in close agreement about the basic facts. A river is central to our lives—whatever its name, wherever it runs. Our fisher bodies beat with the same heart. We share the pain and exaltation. We hate to lose the battle, but we love our quarry and don't want to see it die or become extinct. We want to save the wild fish, but don't exactly know how. This leaves us feeling helpless and angry, for we know the loss is imminent. We recognize doom on the horizon. This is why we are chronically glum and bad company.

It's crazy, this fishing, and what it does to your soul. For instance, I've been camped on the Sauk and watched the Wenatchee rise up in full splendor across the screen of my mind. I can't explain it aside from saying that it's involuntary and fierce. I've stood in the Ronde and had a waking vision of where White Creek merges its flow with the Sauk in a sharp little riff. Each submerged rock and swirl is exactly where it belongs, so I recognize that it is real. I know it by heart and by head.

And now as October ends there is one less month to go in my life. As I leave Merlin's Pool, my legs are stiff from cold, my bad knee aching so badly it barely supports me. It is a recurring affliction, though not a serious one, and in an hour the swelling will be down, the pain nearly gone. Then I will stop walking like a turtle.

My mind is elsewhere, as it usually is. Where am I now? It's August and I'm fishing the Elbow Hole again. It's dry-fly time. The little Deer Creek steelhead are in the river still, not on the edge of extinction. Where else should they be at this time of the year except in the riffles and pockets below the mouth of Deer Creek? I'm fishing classic style, that is, dead-drift floating fly. It links me with the significant past.

Around noon I hook a fish, but lose it on the strike. There are two hours left in the day, in the summer season. If I fish hard enough, make no serious mistakes, I might get one solid take before nightfall. So I bend to the task. It is the most meaningful activity I know with which to occupy an evening, given an hour or so to spend.

Epitaph: Deer Creek Revisited

THE CLOSURE OF DEER CREEK and the restriction of the North Fork to flyfishing only worked well as a conservation measure for a few decades. In the early '60s a handful of us grew fearful for the future of the wild summer runs while observing with alarm the increased logging activity. The first sign was periodic discoloration of the creek and river at times when they used to run clear. Friends from British Columbia had seen their streams near Vancouver deteriorate and lose their summer-run populations; they urged us to release *all* our fish. They were fishing our rivers now because they had lost the fish in theirs.

The chance of our steelhead disappearing through over-harvest or habitat loss seemed remote. Fishing remained good. The reality was a decade or two away. Oh, one year we might have a weak run, but the next generally made up for it. And in some years there was an abundance of bright little fish. We took their return for granted.

Though the North Fork had been discolored most of the year, as a result of a large clay slide half a dozen miles upstream, the fish had accommodated to the dirty water. It was not serious, we believed. Steelhead spent most of their time in Deer Creek and it ran clear even after a hard rain. When it took on color it lost it in a matter of hours—sometimes even while we watched. And the creek's water helped clear the river by diluting the clay from upstream. The creek was pristine and the only "mud" we saw was a few grains of sand in suspension.

The creek was crossed by a railroad bridge just above Highway 530 at Oso. Below it lay a deep pool into which we used to dive, either from the bridge (for the young and the bold) or off the riprap (for those less intrepid). The pool held a trillion steelhead parr that thrived because they couldn't be fished for. And sometimes we spotted slender adults gently finning among the boulders just downstream. The steelhead behaved as though they knew there was no longer any threat to them, at least not from men with rods and flies.

Then the creek began to take longer to clear after a rain and it needn't be a hard rain, either. It quickly took on the peaty color of steeped tea. Logging was the chief economic activity of the region, but logging had been conducted since the turn of the century and had caused no real damage. Roderick Haig-Brown had been a logger here, and he wouldn't do a river any harm, would he? Often the creek turned as gray as a battleship. It was from clay slides the rain caused to reactivate. There was much stratified blue clay in the Stillaguamish basin; up on Deer Creek the gradient was steeper, the effects more pronounced. Still dirty water seemed only the seasonal norm and we were used to catching steelhead in it on brightly colored flies and (in winter) on daylight-fluorescent lures. So we did not panic, not at first.

But conditions did not improve. They worsened. In winter the creek stayed muddy, even after a week of cold nights, and we lost whole weekends—sometimes longer—awaiting the next fishing opportunity. In summer we brought our drinking water in jugs from the city. The swimming hole had grown shallow, clogged with silt; boys no longer dove off the railroad bridge. If they did they would have stuck in the muck like so many flung spears. Even in mid-summer people shunned the creek and began swimming in the river. Who wanted to wallow in a mudhole?

On the heels of a winter flood great piles of logging debris choked the main channel of the North Fork. The creek was filled with the same woody waste. Between the two it looked like a catastrophic event had taken place. What could have happened? All winter long the river ran slate-colored. Its pool-riffle configuration had disappeared.

Because I—as a fisher—kept a close watch on the river and always had my weather eye out for changes, I was among the first to realize the seriousness of the situation. My favorite fishing hole was the Flat Water just a couple of hundred yards down from the mouth of the creek. To fish it I parked by the Oso Schoolhouse and walked down to the property of my friend, Ken McLeod, and slipped into the water off his low bank. There, even when the water was so dirty I couldn't see bottom in a foot of water, I would wade out and make a few futile casts before I turned for home.

I discovered a big change to the river bottom. It was filled with sand and gravel where in the past it was rocky and difficult to wade. I could walk anywhere I chose now, for beneath the quickened surface was a path of coarse gravel. Now pea gravel is coarser than sand, but it comes from the same source. I determined that a slide of some consequence had occurred. But where? I needed to consult the authorities—but whom?

I racked my mind. A year earlier I had attended a conservation committee meeting of the Federation of Fly Fishers. A friend, John Farrar, chaired it and expressly invited me because of my long association with Deer Creek and the North Fork. The program included a presentation by a fish biologist from the Forest Service, Jim Doyle. His subject was the deterioration of Deer Creek.

Doyle was a wiry, fair-headed man of early middle age. He reminded me of Dennis Day on the old Jack Benny Show and at any moment I expected him to break out in lilting Irish tenor. Instead he proved dead-serious about the matter at hand. He showed us slide after slide documenting the logging destruction of the upper Deer Creek watershed. The amount of clearcutting and the volume of post-logging debris left behind were awesome. Not a tree was left standing for as far as the eye could range. Dead wood covered the ground. The groundcover had returned in a few places, but was advancing glacially because of the altitude.

We sat in shocked dismay. Finally the slides stopped coming and the lights went up. Doyle began answering our questions. I asked most of them. Some he didn't know the answers to and said he would find out. He was just beginning his study. He had reached no conclusions, for he was still in the fact-gathering stage. When he was done I introduced myself. I told him of my concern. He was friendly, accessible. We exchanged phone numbers. I had to admire him. He was the kind of guy who spent all of his working hours in the woods, by lakes and rivers, then on weekends returned to the same locations with his young family to backpack and camp.

If Doyle was alarmed, then I was, too, but I hadn't yet grasped the enormity of the problem. I thought it was temporary, short-lived. We talked occasionally on the phone and offered each other a sympathetic ear. We added to each other's river knowledge.

As a result of knowing Doyle I was invited to a Forest Service workshop held at the Mount Baker district headquarters in Sedro Woolley the following January. This was 1983. Again the topic was Deer Creek and Doyle showed the same slides to a different audience. In the group I saw Ken McLeod's son, George. He was an expert fisher whose roots on the North Fork went back farther than mine. We had independently planned to fish the Flat Water after the meeting, as we often did. We waved recognition and exchanged looks of befuddled amazement.

I knew practically none of the other people in the room. Many were from agencies. Later I learned there were fisheries biologists and Indians from the Tulalip and Stillaguamish tribes present; they were the ones who arrived an hour and a half late and missed Doyle's presentation. Some of the somber faces belonged to timber managers from Georgia Pacific, Scott Paper, and the State Department of Natural Resources. There were also Snohomish and Skagit County people in attendance, plus ones from federal agencies and the two area biologists from the Departments of Game and Fisheries, both of whom I recognized.

The day belonged to Doyle, however, and his message of habitat loss. Deer Creek was in sad shape, he said. Logging had left the upper watershed in critical condition. Just as bad was the sloughing from road-building for hauling out logs. This was Forest Service land. Doyle was risking his career by pointing with an angry finger at his bosses. It was a brave feat.

When the meeting broke up George and I separately headed for our favorite fishing holes just below the mouth of Deer Creek. In spite of the cold snap the river ran muddy and there was no fishing to be found. It was how it was going to be in the future. But now we had an idea of the nature of the problem. We turned upstream to fish other reaches where the river still ran clear. At least we had these left. And we found fish there most of the winter.

The following year, 1984, the situation worsened. Creek and river became a vast wasteland. Both ran shallow and wide. The North Fork was clogged with logging debris, and the woody piles caused the channel to braid and form shallow branches of dirty water that extended over the landscape like greedy fingers. Something more had happened, something worse. I contacted the Forest Service—because they seemed to care more than anybody else. I described the situation to them and asked if they would assess the problem. I did this in the form of a letter to the district ranger, Bernie Smith, who had seemed a likeable, knowledgeable man at the earlier meeting. "Help," I said, or words to that effect.

The ranger sent his deputy, Al Zander, to meet me at the mouth of the creek. Zander, like Doyle, was a dedicated professional, a man who often found himself in a difficult situation. His advanced degree was in hydrology, but he had a working knowledge of fish biology and knew intimately how timber-harvest was conducted. He was slender, but muscular, without an ounce of fat. His wire-rimmed glasses gave a military cast to his somber countenance and for a time I thought of him as a career non-commissioned officer, one with expertise in a field shared with not many others, such as ordnance. He smiled seldom and when he did it seemed a major event, his voice so soft-spoken that I and others leaned forward in order not to miss a word. He wasted none. Besides asking the Forest Service to send a representative I asked the two tribes to come—remembering them from Sedro Woolley and knowing that they were sovereign entities with legal rights in land matters—but they didn't show.

Zander drove across the bridge at Oso to meet me at the General Store. He immediately saw that something serious was wrong. A healthy stream isn't milky nor does it have a channel drowned with trees. It doesn't have a broad flood plain where normally it is narrow and well defined. A healthy creek rises and falls, colors and clears; it doesn't drop slash at every turning or each time it slows. Zander said he was sure a major problem lay far upstream. But in winter, with continual rain and snow, people rarely went into remote areas. He would, however, and check it out. Then he would let me know what he found.

The next day he took a four-wheeled vehicle into the upper watershed. The searching process was much like trying to locate a short in an electrical circuit: first you check at various random points high and low in the circuitry (or in the watershed), looking for clear water, then for dirty, until you come to the point where one reach is dirty, the next one clean. Thus you home in on the area where the problem is. Finally you get out of your vehicle and search on foot until you find the source.

Zander knew the area well and its maze of logging roads that start and stop, then sometimes dwindle off into game trails. It didn't take him long to find the source. In back of his mind was the fear that a bad slide had occurred on Forest Service land. This wasn't so. The slide was on State land and it was a bad one. The fact that the Forest Service wasn't responsible came as a relief to Zander. Even when it became clear that his agency was not to blame he maintained his interest in the problem and was a key player in trying to find a workable solution.

A "mass-wasting event" had taken place about 12 miles above Oso. That's a fancy word for a big mud slide. It was in the vicinity of DeForest Creek's entry into Deer Creek. DeForest Creek was tiny, practically disappearing in summer. It entered Deer Creek about a mile upstream from the principal tributary, Little Deer Creek. An additional water source trickled through an unstable area nearby, then poured its flow of mud and clay into DeForest Creek. In winter, especially during times of snow runoff, both flows became heavy. Whenever hard rains fell, creek and creeklet ran at torrent strength. They swept muck and jackstrawed trees into Deer Creek. At first the stuff was mainly slash, the waste from ancient logging, but it was only a matter of time until green trees toppled over and were washed in, too, as the walls of the slide collapsed, time and again.

The area had been logged by the State many years ago. One part had been clearcut about 13 years previously, the other about 20 years ago. I read up on the process of mass-wasting. Swanson and Swanson is a good source. Thirteen to 20 years is about the length of time it takes the root masses of downed Douglas firs to rot away. When the network of fibers is gone there's nothing left to bind in the soil. It is then subject to erosion on a grand scale, if the conditions are right—unstable soils, steep terrain, hard rains, melting snow, and, the worst, the infamous "rain-on-snow event." Any and all can trigger a serious slide. Deer Creek experienced each of these many times each winter. The blue clay and unstable-when-disturbed soils endemic to the region made the creek susceptible to the erosion events that follow in the wake of logging.

Originally I thought that all that was involved was periodic dirty water that ruined my day's fishing. I didn't realize that what was at stake was Deer Creek's wild summer steelhead and its coho salmon. If the slide got too bad it would endanger all the salmonids in the Stillaguamish basin. The impact would reach all the way to its mouth, 35 miles to the West.

Zander said he would inform the DNR of the problem. Not being on Forest Service land he could do nothing about the slide. Somebody else must point out its severity—somebody personally concerned. That meant me, I gathered, since the agencies were pledged to stay off of each other's turf. Me, also, because nobody else knew enough about the slide at this point to stress its urgency.

Frankly I didn't want the job. I wasn't the public-spirited type. But before I begged off I gave Doyle a call. He was not surprised at what Zander had uncovered. He had expected the worst in a watershed so ravaged. But he was powerless to act for the same reason Zander was; it wasn't a Forest Service matter. He would help me, however; Deer Creek was our common concern. His many transparencies on Deer Creek were available to me to help others visualize the problem. Maybe he could get up to the slide and take some fresh pictures, in spite of the snow. If people understood the nature of the problem they might get involved in seeking a solution. It was worth a try.

So he took his pictures, showed me the results, and I scheduled a public meeting to present his findings to whomever was interested. I didn't know who these people might be. The populace of Oso, surely, and maybe some anxious flyfishers. The meeting was to be held at the Oso fire station, 10 days hence. This was early April. I had been a nonparticipating member of the Federation of Fly Fishers for a long time, so I used their name as co-sponsors of the event. The Forest Service (that is, Doyle) was the other one. Whoever the FFF turned out to be — I knew none of them—they couldn't put me in jail for misusing their name, now could they? I mean, we had a common matter of concern.

I sent announcements to the press, TV stations, Indian tribes, agencies, and fishing groups. I hung posters on the walls of the four general stores that stretched between Arlington and Darrington. And I made a lot of phone calls to people I didn't know but hoped would be interested in attending. I had no way of knowing if they would show up. Doyle and I might have to spend an evening in just each other's company. I could imagine a worst fate.

The meeting was on a Monday night at seven. It was pouring. By 10 minutes after seven 125 people had jammed the fire hall. The big room grew hot and damp as people entered and shed wet coats. A lot of the faces were familiar. Most of the locals came—perhaps for lack of any other entertainment. Some I recognized as fishers from the Seattle and Everett areas. There were agency people I now knew and many faces unfamiliar to me. People from the tribes had come and so had the press. I spotted a TV crew. It was more than Doyle and I had hoped for.

I made a few nervous opening remarks and introduced my partner. The lights went down and slides already familiar to me began flickering across the screen. An angry murmur filled the room as the destruction revealed itself—acres and acres of barren ground and sun-whitened slash. And this was just the old stuff. Doyle showed his new material on DeForest Creek and some shots Zander had taken only a week ago. The area looked like the aftermath of a volcano. Mud flowed like lava. The group became angrier, noisier. People shouted out words of rage. Who was responsible for this travesty? The lights came up, the show was over. And it was at this point that Doyle and I realized we had lost control of the group. What we had before us was an angry mob.

But wasn't this precisely what we had hope for when we scheduled a public meeting? Secretly? We *wanted* people to get mad. Out of their anger might come a plan for action. In fact it might arise tonight, out of the group dynamic. But it didn't work out this way. What we did was make them angry, without giving them a recourse for action. It was probably a mistake.

I remember Steve Raymond and Walt Johnson in the audience. And Ken and George McLeod. The Pederson clan. Nearly the entire Evergreen Fly Fishing Club. With Raymond was a young, dark-haired man I had never seen before. He was Dave Round, president of the Washington Council of the FFF. Not a steelheader, he had ridden up with Steve on this wet night out of curiosity. Who was using the FFF's name so freely? As president hadn't he ought to know the person? (Later Dave and I got to be friends, and he and the FFF were key supporters of our early efforts to save Deer Creek.)

Fishermen demanded to know who in the room was responsible for the slide. I too was interested and looked around for a person from the DNR to identify himself. A tall, slender man with a quick demeanor held up his hand and frantically identified himself as Jack Hulsey, assistant area manager for the agency. He was gaunt, angular, and looked a little like a wolf at bay. Clearly he didn't like the position we had put him in—or the people who had put him there. In a deep, bass voice he announced that he'd "look into the matter" and "report back." How he was to do this, and whom he would report to, were left up in the air. He was anxious for the evening to end and frankly so was I. I told the group and Hulsey that I would follow up on it. (Afterwards Hulsey told me that the Oso meeting was just about the worst moment in his life. He felt like he was being lynched. This was nowhere near the case, however.)

The fishermen wanted a quick fix and so did I. Nobody had any idea of the slide's magnitude. We thought that maybe a Cat and some men with shovels would take care of it. George McLeod urged that it be "cemented over." The projection transparencies lacked a sense of proportion. We had heard the slide described as big, but big was a relative word. How big is big? We were about to learn.

As we were dispersing Dave Round came over and introduced himself. He told me to keep up the good work; he and the FFF would back me up. It was just what I needed to hear. I had no intention of going away at this point, but it was great to have the moral support of an organization with some clout. So I scheduled a meeting of the agencies, tribes, and the FFF (myself now) two weeks hence. That would give the DNR time to study the problem and come up with a recommendation. Of course I had badly underestimated how long it takes an agency to do anything—even something that seemed to me so simple.

I remembered how the two tribes had come distressingly late to the Forest Service meeting a year ago and how they hadn't showed up for my field trip with Zander to the mouth of the creek. So I developed a strategy to guarantee their attendance. I called Terry Martin, the head fish biologist for the Stillaguamish Tribe and a man with whom I had spent many an hour talking over fish problems, and asked him if we could hold the meeting at tribal headquarters just off Interstate-5, which would be handy for everybody. He agreed. So now one of the tribes would be there, for certain. The tribes were important, for they were a political entity with legal authority in land and water matters. As it turned out I needn't have worried, for their fisheries director—an Indian, Gary Tetro—was present and the Tulalips, who were highly organized and influential, sent several representatives.

In fact everybody came; I learned the one thing that all budding environmentalists discover: If you call a meeting the agency people will come—they dare not. Something might be decided that would work against their agency's best interests. Besides, what do they do all day long but attend meetings? It's the nature of the job.

I chaired the meeting, since I had called it. It was a heady experience. What power I had achieved overnight—me, a mere fisherman. Zander introduced me to his boss, not knowing I had already met him in Sedro Woolley a year ago. This was the Forest Service's district ranger, Bernie Smith. There were a couple of other Forest Service personnel present and of course good old Doyle. The DNR sent many people, including their environmental specialist, Noel Wolfe, who was a field geologist. Jack Hulsey was there, of course. And I recognized the pair of fish biologists from Game and Fisheries. One was Curt Kraemer.

We sat in a ring and introduced ourselves clockwise, as people now do at meetings everywhere. Hulsey, looking a little more relaxed than on that rainy night in Oso, was prepared for our questions. He had his answers ready. They pretty much put him in charge. My power base quickly eroded and I prudently turned the meeting over to him.

The DNR was anxious to solve this problem in-house, he said. I gathered that knowledge of a slide of such magnitude, one that had to be pointed out to them by their arch rival, the Forest Service, was an embarrassment. They too were in the logging business and knew a thing or two. They had a mandate from the State Legislature to log their lands hard and obtain maximum revenue for the common-school construction fund. But a set of forest practices rules and regulations governed how they (and the private timber companies) were to do it. Cut, yes, but they weren't supposed to lay waste the land in the process.

The DNR would assign a study team of staff professionals—geologists, hydrologists, engineers, etc.—to the slide. They would give us a report on what they found. And they would tell us what they intended to do about it. Hulsey stopped talking, signifying that the meeting was over, the matter closed. Wait, I said. When might we expect to see the report? June 15, he replied. Good enough, I said.

The report was completed and reviewed internally and issued to the public at the start of August; the short summer work season was two-thirds over. But the DNR surprised me. They had gone right to work repairing the slide while the report was in preparation. They constructed a series of holding ponds and ran the muck into them, where it settled and the water evaporated under a hot summer sun. (When I went up there to check, it looked like fudge icing.) Then they diverted DeForest Creek back into its original channel so that it ran clear again and did not mix with the thin line of slurry.

I visited the site several times. It was a long drive over rough roads. DeForest Creek at mid-summer was barely a trickle. The rivulet of slurry had shrunk, too. It was but a yard across and ran paper-thin. The ambient groundwater feeding it had nearly dried up. I thought the slurry creek needed a name. "Hulsey Creek," I called it, with a grin.

The report was professionally done. As an engineering editor I knew a good one when I saw it, but I couldn't refrain from pointing out a few factual errors. For instance the DNR placed the slide's occurrence at the same time it was brought to their attention. This was self-serving and wrong. I had seen Forest Service aerial photos revealing its beginning two full years earlier. It was important to establish the correct time in case we went to court, I said. This was largely bluff, for the FFF had no money for attorney fees and was not known to sue anybody. What I was after was getting the slide fixed as soon as possible. If it required a legal threat I would provide one. I wanted clean water, my good fishing back.

It was not that easy. The slide was more active than we had imagined. And it was growing bigger daily. It was so alive, so susceptible to expansion, so determined to advance both North and West against its headwall, that efforts taken that summer and fall proved puny and futile. The acres of settling ponds slowly filled with muck. By fall they were full. Deer Creek and the North Fork downstream from the confluence cleared nicely, as the silt flowed into the ponds far upstream and was held there all summer long. The channel of the North Fork, however, remained clogged with logging waste, the substrate buried in silt, for there wasn't enough current to carry it away. Still we had good fishing for the remainder of the summer and the return of clear water gave the river the illusion of health.

Nobody who had seen the slide believed we had found a permanent solution. It was too big for a couple of shallow ponds to suck up all the slurry it could produce. In fact, the work was known to be of such a temporary nature that the two tribes, Trout Unlimited, FFF, and Washington Environmental Council called a joint meeting in the fall to seek a lasting solution. We feared what would happen when the rains arrived. The DNR said they had done all they could and had no money to pursue it further. We felt the public resource required more effort.

At the meeting we drafted a letter to the Land Commissioner, Brian Boyle, who headed the DNR, demanding he develop an action plan for the coming work season. It was an election year and he was up for re-election in a couple of months. He was in no position to refuse our request, not if he liked his job. So he appointed a second study team. It didn't seem to me to be the answer, but it is how agencies work and maybe the team would come up with a permanent fix. I was getting used to an agency's snail pace.

Late in October the DNR held a hurry-up meeting in Seattle. The Land Commissioner was worried about our letter and the public uproar. At his urging the DNR organized a work party to shore up the retaining ponds so they would last through winter. This seemed a good idea. But it required volunteer labor, since the DNR had no more money or staff to expend on the problem. The fishing and environmental community responded in numbers. The cooperation was excellent. The Department of Fisheries furnished steel gabion baskets and plastic sacks to hold sand, and labor was supplied by the tribes, fishermen, and environmental organizations. Work was scheduled for a Saturday and Sunday late in October, a time of historically bad weather.

Fresh snow brushed the hills on the Saturday of the two-day event and at a lower altitude it was raining; the second day it rained even harder and the snow line dropped. The work continued. It was a wet, slippery, unglamorous affair, but it was worthwhile, we believed. When it was over people washed each other off with big grins. A few days later a Chinook wind moved in from the East, the snow turned to rain, the downpour increased, the creek rose, and the holding ponds overflowed. The creek and the river filled with the summer's accumulation of muck. And the slide slumped further. Sloughing continued through the winter of 1984 and '85. We had no winter or spring fishing. The river ran continuous brown-gray. Its bottom was solid sand.

Many of us believed we would lick the slide the following year. We waited for the study team to call a public meeting to announce its findings. Time passed. Now that the Land Commissioner had been re-elected there seemed less urgency. I kept bugging them with letters and phone calls. Suddenly in June the DNR began soliciting *our* opinions. What should they do? They had no money, of course, but they were listening, they said. Last year's work had been financed from their fire-fighting fund and would have to be replaced through a special legislative appropriation; would we help them get more money? Well, sure; maybe. A new study team was appointed, this one inter-agency in nature but strictly State. Advisory representatives from the timber companies who had holdings near the slide were included. The Forest Service was not invited. Several plans emerged. They were in deep conflict. A promising one had been put forward by Georgia Pacific and the Forest Service. It would place a rock blanket and French drain at the neck of the slide and filter out the slurry. This was dismissed out of hand. We were not told why. (Perhaps it was NIH—Not Invented Here.) But at a public meeting called by the Land Commissioner the team leader—a man from the Department of Transportation—wouldn't personally endorse any of the proposed action plans, including the GP-FS one, so the DNR wouldn't either. It seemed an orchestrated response. The Land Commissioner wouldn't give his approval if his agency wouldn't support the plan. So we were stymied, stalled again. And the year's work season was well upon us.

The DNR couldn't stand idly by, though. Too many people were pressing them for action, especially the tribes, whose fishery was threatened. (Ours didn't matter so much to them.) The DNR turned to the private sector. They put out a request-for-bids on a contract for study and remedial work to several geotechnical engineering companies. The shortness of time enabled them to bypass the normal bidding process and award it to a company they had done business with before. This was Hart-Crowser. The company was paid a premium of $40,000 to meet the close deadline. The work to be performed (also by them) would cost $180,000 more. It entailed grading the slopes above the slide in order to reduce their steepness and to hasten the "angle of repose," as they put it. This was the point when the slide would stop disgorging material. Then a plug, or dam, was to be placed at the neck of the slide. Instead of using quarry rock, as both GP and the Forest Service had recommended, the company would use indigenous soils. I heard this with alarm.

I greatly preferred the GP-Forest Service plan and thought quarry rock was the only material that might hold up under heavy rain. I had a pretty good idea how far it would travel if the slide collapsed and another wall of slurry came roaring down. It was not far. The use of handy indigenous materials—sand and gravel, which comes trapped between layers of blue-clay—would produce a slithery mass that would be carried by flood waters the length of the creek and into the Stillaguamish River, I feared. It might end up in Puget Sound. It was the worst possible scenario. But I was no engineer and maybe I was wrong. Most of the group went along with the plan. Those of us with reservations agreed not to protest in public; it was our only chance of getting any work done this year. So we bit our tongues.

The labor began. It entailed bringing in huge D-8 Cats and restructuring the slopes of the slide. The amount of earth-moving that took place was comparable to the site preparation for a dam. The slopes were so steep that sometimes one Cat had to be lashed to another to pull it back up the side of the gully. As the work proceeded layers of sand, clay, and gravel became intermixed and lost their integrity or natural bonding quality. The earth grew loose and dangerous, its movement unpredictable. All day long now heavy equipment churned across the face of the slide as workers hurried against the advancing season and the prospect of rain. In the city we heard tales of great balls of slurry tumbling down the slopes and just missing workmen, who scurried out of the way just in time. It sounded like a nightmare movie. Once two men escaped by seconds being buried in a huge mud ball. The DNR became so worried that they halted the work for the year.

The rains came. The DNR decided not to attempt placing the dam and filter at the base of the slide, which were the key components of the design concept. All the early work was in preparation for it. A small gravel blanket was installed instead. It soon proved inadequate. The gabion structure and reinforced geotextile fill called for by the geotechnical engineers were never started. It was too late, too dangerous, the DNR said. The net result was that the area had been extensively graded, but nothing put into place that would hold back all the loose soil.

It began to rain in earnest, which was only normal. The engineering consultants, who had remained on the job to oversee completion of the work under a further contract, now gave it a 50/50 chance of holding through the winter. (Why hadn't they told us this earlier?) But even if the year's effort failed, they said, it would speed up the slide's "natural stabilization"—whatever that meant. It was the time when there was no more slide material to come down. The idea sounded hokey to me.

The stage was set for a debris torrent on an enormous scale. It wasn't long in coming and arrived at the most auspicious time. It was ironic, too. Upon completion of the year's work the Land Commissioner led the media and the most influential legislators on a field trip to view the slide and examine the product of the work effort. He was anxious to recover some of the DNR's large investment. His fire-fighting fund was depleted by his redirection of its moneys to the slide. The work was conspicuous and impressive. Photographers were invited to record the visible results and the grand political occasion.

That morning one of the DNR employees—driving a van full of visitors—remarked, as the vehicle pulled within first sight of Deer Creek, "Funny, but yesterday the crick ran clear. I wonder what has happened? There hasn't been enough rain to muddy it up like this." Yet the creek ran a rich brown. Here and there could be seen slash and newly uprooted trees—fresh because their leaves and needles were bright. When the caravan of vans reached the slide area the sight was one of fresh desolation. Raw earth and muck had tumbled into the creek. It was as if an atom bomb had been dropped.

Both slopes had collapsed. Blue clay, mixed with sand and gravel from the grading operation, had provided the perfect lubricant to transport the loose soil directly into Deer Creek. A dam had quickly formed, then blown out. The damage couldn't have been worse if it was planned. Several dead adult steelhead were found just upstream, off to the sides of the creek where the slurry had overcome their holding area. More were believed to be buried downstream, perhaps the bulk of the run.

An estimated 200,000 cubic yards of soil had entered Deer Creek, all at once. This was the equivalent of 20,000 10-yard dumptruck loads full. Previously about 2,500,000 cubic yards of muck had eased into the creek and drifted into the river downstream. This was equal in volume to a river of silt 100 miles long, 60 feet wide, and three feet deep. Since the start of the slide one million cubic yards had been deposited in the creek and river. As these numbers came to light we began to recognize the enormity of the slide and its long-term consequences.

Meanwhile the group that had met originally to draw public attention to the slide became organized and began to hold regular meetings—monthly at first and ultimately quarterly. Terry Williams, Fisheries Director of the Tulalip Tribes, was instrumental in getting it started and in obtaining financing for a part-time facilitator, Connie Miller. Money came from two participating timber companies, Scott and Georgia Pacific. Consequently, some of us felt that the group had a built-in bias.

We called ourselves the Deer Creek Policy Group and we had a counterpart organization made up of professionals with specific technical training; they were solely advisory to the policy people and protocols were severe. If technical people were to sit at the "big" table, they were instructed to keep their mouths shut except when requested to furnish technical-specific data that might lead to policy "decisions."

Only no decision was ever reached, not in years of meetings, for we operated under a consensus plan, then popular and having a basis in tribal government. If not everybody was in agreement on a given matter, no action could be taken. The most that could happen was that some landowner might take unilateral action on his own timberlands that might benefit the group as a whole. Except in one instance—an important one—this was wishful thinking.

Quickly we divided into three interest groups: agency people, environmentalists (including fishers), and timberland owners. Mostly we stood at deadlock. Marcy Golde, of the Washington Environmental Council, and Alec Jackson, a flyfisher with a background in forestry and the technical team member of the FFF team headed by myself, petitioned the USFS to halt logging in the Deer Creek watershed. Both Bernie Smith and his successor, Larry Hudson, district rangers at Sedro Woolley, had already such a plan under consideration. The timing was perfect for us. They said okay.

This was a monumental event. Since that day nearly ten years ago, the Forest Service has done penance for earlier ravaging of their large portion of the watershed by issuing a moratorium on cutting timber and conducting extensive annual road repairs adjacent to former cutting sites that had badly slumped and were pouring tons of clay and woody debris into the headwaters of Deer Creek.

Impressed with Marcy and Alec's victory of sorts, I tried a similar tactic with the DNR, but was nowhere near so lucky. We scheduled a series of meetings over one Christmas holiday and in each case I thought I would go into negotiations with a single member of the agency, Bill Wallace, who was assistant manager for the Northwest area. Each time I, alone, was met with a team; these varied from two to five. At one Wallace agreed to a tentative three-year halt in timber sales in all of Deer Creek. They would not agree to the use of the word moratorium.

Whatever timber sales had already been signed by the state would proceed. However, our technical team representatives were welcome to visit the site of contracts in preparation and offer advice on how they might be mitigated environmentally. The DNR would make the final decision.

Such timber sale inspections were previously unheard of and constituted an important breakthrough. Three sales were about to be let to gypo outfits and as a result of recommendations of the technical team were greatly modified. One unit of a three-part sale was removed from harvest because it was located on an old slide. In another instance a cut along Deer Creek was made smaller and the cut line moved about 300 feet away from the edge of the stream.

The technical-team inspection process also had failures. Most notable was the cut of 60-year-old second growth conifers a mile above the mouth of Deer Creek, near Oso. The land was owned by Scott and Scott executives were in the process (unknown to the rest of us in the Deer Creek Policy Group) of divesting themselves of all their timberlands in the state. Consequently they were anxious to sell as much timber as they could before they sold the land itself. And the price for timber was high.

The technical team inspected the site of the sale and saw a quarter mile of undercut bank that was beginning to slump into Deer Creek with each high water. The recommendation of the technical team as a whole was negative. My team's recommendation (the FFF's), which had Alec on it and also Tom Crawford, a fisher with a M.S. degree in salmonid fish biology, was not to cut the land at all, but if our good advice was not to be followed to allow at least a 300-foot no-cut buffer back from the creek.

Scott said, "No, thanks," and proceeded to harvest the unit within the letter of the law, which permitted cutting to within 50 feet of the water's edge and even the taking of certain large, "marketable" conifers within that zone.

The Deer Creek Policy Group collapsed into chaos and dissention. Never again was it to function with any degree of confidence and coherence. Meetings were held to hear technical reports on the sedimentation problem and no discussions of substantive matters were attempted. For practical purposes, the group was dead.

Meanwhile negotiations on a state-wide plan modeled loosely after the Deer Creek Policy Group were held in various think-tank locations and at marathon sessions in which participants came up with a consensus plan. It was called The Timber/Fish/Wildlife Agreement and the word order of the components is important. No attempt was made to stem the amount of clearcutting or the method of harvest; these were prior restraints on the decision-making process that all had agreed to. The policy members were heads of state agencies and executives of timber companies; again there was a technical team whose role was solely advisory.

Sound familiar? It was. The irony of the birth of TFW was that it was modeled after a pilot program that had just failed. No matter. It was well-funded and carefully publicized. It took about three years before it too fell apart. There was only one environmental agency allowed to participate—Marcy Golde and the Washington Environmental Council. They were presumed to represent all fisheries, wildlife, and environmental interests other than those of the appropriate state agencies. During these three years and longer clearcutting took place across the state on an unprecedented scale, for the price of timber was high. Much of it was exported in the form of raw logs to markets in the Far East.

Protection given by TFW to streams and the woods I'd say was minimal: A tree here, a slump area there, a risky road, a pile of rocks on which no trees would grow now called a Wildlife Habitat Area. The clearcutting raced on, even across lands that were deemed unstable and with clear evidence of slides. And state and private timber harvest in the troubled Deer Creek basin continued, although abated.

Early in the process Georgia Pacific clearcut its lands on both sides of Little Deer Creek upstream for more than a mile from its mouth; scarcely a whip was left standing. Earlier the USFS had clearcut much of the tributary's headwaters. This small stream provides most of Deer Creek's sanctuary water now that the canyon is badly silted from sources above. And Little Deer is where most of the restoration activities have been centered since then, led by Alec Jackson and the Fourth Corner Fly Club of Bellingham, who have adopted the stream.

Annually stream-protection efforts take place, with the club furnishing the labor under a hot sky, Georgia Pacific lending its helicopter when it is available to carry in heavy materials, and the USFS furnishing technical expertise in stream-channel work. Sediment fences are installed, Jersey barriers are put into position, and large logs are anchored into place to give the surviving fish a better chance at spawning successfully and rearing the next generation of wild steelhead.

In the years to follow both the creek and the North Fork have lost their natural pool-riffle configuration. They are so choked with silt that they run at a uniform depth and speed nearly their entire course. They resemble rivers with a glacial source. They no longer are naturally flowing. Widening and shallowing, they have increased their capacity for retaining solar radiation. This means they are much warmer, summer and winter. And they have lost much of their ability to spawn and rear fish.

The following year the DNR publicly announced it had surpassed its budget limits for remedial work and would do no more. Fishermen and the tribes heard the announcement with mixed sympathy and anger. Work to date had only exacerbated the slide and the problems associated with it. It might be best to do nothing for a while, we agreed. "Benign neglect" couldn't be any worse than what had already been caused to happen. But given the nature of agencies they could not quite leave it alone. New study and monitoring teams met, oversight committees were formed, "new players" brought into the "game" and solicited for "fresh" opinions. Committee meetings of a policy group were scheduled quarterly. Nothing happened except talk and formal requests were submitted for funding pet study projects, mostly by the tribes.

The slide continued to gnaw away at its headwall, slowly enlarging itself. Nothing dramatic occurred, no great blowouts. The slide stayed out of sight and out of mind to most people. Thus it remained through the end of 1985, all of 1986, and into spring of the following year. Sometime between March and June of 1987 another mass-wasting event took place in the same general area; this was revealed by the annual helicopter overflight by the Stillaguamish Tribe and was documented on videotape. Such flights provide an important yearly assessment of the slide's condition, now that remedial work has stopped. Incensed, the tribe applied for and received a two-thirds million dollar grant from the state's Centennial Clean Water Fund to continue seeking longer-lasting solutions. They selected a new geoengineering firm—no surprise. The study dragged on. The final recommendation to the tribe, late in 1991, was to do nothing. The tribe concurred.

In 1987 the summer steelhead fishing was fairly good and I did well. I caught and released 23 wild fish, including 16 in a row. (The rest were hatchery fish, a couple of which I kept for the table.) The Department of Wildlife's annual electroshocking of selected reaches of Deer Creek showed no improvement in juvenile counts. These efforts were led by Curt Kraemer. Only about half the number of one-year steelhead were found as in the previous year. And there were no baby coho.

The following summer, 1988, was worse, and most of my friends caught and released no steelhead bound for Deer Creek. Luckily I took a few, for I knew the river well and the odd places where they might be found. They seemed even more special to me now. That year most of my fish caught below Deer Creek were hatchery steelhead. Though I enjoyed catching them the absence of wild fish was distressing.

In 1989 I caught but two adult summer steelhead there and both were hatchery fish. A July fish weighed 16 pounds and was released after a great fight. I thought that a fish of such size deserved to go free, even though not wild. It was hooked a few yards above the mouth of Deer Creek and landed more than 200 yards downstream. Walt Johnson reported a four-pound Deer Creek fish from the Pocket. The following month I caught a hatchery fish that went 18 pounds in my beloved Elbow Hole. It too went free. It was a big male and the water was warm. I tried to lift the fish out of the water to show Chris Crabtree and his son, but it twisted free and swam off. Two big hatchery fish hardly compensated for the loss of the Deer Creek run, however. It was important to put the two big-fish matter into perspective.

In the fall Wildlife conducted its annual electroshocking. Once more Curt reported about half the number of juveniles as in the past year; the run was decimating itself by halves each generation. It was an unusual fall, with clear water lasting late in the season, so the department was able to count adult steelhead from a helicopter for the first time. Curt spotted 88 "adult salmonids"—probably all of them steelhead, though there was a statistical possibility of coho—between the mouth and the anadromous fish barrier, a steep waterfall many miles away. This probably comprised the bulk of the run.

In 1990 I caught only hatchery fish below Deer Creek and not many of those. They were average size. George McLeod caught a seven-pound unmarked fish probably headed for Deer Creek on May 31. This was very early in the season and the fish might have been a winter run—though George knows his fish about as well as anybody and maintains that it was a wild summer fish. By late summer I had heard of only a few fish caught in the vicinity of the mouth of the creek—maybe six or eight, all told.

In the fall Walt Johnson caught another one while fishing for cutthroat. Electroshocking a month later showed the juvenile count down by half once more, with the best concentrations in Little Deer Creek region, which had the healthiest habitat. It is where restoration efforts had been centered.

The following year, 1991, I caught four fish headed for Deer Creek, two pairs, each pair bunched on consecutive days a month apart. I found a few rocks in the river that would shelter steelhead, but only while the

Epitaph: Deer Creek Revisited

water remained high, and I fished hard but with no success for more wild summer runs. The annual electroshocking showed the numbers down by the usual amount—one-half. In 1992 my wild-fish catch was five and the substrate looked to be somewhat improved. But this might be a fluke.

As Curt sadly notes, "At this rate by the turn of the century we will be down to the return of a fractional fish."